Automobile
Year

PHILIPPSEN

Automobile Year is published by

Christian Philippsen
19, boulevard de Suisse
MC 98000 Monte-Carlo – Monaco
Telephone + 377-9350 9610
Facsimile + 377-9350 9612
E-mail CP@ChristianPhilippsen.com
www.automobileyear.com

Automobile Year is published
in French as *L'Année Automobile*
(www.anneeautomobile.com)
and in German as *Auto-Jahr*
(www.autojahr.com)

ISBN 2-916206-08-6

Contents

WHAT DO YOU
WANT TO DRIVE?
A LOGO? OR A CAR?

What drives you? A car should be more than just a symbol of status and
possession. Infiniti has arrived and introduces Inspired Performance; an
exhilarating experience delivered in our V6 and V8 engines.
The new Infiniti FX, EX37, G37 and G37 Coupé.

Discover what really matters.
www.infiniti.eu
00 800 463 464 84

Infiniti is made in Japan.

Inspired Performance

Automotive Fine Art Paintings of your Design Studio or your machine At Speed. These could include a portrait of you, your childern or a love one.

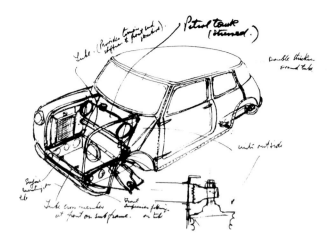

Whether we're helping you to define your next concept, benchmarking your product or planning your launch strategy, Car Men has the experience and resources to make it happen.

Contact us to see what we can do for you.

Automotive Design Strategy | Design Benchmarking Database

Pure emotion

300V motorSport

High Tech solutions when racing is your job or passion !

Motul is involved at the highest level of car racing. Where performance is all that counts, Motul earned its reputation with the most prestigious teams worldwide. Motul matched its drive for innovation with an unrivalled test facility. Once fully developed, experimental formulas are made available to our most demanding customers for further field testing.

This motorsport range, created by the Motul R&D laboratory, exceeds all existing international standards. This new generation of 300V engine oils is quickly becoming the premier reference at the motor racing

Weltweiter Partner

Global Player

Représentation mondiale

Wir im Allgäu.

▶ **Fahrzeugprüfung auf höchstem Niveau**

▶ **Vehicle testing at the highest level**

▶ **Contrôle technique au plus haut niveau**

Vertretungen und Niederlassungen in mehr als 130 Ländern dieser Erde sichern die optimale Versorgung der Kunden vor Ort. So sehen wir uns nicht nur als System-lieferant für die Fahrzeugprüfung und Wartung, sondern sind zentraler Ansprech-partner für die Planung und Umsetzung länderspezifischer Prüfkonzepte. Hochent-wickelte Software-Anwendungen werden auf die Bedürfnisse und Anforderungen der Kunden und der jeweiligen Standorte bzw. Länder abgestimmt.

Customers are optimally served on location with subsidiaries and dealers in more than 130 countries. We see ourselves not only as system provider for vehicle testing and maintenance but also as a pivotal contact partner for the planning and execution of country-specific test concepts. High-tech software applications are adapted to the needs and requirements of customers and the respective locations or countries.

Avec des représentants et des filiales dans plus de 130 pays à travers le monde, nous disposons d'une couverture optimale de la clientèle locale. Ainsi, nous ne sommes pas seulement un fournisseur de système pour le contrôle technique et la maintenance mais aussi l'interlocuteur principal pour la planification et la mise en œuvre de contrôle spécifique au pays. Des logiciels d'application de haut niveau sont adaptés aux besoins et aux exigences des clients ou des pays respectifs.

- Brems- und Fahrwerktester
- Leistungs- und Funktionsprüfstände
- Abgas- und Diagnosegeräte
- Hebetechnik

- Brake and Suspension Testers
- Dynamometers
- Emission Testers and Diagnostic Units
- Automotive Lifts

- Banc de freinage et de suspension
- Banc de puissance et de fonction
- Analyseurs de gaz et appareils de diagnostiques
- Système de levage

MAHA Maschinenbau Haldenwang GmbH & Co. KG
Hoyen 20 · 87490 Haldenwang
www.maha.de

Premium Workshop Equipment

Innovation has good prospects whenever it is cleaner, safer and more efficient.

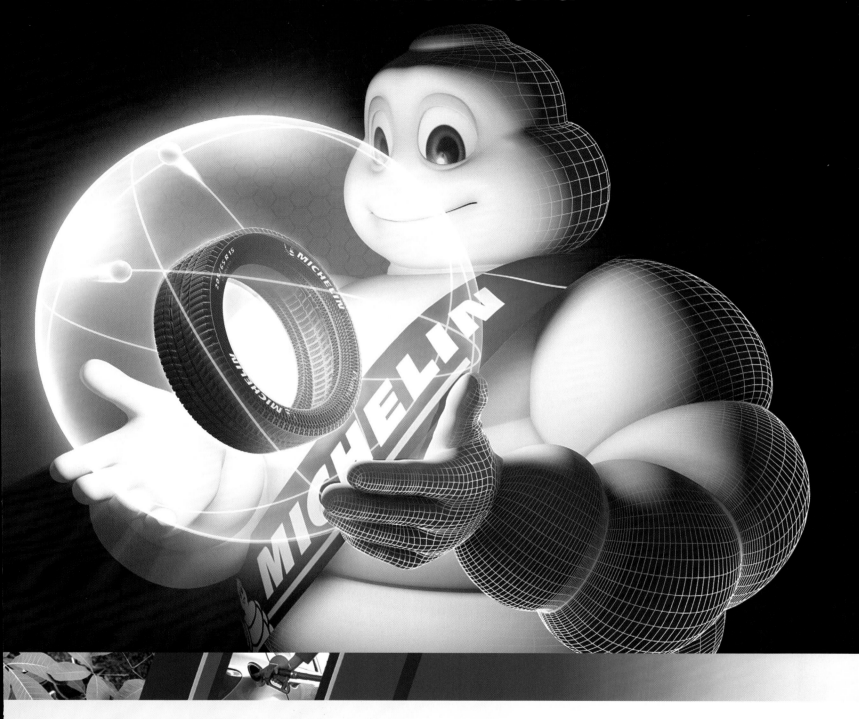

The new MICHELIN® ENERGY™ SAVER tire saves almost 0.2 l of fuel for every 100km* covered, i.e. CO2 emissions cut by 4g per km*. With this tire you can cover 40% more km* and, on wet surfaces, its braking distance is under 2.40m*. This tire has the GREEN X label for MICHELIN tires that are particularly fuel efficient.

* Compared to the tires of competitors' major brands, ISO test conducted by TÜV SÜD Automotive in 2007 on the dimensions 175/65 R14, 195/65 R15 and 205/55 R16.

www.michelin.com

BMW Classic

quality is our
style™

1937 Bugatti Type 57SC Atalante Coupe

SOLD $7,920,000

Pebble Beach Auctions . 2008

Pebble Beach . California . USA

GOODING
& COMPANY®

+1.310.899.1960   general inquiries: info@goodingco.com   goodingco.com

GRAN TURISMO™
THE REAL DRIVING SIMULATOR

Gran Turismo Celebrates 10th Anniversary.

The Gran Turismo series has now shipped over 50 million units worldwide.

Thank you for your support over the past 10 years.

www.gran-turismo.com

POLYPHONY
DIGITAL

There are journeys that turn into legends.
Bahamas Islands. 10:07

LOUIS VUITTON

Editorial

Nothing reveals talent like adversity. As I write these lines, I am watching the British Grand Prix unfold in atrocious conditions; but my thoughts are on the predicament faced by the heads of the car industry. Because the stage is now set for a drama that will undoubtedly sort the winners from the losers.

First, there's the economic crisis. It's never good practice to lend money to borrowers who can't pay it back. And it's even more dangerous to mix bad loans with good ones, bundle them all together in attractive packages and dish them out to profit-hungry investors. It is a bit like a supermarket slipping a slice of rotting salami into every pack of fresh sausage it sells. Which is why the world economy now has an acute case of indigestion.

Then, there's the role played by oil. Oil is the energy best suited to transport applications, which account for roughly 50% of global consumption. The needs of fast-growing emerging economies, combined with the needs of mature markets, has – with the help of a little speculation – increased demand and put upward pressure on prices. And what's true of oil is true of raw materials, so the cost price of cars has shot up.

It is understandable in these conditions that political powers should intervene, and this is the third part of the equation that manufacturers are left to solve. Recession, inflation and the desire for energy-independence, not to mention concerns about climate change and the environment, bring a cacophony of short-term decisions in their wake, which contribute precious little in the way of guidance for industrialists.

So cars are selling badly. Let's not forget that even the most recent models were conceived four of five years ago, when the global mood was one of unbridled optimism… Nowadays, by contrast, when it comes to communication campaigns, manufacturers have only one option: to underline reduced fuel consumption, alternative energies and environmental protection. But beyond the fine words, engineering departments are in disarray. Because they're snowed under, you might think. But that is not the problem. The problem is that they are awaiting instructions. Put yourself in the shoes of the Ghosns, Wagoners, Watanabes and Wiedekings of this world: you obviously need to prepare for the future, and the future will inevitably be different from the present, but where and in which technologies do you invest? It is not about dreaming and it is not about following fashions, it is about safeguarding the future of businesses, the jobs they provide, and about providing a decent return on the invested capital. So what is it going to be? Batteries? Solar? Hydrogen? Biofuel? Or are we just going to perfect the petrol and diesel-fuelled combustion engines? This simple statistic illustrates the progress made by the latter: Martin Winterkorn, Chairman of the Volkswagen Group, recently stated that if the average age of Germany's national fleet fell from nine to eight years, this alone would save 800 million litres of fuel per year…

The time is ripe for new players to take the stage and accelerate the pace of change. Here in Monaco, in my own back yard, the small company Venturi is making some interesting creations, thanks to its mastery of the latest state-of-the-art technologies. On the other side of the world, the Indian company Tata has turned conventional thinking on its head by launching a real car with a 2500 dollar price tag… while still treating itself to Jaguar and Land Rover! Michelin, which gives constant consideration to the future of the motor car in order to ensure the future of its tyre business, not only organises the Bibendum Challenge dedicated to sustainable mobility, but is also working directly on their Active Wheel, incorporating piloted suspension and an electric motor.

We already know who won the British Grand Prix: Lewis Hamilton, in the style of a true champion! His victory took just under two hours to achieve. But to find out which of the car manufacturers is making the right strategic decisions today, we'll have to wait 10 years or more… You can bet that, between now and then, the automotive landscape will change dramatically.

Happy Automobile Year!

Christian Philippsen

Christian Philippsen
Editor

Industry

RoboCar 2057

The Los Angeles region, long hailed as a leader of creativity and consumer trends, is home to the world's largest concentration of manufacturer design studios, representing automakers from North America, Europe and Asia. It is also the home of the Art Center College of Design, one of the foremost transportation design institutions where many of today's leading automotive designers graduated. The Design Los Angeles Challenge has evolved into an integral element of the Los Angeles Auto Show, held in November. Now in its fourth year, it is a unique annual contest open to the many local car design studios. The 2007 theme, "RoboCar of 2057", asked to form a vision of the future by depicting a vehicle that incorporates artificial intelligence engineered to make life easier and more attractive to consumers 50 years from now. **Christian Philippsen** introduces the most significant entries, beginning with the winning Volkswagen Slipstream.

VOLKSWAGEN SLIPSTREAM
Volkswagen/Audi Design Center California
Design Team: Ian Hilton, Derek Jenkins, Patrick Faulwetter

In the year 2057, population centers have become unimaginably dense and the roadways have reached the point of total saturation. Volkswagen's solution is an advanced autonomous vehicle that dynamically adapts to minimize its footprint in the city and its drag coefficient on the highways.

When in the city, these two-wheeled, teardrop shaped pods travel in an upright orientation that occupies one fifth the size of a traditional vehicle. When on a special freeway lane called the "Slipstream", it tilts to a horizontal orientation optimizing its aerodynamic shape. Rear fins slide out to allow the rear of the vehicle to float like the tail section of an airplane to achieve speeds in excess of 250 mph.

The skin of the vehicle is made of hyper-efficient solar panels that power the vehicle.

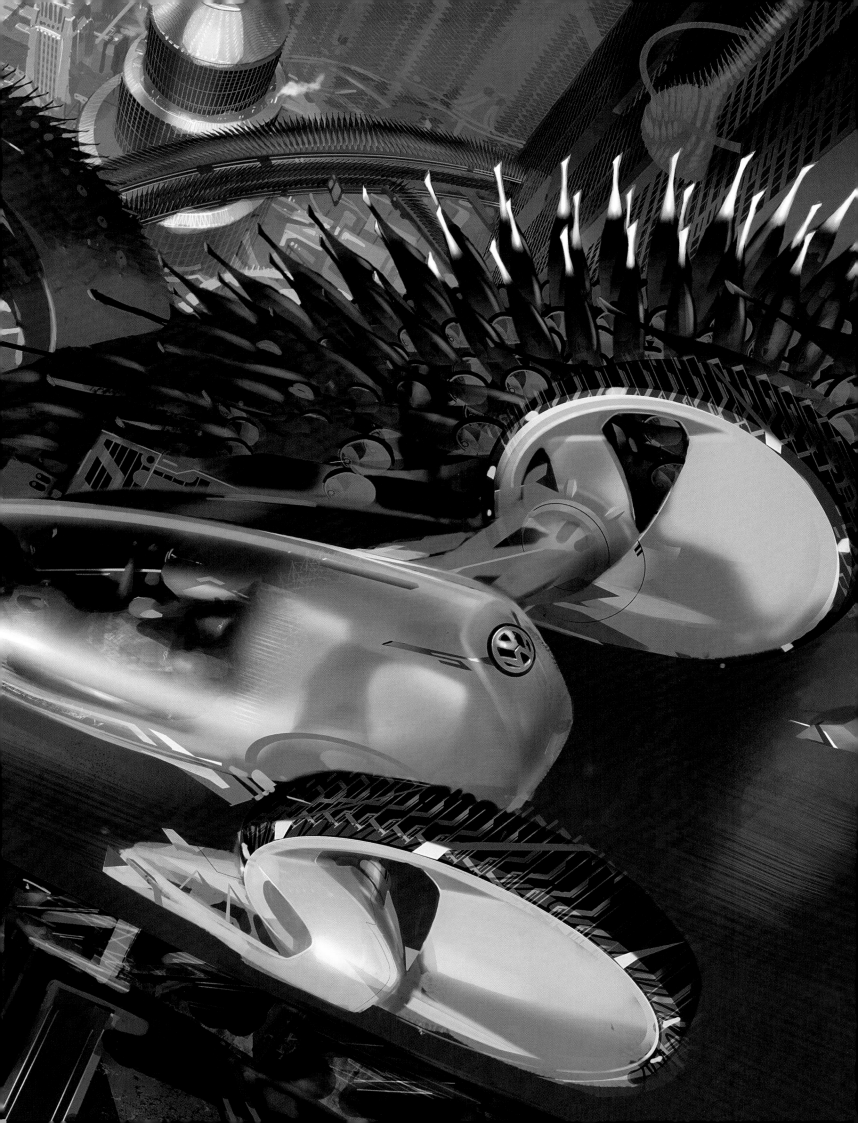

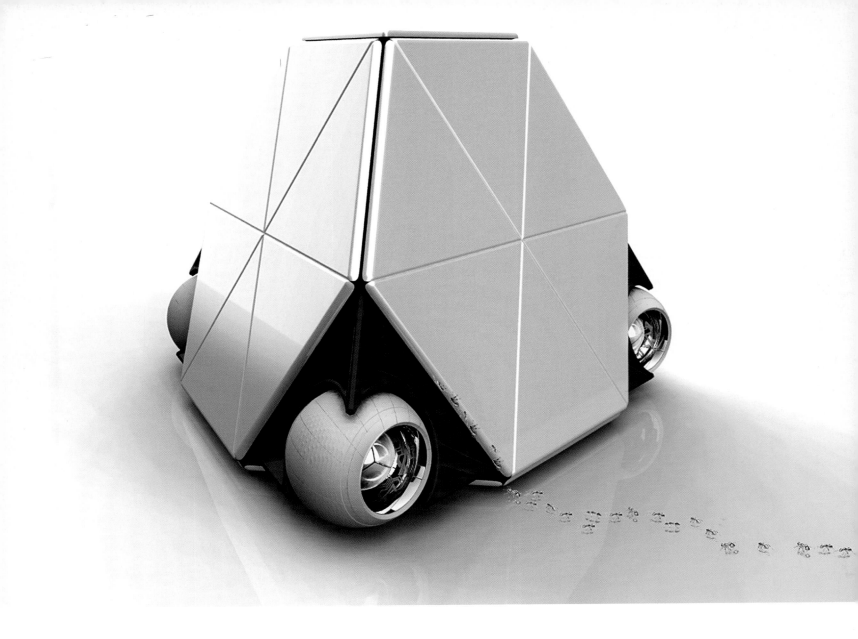

GM ONSTAR ANT

General Motors Advanced Design, California
Design Team: Frank Saucedo, Steve Anderson,
Jussi Timonen, Jose Paris, Lorne Kulesus,
Tony Liu, Jay Bernard, Phil Tanioka

Much like the self-regulating traffic system found
in nature's best commuter, the ant, OnStar enabled
vehicle-to-vehicle communication and ubiquitously
embedded intelligence allow GM's ANT to act
independently yet communicate with other vehicles
to optimize traffic flow. Quantum computing power
also allows each ANT to virtually recreate a highly
personalized space for any occasion or personal need.
Omni-directional propulsion, provided by three
independent Nanorb wheel systems, operate as
independent robots and can arrange themselves in different
configurations, turning virtually anything into a mobile
device. Layered, environmentally friendly, single-walled,
carbon-polymer nanocomposites form the flat surface
panels, which incorporate the carbon nanotube battery.
All body panels are connected with electro-
active polymer actuators (a.k.a. artificial muscles),
allowing the easy and silent reconfiguration of body
panels, depending on their optimal street use.

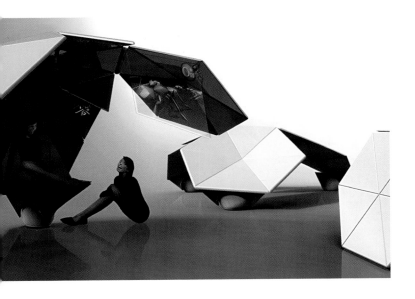

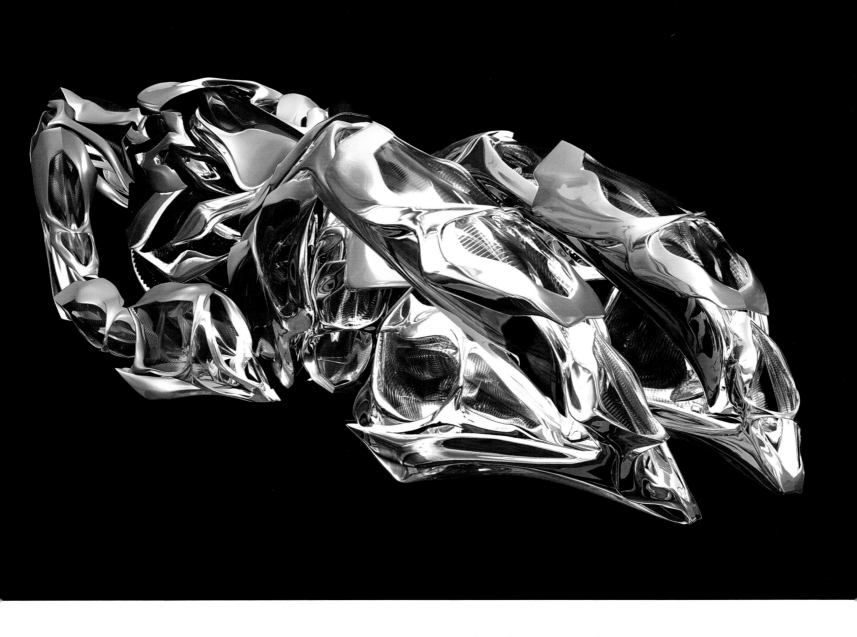

MAZDA MOTONARI RX
Mazda R&D of North America
Designer: Matthew Cunningham

The Motonari RX, named after legendary Japanese
warrior Mori Motonari, non-invasively integrates the
driver with the vehicle making each indistinguishable
from the other. A driving suit serves as the primary
interface between the occupant and the vehicle,
which contains millions of microscopic actuators
functioning as a haptic envelope. This allows the driver
to experience the road psycho-somatically, receiving
electrical stimulation to specific muscle groups.
The entire structure of the vehicle is comprised of
a 100% re-prototypable, carbon nano-tube/shape
memory alloy weave with a photovoltaic coating.
This enables programmable tensiometry and fluid
movement while insuring efficient energy transfer
to the in-wheel electro-static nanomotors.
The four omni-wheels allow 360 degree movement.
Acceleration and direction is determined by two
armrest mounted control points. Occupant positioning
controls the effectiveness of cornering and is comparable
to street luge maneuvering in appearance.

TOYOTA BIOMOBILE MECHA

Calty Design Research
Design Team: Edward Lee, Erwin Lui,
Yo Hiruta, Kevin Hunter

It is the year 2057 and due to limited ground space, vertical architectures have caused the transportation industry to create new pathways that also explore vertical space. An innovative solution is discovered in biomimicry. Inspired by life found in nature, the vehicle is powered by pollution with dynamic driving instincts and structural adaptations to accommodate the user's need for space. This vehicle's unique capability to extract pollutants in the air and utilize it as an energy source restores balance to our atmosphere. It is able to autonomously adapt to its driving environment by utilizing its four nano-laser wheels. Nanotechnology also enables the structure of the vehicle to expand and contract horizontally and vertically to serve as a compact commuter, an aerodynamic performance vehicle and temporary dwelling.

RENAULT
Renault Design, Paris and Barcelona
Designers: Eric Diemert, Anthony Villain, Ken Malville

With no presence on the American market and thus absent from the Los Angeles Auto Show, Renault nonetheless took up a similar challenge when the Russian magazine Za Rulem, which is celebrating its 80th anniversary, asked the company to imagine what cars would be like 80 years from now.
So here we are in 2088. Having freed itself of traditional means of propulsion over the course of the 21st Century, the car has finally harnessed the energy of the sun and wind to become a self-powered vehicle running on electricity. Adapting to its context and desired use – whether intra-city transit or long-haul travel – the car has become an object of variable geometry. While remaining compact in town, it has developed the ability to extend its length, and shape its contours for very high speed travel. It has traded its bodywork of yesteryear for a skin made of ultra-high strength lightweight alloys, providing opaque visual protection zones and translucent areas for a view of the outside world. Driver-operated in town, it makes long journeys on autopilot with automated flow management, using elevated infrastructures bearing electromagnetic rails. Sometimes supported from the ground, sometimes suspended from overhead superstructures, these infrastructures are also powered by wind and solar energy, and blend harmoniously into the environment. Mountainous terrain and water are no longer obstacles, but a spectacle for the vehicle's occupants, who dart from one place to another in direct lines and absolute silence, without any contact with the ground.

Laurens van den Acker creates a new type of beauty for Mazda

Laurens van den Acker, General Manager of Mazda's Design Division, was officially presented with the Louis Vuitton Classic Concept Award for the Ryuga (see AY 55). The prize rewards a design that has the potential of winning a major concours d'elegance in 40 years from now. The ceremony took place at the North American International Auto Show in Detroit in January 2008, in the presence of Yves Carcelle, President of Louis Vuitton. Laurens is Dutch, was born in 1965, and now lives with his wife and daughter in Hiroshima. **Christian Philippsen**, who chaired the judges' panel, submitted him to the Automobile Year questionnaire.

AUTOMOBILE YEAR: You won the Louis Vuitton Classic Concept Award, what does it represent for you?
LAURENS VAN DEN ACKER: It is a tremendous honour of course as it is a very prestigious award. To be a 'potential best in show 40 years from now', must be one of the most demanding criteria for a design award. What makes it very special too, is that we are the first Japanese car company to ever win this award.

AY: How did your passion for cars start?
LVDA: My passion for cars really started with a love of drawing. My father was an architect with his studio at home, so I spent many an afternoon drawing away at his desk. The step from sketching houses to cars then was a very small one.

AY: What is your educational background?
LVDA: After graduating high school, I studied Industrial Design at Delft University of Technology in the absence of a proper automotive design course. However, the passion for cars was strong enough to overcome that initial disadvantage.

AY: What was your career development?
LVDA: I've learned by doing. First starting out as a young designer in a small studio in Torino called Design Systems. To my surprise the first project we worked on was the interior of the Bugatti EB110, so I had a chance to observe one of my all-time heroes, Marcello Gandini, from up close. Then I moved to Ingolstadt to work for Audi, who were just about to break through with their Bauhaus design style. A magical period with many very talented designers, one of whom was J Mays. After J had left Audi to start up

a new design studio for SHR Perceptual Management in California, he enticed me to join. This story repeated itself when he moved to Ford where I ended up working seven years, five years in California as Chief Designer of the Brand Imaging Group, a sort of think tank for brand strategy and advanced design, then two years in Detroit, heading up the Ford Escape/Mercury Mariner production program. Somehow, this varied background proved attractive for Mazda when they were looking for a new Design Director, and as of February 1, 2006, I've been living in Hiroshima, Japan.

AY: What was the best moment in your career?
LVDA: October 24, 2007 Tokyo Motor Show. We unveiled not only the Mazda Taiki, but had the complete Nagare Series on display, including the Mazda Ryuga. It was a tremendous amount of creativity, created by all of Mazda's four global design studios.

AY: What was the most difficult moment in your career?
LVDA: As an aspiring car designer I was rejected a lot, be it internships, thesis projects or real positions. Now I think it comes with the territory.

AY: Which is the favourite car you designed and why?
LVDA: I am most proud of the Nagare Series, because I think we managed to create a new type of beauty. Something people had never seen before, but nevertheless intuitively liked.

AY: How do you see the car evolve in the next 20 years?
LVDA: On the one side, the importance of the car as one of the more important things in people's life will diminish, at least in the developed world. But I also think that cars will become

LAURENS VAN DEN ACKER, YVES CARCELLE, CHRISTIAN PHILIPPSEN

more and more specialized and diverse, aiming to be very good at particular things, be it price, fuel economy, long distance travel, or as a communication pod on wheels for in the city. This will make the future very interesting for us designers.

AY: Which cars are in your garage?
LVDA: Mazda RX8, Mazda6 Stationwagon.

AY: Which are your favourite car events?
LVDA: The classic races in Laguna Seca on Saturday, followed by the Pebble Beach concours d'elegance on Sunday. I love the contrast. First drinking cans of beer in the hot sand watching the action at the corkscrew, then sipping champagne at the 18th hole.

AY: Apart from cars, do you have other interests in life?
LVDA: I like visiting art musea on my travels, hiking in the mountains, I love modern architecture and tickling my daughter.

AY: What do you do in your free time?
LVDA: Spend time with my family, keeping a diary with photos of past experiences.

AY: Which is your favourite place in the world?
LVDA: At the moment Beijing.

AY: Which is your favourite hotel/resort?
LVDA: The Iori *machiya* in Kyoto. These are old, beautifully restored townhouses in central Kyoto.

AY: Which is your favourite restaurant?
LVDA: Nobu, creative sushi, just around the block from our apartment in Hiroshima.

AY: Which is your favourite dish?
LVDA: Rainbow roll.

AY: Which is your favourite music?
LVDA: I grew up in the 70s and 80s. That says it all.

AY: Which is your favourite movie?
LVDA: Delicatessen, Life of Brian, Deerhunter, Amadeus, Monsters Inc, Ratatouille.

AY: Which is your favourite book?
LVDA: De Ontdekking van de hemel (The Discovery of Heaven), by Harry Mulisch.

AY: Do you have a hero?
LVDA: Brian Eno, Marcello Gandini.

AY: Any advice to youngsters?
LVDA: Am I getting that old already? If there's anything, I'd say leave the nest and try to find a job abroad. You'll experience so many new things and find out what you're made of.

AY: Thank you.

Considerations for the future of the worldwide auto industry

Manufacturers' and brands' competitive positions, which have grown and become familiar over decades on the international market, are about to make way for a new order. Comprehensive awareness of resources is growing worldwide and is increasing rapidly in every sector of society. A company can paralyse itself if it has the potential to offend. The subject matter has taken root. Generally speaking, revolutionary innovations will become rarer only to be replaced by a multitude of gradual developments. These are no less complex and will require even greater investment in communications to publicise the difference between products in a sales-effective way (cf. the PR success enjoyed by BMW's Efficient Dynamics). Innovative progress now remains exclusive for an ever shorter period. The long-term tendency towards individualisation needs to be countered by an ever more extreme acquisition of niches. At the same time, one-off charges and production costs are constantly growing as are potential customers' overall expectations of the product. The above are some considerations developed below by **Karl-Heinz Kalbfell**, a consultant for auto-industry projects and formerly the director for many years of product and market strategy for the BMW Group, Chairman and CEO of Rolls-Royce Motor Cars, and CEO at Maserati.

The structure of competitive conditions in the auto industry is currently shifting dramatically. The term 'dramatically' needs to be seen from the point of view of the particularities of this industrial sector. The relatively long development cycles (three to four years as a rule) based on the average model's shelf-life (five to ten years) and the huge investment requirements mean a supervisory overview of at least 10 years is necessary. Accordingly, the situation in the auto industry today is largely the result of the planning findings, decisions and also failings of years past. The foundations for success or the lack of it far into the future are similarly being laid here and now.

CONSERVING RESOURCES WITHOUT LOSING FASCINATION AND DYNAMISM

What stands out today is in some ways comparable to the turning point approximately 30 years ago that led to the Europe-wide move towards the catalytic converter. The challenge, however, is dissimilar in its complexity. Whereas environmental issues were hardly taken seriously for many years and seen as the domain of more marginal political groupings, awareness of resources has now become a truly comprehensive part of our daily lives. The fact that the price of fuel is currently rising drastically is consolidating the trend considerably.

Expertise and credibility in the framework of this new environmental awareness present perhaps the greatest future challenge for the auto industry. It is worth pointing out that this was predictable years in advance! The EU is currently debating a policy whereby new cars would be obliged to reduce emissions to no more than 120 g/km. This affects the manufacturers of high-performance SUVs and powerful sports cars the most severely. And there are fears that even stricter CO_2 limits are in the legislative pipeline. To what extent exemptions can be achieved is tactically important but it can't be counted on too much from a strategic point of view. This means that the manufacturers' current marketing policy is bound to enter a period of turbulence. Businesses should, at the very least, plan consistently for the worst case scenario. As the motor car is perceived not just rationally but also holds special fascination for people, purely rational solutions are going to have little chance of market success in future. Current efforts in the electric vehicle sector show that very clearly. The solution to this conflict of objectives: maintaining the usual performance level with inspiring dynamics whilst meeting statutory emissions levels and keeping the brands' values, means both product strategists and even more engineers have challenging and pioneering tasks ahead of them. It is wrong to think that only a huge breakthrough can achieve a success in sales and public opinion. On the contrary, it is small, continual and professionally marketed steps which reap rewards. This is also why Toyota

was able to post a partially unexpected success with its hybrid technology. When push comes to shove, reality convinces the market more than vision. European manufacturers really missed out by not marketing the accomplishments of, for example, diesel technology in a convincing and timely way. Hybrid schemes were arrogantly branded half-baked. But one ought to remember that most ground-breaking schemes were not always recognised by the establishment as such in their early days. Today, offers such as hybrid vehicles that one can buy are appreciated as they allow people to at least think they are not one of those polluting the environment. This, incidentally, regardless of tactical sales comparisons. The first step matters. This surely cannot be explained away purely rationally. But psychological legitimacy plays an important role where this topic is concerned. On the one hand we have the petroleum industry declaring that oil and gas reserves will keep on increasing and that there are no cutbacks on the radar screen. The risk is more due to the fear for insecure producing countries. On the other hand, research into new forms of energy continues unabated, regardless of such statements. What will finally be enforced as regards petroleum in the future depends largely on political decisions. But car-makers must propose the technical solutions. I think that the current competition between concepts, whether it be electricity, bio-fuels or hydrogen, is important to help determine the new general direction. But one must not

forget that the world's infrastructure is built on oil and that the internal combustion engine still has great potential too. It is amazing that this sector's communications skills are not better. Based on infrastructural factors, it is highly likely that alternative fuels will only get anywhere for the foreseeable future if they can be sold at today's petrol stations.

EVOLUTIONARY, NOT REVOLUTIONARY

The technical requirements for ground-breaking cars are ever-increasing. Interlinked aspects such as security, electronics, lightweight structure, fuel consumption, emissions, production costs and legal requirements are leading to significantly increased "conflicts of objectives". New professional categories are thronging to the as yet mechanical auto-world. Mechatronics is a valid example. A fundamental and thus far neglected task has been organising current traffic flow. There is significant potential for conserving resources in the area which would, furthermore, be quicker and easier than many detail improvements on a car. Some habits that we take for granted would have to be put up for grabs, though. No-one would think it was a good idea to let air traffic go unregulated, for example. Maybe allocating individual slots at peak times could keep the traffic flowing. The fast-growing development costs are also leading to formerly untouchable fields of competence having to cooperate across the competition. This is especially the case when the in-house creative potential is being systematically dismantled. When even BMW is openly considering Peugeot engines in their own cars, the old dogmas seem to have been resoundingly displaced! Individual development projects for particularly complex systems such as hybrid solutions appear to only be possible in firms the size of Toyota and Volkswagen. Nor must we forget the concentration effort of the supplier industry which led to the skills required to make a complete vehicle. If these suppliers have efficient structures for reasonably-priced vehicle production and display a high level of system competence, some manufacturers could in future have nothing left to do but manage the brand. Magna leads the way. Bosch has also announced a new business sector which will deal with new forms of energy. In future, developers won't have the luxury of optional animosity. Electronics, mechanics and material science will only be able to achieve continued solutions together. I would go so far as to say that whichever manufacturer is the quickest to conquer these internal optional divides will have won a considerable advantage over the competition. It will be interesting to follow how much further back the current physical barriers in the interplay between mechanics and electronics and new areas of research can be pushed. The big questions remain more than ever the feasibility from the point of view of cost considerations, and the new approaches' chances of securing a majority of the market. It is largely unknown but worth mentioning that a large part of development capacity is already bound by international legislation and national registration regulations. This will increase. The competitiveness will be determined by a company's size, a size not too many manufacturers can boast. The multi-brand policy of firms such as Volkswagen and BMW is paying off.

CHARACTER IN SPITE OF MODULAR DESIGN

Platform strategy and modular design are almost common knowledge these days. The long-term trend towards individualisation with lower quantities per model requires a sophisticated component strategy. The new technologies which have been developed with huge effort must, for economic reasons, be put to use as often as possible. Without a deep understanding of sustainable, customer-oriented solutions and persuasive vehicle character, any component strategy will definitely be a non-starter. The product categories that have already established themselves, such as hatchbacks, limousines, coupés, station wagons, SUVs, cabriolets, vans and sports cars, will hardly be added to. But weight will shift within the categories and new crossover vehicles will establish themselves, though in manageable quantities. This will give contract manufacturers like Magna new opportunities. In all these developments one may observe that the majority of motorists prefer concrete, conservative offers.

Trendsetting features only find their way to mass approval after a certain time; in some senses this is an advantage as it gives the large car manufacturers greater planning security. Because what Californian surfers find hip catches on only slowly or not at all and can be systematically measured, one knows which style and which technology need to be at the cutting edge and where it's enough to follow the crowd. Designers have a particularly large responsibility here! Sadly, it seems to me that in the face of multiple concepts, the love of detail, especially in interiors, has partly been lost. It is always more interesting for designers and engineers to design and develop complete cars than to go for increased customer value through obsessive attention to detail. Admittedly, working on the detail is complicated but it pays off in the long run. At the same time, not everything that is feasible today is necessarily of help to the customer. The surplus of electronic gadgets is partly considered thoroughly dispensable. I think that a responsible choice of the fitments on offer will in future become more important as a set-up discipline.

INNOVATIVE POWER AND THE NEW CENTRE

Since room for manoeuvre as regards pricing for premium brands may largely have been exhausted, required volume growth will only be generated by entry into lower-priced sectors. And manufacturers from the lower-price range are now aiming upwards. A consequence of this is that the distinct classification of mass- and premium-producers is gradually blurring. Whereas a few years ago we were still speaking about the "loss of the centre", which affected brands without great charisma like GM, Ford and Chrysler especially badly, now the lower and upper sectors are growing ever closer, overlapping and forming a "new centre". Due to the increase in international earnings, this new centre will be noticeably higher than the former centre. Volkswagen, Audi, BMW, Mercedes and Toyota/Lexus will constitute the "new upscale centre" of these developments. The tendency in the financial data from, for example, BMW (increased sales and stagnant earnings) delivers just as clear a message as the increased growth and earnings figures from Toyota and Volkswagen. These shifts mean new opportunities for growth and positioning for all competitors. Volkswagen is following Audi on the upwards trend and is consistently gaining ground with its attractive models, persuasive technology and favourable cost-to-performance ratio. An outstanding example is the Tiguan, second to none when compared to corresponding models from the premium manufacturers. BMW is following Mercedes on the way down. And that at a time when the lower segments are no longer synonymous with natural high volume. Closer examination of quantities per segment shows the BMW 3 Series, with 500,000 vehicles sold, slowly moving into the Volkswagen Golf category numbers-wise – an effect of rising disposable income. An interesting and prospering business area has developed between the so-called Golf class and the entry to the, say, BMW 3 Series: the classless premium compact vehicles. The revived MINI has managed to establish itself as an impressive forerunner. The thread is currently being picked up by the Fiat Group with its new Cinquecento and consistently taken up further down the scale. Furthermore, Japanese brands, which were never formerly established in the premium segment, are once more gaining a reputation as an alternative. This is how Toyota, with its phenomenal product quality, has managed to gain and hold on to many customers (in spite of the odd slump). The consistently marketed hybrid has contributed to an improved position in Europe in addition to the pre-eminence it had already achieved in the U.S. Far more dangerous from Western vendors' point of view is the fact that the now widely recognised power of innovation has become a significant element of decision for social climbers. Current mass manufacturers will upgrade and eagerly serve new markets and new consumer categories with enhanced offers. Fiat, Mazda, Kia and Hyundai serve as examples of this.

EXCLUSIVITY

Premium manufacturers are fighting doggedly for the last remaining market share in their segments and will have to face up to the challenge of all-round competition. The upper measurement for a car is just above five metres. But with each new generation of models, all cars are growing! This means that in the medium-term, model categories will disappear. The top end of the premium range, currently dominated by BMW, Mercedes and Audi, will, in the not too distant future, be topped by brands underlining their difference. A BMW 7 Series or Mercedes-Benz S-class is less and less exclusive because of the numbers sold today, the vehicle population and easier accessibility. Porsche could take over the leading position here. The Panamera will clearly hurt the establishment when it appears and put Porsche into a new position of growth, as has already happened with the Cayenne. The more BMW, Mercedes and Audi battle it out exhaustingly in the lower price range, the less they will shine in the upper price range. Bentley, Rolls-Royce, Maserati and Mercedes-AMG can dominate the 100,000 to 200,000 price range in future with their attractive but still socially compliant differentiation potential. Maserati and Jaguar also have a particular opportunity if they consistently regenerate and think over the true strengths of their brands. Ferrari and Rolls-Royce will continue to cover the absolute top of the range.

MARKET SHARE ADJUSTMENTS EMERGING

A successful company or one that will be can be spotted today because it is either already completely international or is at least concentrating its efforts on gaining a foothold in all the world's markets. Anyone who either cannot or does not want to play game will, with a more regionally limited market

position, hardly be one of the winners in the long term. This has come about from the pressure for growth in the face of rising costs, stagnant prices and the increased fitment requirements in all vehicle classes. BMW and Mercedes-Benz are the stars of this show. The internationalisation of both companies was pushed through decades ago (but Mercedes and Chrysler going their separate ways demonstrates that growth has its limits dependent on the core competencies of the relevant companies). In the past, mass-producers were rather oriented towards their domestic market. A serious signal is the global response to the 'provocative' Tata Nano. There are also shifts in the size of the sales markets. Last year, China already took over third place in the international list from car-making Germany. Predictions have it that China could soon displace Japan for position No. 2. And in an atmosphere of rapid departure, Russia is already lurking in the wings. There is already talk of up to 4 million cars. The manufacturers' importance in the respective markets is also shifting. Thus the market share of, for example, GM, Chrysler and Ford could conceivably sink below 50% on the domestic American market for the first time. In 1974, U.S. car-makers still had a market share of just under 75%. Now, in contrast, the American share of Far East car-makers stands at almost 45%. Toyota alone accounts for 17% of that sum. This demonstrates very clearly that consistent international activity is essential to survival.

Clever policy as regards the models themselves won't be enough to be successful in future. Only internationally-minded companies with brands known to be forward-looking and an actively communicated claim to sharing the shape of politics and infrastructure can hope to succeed. Which means that "Blowing your own trumpet!" – and in good time – will become significantly more important alongside the required technical expertise.

Tokyo puts a playful slant on a serious game

October 2007. The atmosphere of the Tokyo Motor Show is always more playful than that of its counterparts, and every other year the show unveils some of the more unexpected directions that the automotive industry could take in the future. Forgoing real-world prototypes, Japanese industrialists tend to express their views through unashamedly futuristic concept cars, of the type presented here by **Serge Bellu**. In so doing, they display a marked talent for meeting the perceived expectations of tomorrow's consumers. Even with serious issues at stake, they express themselves with a lightness of touch that gives priority to charming visitors to the event, which is still the world's second largest by attendance, after the Mondial de l'Automobile in Paris. In the land of the rising sun, it's already universally accepted that the time has come to start thinking up some radical solutions for replacing the conventional car. Undesirable in cities, and forced to embrace profound change in order to preserve what's left of the environment, the car is being re-evaluated in Japan more than anywhere else in the world.

MAZDA TAIKI

The car seems caught in its own contradictions, as it's forced to meet the conflicting demands of inspiring the public with outlandish propositions, while simultaneously offering pragmatic solutions. Mazda uses design as a strategic weapon and continues to retain its place at the forefront of contemporary Japanese style. The Taiki concept car, propelled by a new generation of the Renesis rotary engine mounted at the front, crowns a succession of stunning studies made under Laurens van den Acker, Head of Design since May 2006. The organic contours of the model, its bird-like profile and its undulating surfaces, like those of a manta ray, are reminiscent of the golden age of American dream cars of the '50s.

HONDA CR-Z

Keen to hold on to its reputation as a pioneer, Honda never fails to arouse passions with its projects that promise sparkling performance combined with care for their environmental impact. The CR-Z coupé (for Compact Renaissance Zero) is an effective proposition, which accentuates Honda's aggressive house style in a manageable format (4.08 m long). The CR-Z offers sporting spirit with a clean conscience, by using a hybrid power-plant like the one in the company's standard commercial catalogue. Special attention has been paid to the display of information on the dashboard, with particular reference to lighting.

NISSAN ROUND BOX

With its open top, two doors and four distinctly separate seats, the Round Box gives priority to communication. The studied intimacy on board is generated by the car's deliberately reduced length (3.65 m), which forces a kind of positive interaction on its occupants! The project is clearly aimed at younger buyers, and its style, summed up by the 'round box' formula, may lack grace but has spade-loads of individuality. And of course there's the inevitable aircraft-style steering wheel!

MITSUBISHI i-MIEV SPORT

Finally out of its financial difficulties, Mitsubishi is sending out signals of optimism with a compact, lowered, streamlined, sporting concept. As a continuation of its electric vehicle programme, the i-MIEV Sport coupé draws upon the mechanical components of the EZ-MIEV concept car created in 2006, with its motors housed in the wheels. These deliver 20 kW to each of the front wheels and 47 kW to the rear wheels. The four-wheel drive system provides anti-skid and stability control capability. Of almost one-piece construction, the car comes in a package measuring just 3.45 m in length, featuring an exceptionally forward-located driving position.

TOYOTA HI-CT

The marketing men have their sights set on the demographic of the famous 'parasitic singles', who are proliferating in Japan. For this target market, the car will have to change posture while also evolving in use: hence the raised volumes, cubic shapes and often ungraceful contours, which represent a marked departure from accepted aesthetic conventions. Behind its truck-like structure, the Hi-CT (pronounced "City") project conceals built-in electric rollers.

NISSAN NV200

Not many manufacturers choose utility vehicles as a focus for experimentation. Nissan, by contrast, are specialists in the field, but even they have surpassed themselves with this small van measuring 4.38 m in length. The realistic aesthetic solutions will no doubt be deployed to the credit of a mass market model, but for the purposes of this exercise in style, the vehicle is fitted out for oceanographic exploration, with a retractable compartment housing accessories and a built-in multimedia suite.

NISSAN PIVO 2

The future of cars in cities is a thorny issue when you realise that the latest architectural programmes in Tokyo (Art Center, Midtown Center, Roppongi Hills) leave barely any space for either cars, driving or parking. Pivo 2 is a three-seater bubble, capable of pivoting through 360 degrees. It's the work of the Creative Box studio, based in the trendy district of Shibuya, and uses an electric motor called "3D", fed by a lithium-ion battery.

HONDA PUYO

According to its creators, the Puyo was designed to neutralise stress. That's why it cultivates a tame look with its "front end that looks as though it could be the face of a pet", and its softened bodywork "which feels like skin to the touch". The idea echoes Japan's sudden love-affair with pets, which has spawned countless businesses offering wacky wardrobes for Chihuahuas, jewellery for poodles and strollers for fox terriers!

TOYOTA RIN

Japanese designers are always happy to draw upon the most traditional aspects of their culture. Hence this compact (3.25 m long), high-roofed (1.65 m) cube featuring an almost vertical driving position, which is supposed to give a sense of "well-being, comfort and serenity, like a room dedicated to the ceremony of tea-drinking".

Some of the finest new designs

North America is the world's largest car market, accounting for about 20 million sales per year.
For a long time its highest profile auto show has been in Detroit, home of the country's 'Big Three' car manufacturers. But the international standing of the Detroit Auto Show is receding, due to the gradual decline of the 'Big Three' U.S. domestic car companies and the growth of the regional shows of Los Angeles, New York and Chicago.

Collectively the 2008 North American auto shows had much the same volume and quality of new production and concept cars as ever. They still reflect the unique glamour that cars and the car industry have in the U.S., and still celebrate cars and car design with more showmanship than any other nation.
So, whilst Detroit this year showed signs of waning relative to shows past, the North American auto shows still had some of the finest new designs of 2008. **Sam Livingstone** reports.

HUMMER HX

Detroit. The HX is far smaller than any previous Hummer design and is aiming to capture a more youthful spirit, which is in part why it was designed by three designers fresh from college. Essentially, the HX shows how Hummer is looking to produce a vehicle which would compete directly with the Wrangler from their arch rival, Jeep. The HX is similarly open, rugged and has two easily removable doors also, although it is more reminiscent of the Jeep Hurricane concept shown three years ago. Four-wheel drive and powered by a front mounted 3.6-litre V6 engine, the HX relates closely with its production siblings with its grille and head lamp design, and also with its upright shallow windshield and its general square aesthetic.

AUDI CROSS CABRIOLET QUATTRO

Los Angeles. Like many concepts presented
at U.S. auto shows, the Cross Cabriolet was
designed in an L.A. satellite studio. It was
also designed as a new type of California
car that combines two of the region's
popular car types: SUV and cabriolet.
Whilst a new idea, the Cross Cabriolet
concept is based on the soon to be
announced five door Q5 that will sit below
the existing Q7 and above the forthcoming
Q3 in the new Audi SUV model line-up.
Beyond its attractive, but relatively orthodox,
overall design, there are some neat details:
the lower chrome strip at the base of the car,
the 'copper sunset' colour, and the abstract
pattern etched onto the white leather seats.

JEEP RENEGADE

Detroit. The Renegade was one of three
compact Chrysler concepts debuting
that showcased strong environmental
credentials centred on electric power.
In this case, two electric motors and
lithium-ion batteries have their 40 mile
range extended by a 1.5 litre 3-cylinder diesel
engine that charges them on the move.
The Renegade concept was designed to be
part of a water-sports lifestyle, with two sea
scooters integrated into the rear, wet-suit
style neoprene used for the seats, and a
water-proof interior. The overall design is
beach buggy meets classic Jeep, but executed
in a simple and modern way with some
great details such as the way both front and
rear lamps are set into black rubber pods.

LAND ROVER LRX

Detroit. The LRX shows to the world, and particularly the prospective buyers of Land Rover how a smaller, more road-orientated, and more environmentally sensitive Land Rover could be. Underpinning this is a diesel electric hybrid power-train which is claimed would produce less than 120 gr of carbon dioxide per kilometre. The concept is far more dynamic than any previous Land Rover, with a shallow side window that tapers rearwards, short overhangs and a near coupé style rear. The LRX proves that the prospect of a smaller Land Rover has a strong appeal – it will be interesting to see how it might be translated into a production version.

FORD EXPLORER AMERICA

Detroit. The Explorer is one of Ford's most important vehicles, selling in huge numbers at considerable profit. In response to traditional SUV buyers switching to SUVs from import brands or to crossovers, the Explorer America shows the more contemporary direction for the forthcoming production Explorer. Whilst retaining classic SUV proportions, the Explorer America introduces a subtle and clean exterior surface that almost shrink-wraps to the core structure of the car – witness the concave surfaces around the wheel arches. This combines with a smaller V6 engine, a unitary body, and lightweight materials, to make it a far more advanced proposition than the current production model.

GMC DENALI XT

Chicago. Not dissimilar in concept to the Toyota A-BAT shown earlier, the GMC Denali XT is a more car-like and dynamic take on the conventional crew-cab pick-up. Powered by a new GM flex-fuel, direct-injected petrol V8 with 326 bhp, the Denali is either four- or two-wheel drive depending on driver choice. Its design is dominated by archetypal show car features: prominent fenders, huge wheels (23 inches!), shallow glazing and a very masculine identity complete with huge grille. The interior uses a theme of deep-section aluminium surrounds for the instrumentation, door inners and air vents and has a similarly masculine feel to the exterior.

TOYOTA A-BAT

Detroit. The A-BAT is a classic 2008 U.S. auto show concept: designed in L.A., having a hybrid power-train (albeit a well proven one, being that this is a Toyota), clear SUV genes, and being a re-mix of vehicle types that create a slightly more environmentally friendly crossover. With it Toyota is showing how the declining small pick-up market might be re-energised with a more dynamic, car-like design. Conceptually the A-BAT is a low-roofed crew-cab pick-up. As well as different proportions, the A-BAT is notable for its unusual use of colour and finishes. The exterior has a polished aluminium appearance and the interior features extensive use of yellow for the soft elements that cover the exposed light alloy structure.

CHRYSLER ECOVOYAGER

Detroit. The eco in ecoVoyager is provided by the same Chrysler electric engine used in the Jeep and Dodge concepts also shown in Detroit, only this time it powers the front wheels and has its 40-mile range supplemented by a hydrogen fuel cell at the rear of the car. The Voyager part is denoted by the simple mono-space volume of the car – more tear like than its production name-sake – and the spacious and airy interior. The ecoVoyager explores a premium direction with white leather, simplicity, and some key curving feature lines, but it is still several steps removed from production possibility.

SCION HAKO

New York. Taking its name from the Japanese word for 'box', the Hako was designed in Tokyo, despite Scion being Toyota's exclusively American market brand. The design is dominated by its lurid orange colour set off by dark tinted windows, and by its boxy profile that is emphasised by a vertical windscreen and front pillar. The interior carries over the orange and black of the exterior and is particularly innovative with its driver's 'gaming' zone, front passenger's 'entertainment' zone, rear passengers' 'lounge' zone, and in the way the seats are all different. The instrumentation runs from the conventional instrument area over to the static wheel hub.

DODGE ZEO

Detroit. The Dodge ZEO is the third of the trio of Chrysler concepts cars presented at the North American International Auto Show that all feature a 268 bhp electric engine, which in the Dodge has no range extending supplementary power source but sufficient lithium-ion batteries for a range of 250 miles.
The compact four-door coupé looks almost cartoon-like with its low orange body sitting on its huge 23-inch wheels! Opening the butterfly-hinged doors out and upwards reveals the white cabin with four separate slim seats each with an orange seat belt.

MITSUBISHI RA

Detroit. The RA takes various Mitsubishi design cues, such as the forward-leaning front aspect, and successfully combines them in a contemporary two-seat sports coupé design to give a hint perhaps of what to expect from the forthcoming new Eclipse production design.
The *raison d'être* of the car is to showcase a new 2.2-litre production turbo diesel, mated to a six-speed twin clutch transmission, that meets the latest stringent emission legislation, and yet with 204 hp and 310 lb/ft has enough power and torque to require the four-wheel drive platform from the Lancer Evo.

MAZDA FURAI

Detroit. Pronounced 'Foo Rye' and meaning 'the sound of wind', the sublime Furai is the latest in the series of 'Flow' design language Mazda concepts. Based on an American Le Mans series Courage C65 racing chassis, and featuring a 3-rotor rotary engine, the car is clothed in a body defined by flowing lines like the ripples on a sand dune. The super compact interior concentrates much of its control interface on the steering wheel – race car style – but is defined by a seamless sweeping front panel covered in a tactile "dolphin suede" material never seen before in a car.

Ecology, luxury and sporting credentials

March 2008. The Geneva Motor Show has always occupied a privileged place in the calendar. In 2008, it took on a particularly green hue, by virtue of being the first European event held since the entry into force in France of a system of penalties and incentives linked with the CO_2 emissions of new cars, involving reduced taxation on the cleanest models and a surcharge on the polluters.

Against this backdrop, the message sent by manufacturers through their concept cars has to take account of what is now an incontrovertible truth: none can any longer omit to refer to the environmental impact of their creations. But at the same time, all must endeavour to preserve the passion, nurture the desire and stimulate the appetite for this irreplaceable tool of individual mobility. Sporting spirit and luxury, therefore, remain the driving forces of their creativity, as **Serge Bellu** had the pleasure of discovering.

ITALDESIGN-GIUGIARO QUARANTA

To mark the fortieth anniversary of Italdesign, Giorgetto and Fabrizio Giugiaro developed a project aimed at expressing the two facets of their profession: style and design. For its panache and architecture, the Quaranta draws upon the Manta, which, in 1968, became the first prototype to wear the Italdesign badge. Like its ancestor, it's a monolithic sculpture with a minimalist style. The same three front seats are there, with the driver in the middle, but a small additional seat has been squeezed in behind him. The Quaranta uses a hybrid mechanical set-up, of Toyota origin, comprising a 3.3-litre V6 paired up with two electric motors. The solar panels built into the roof and bonnet generate 250 W – enough to recharge the batteries and power the air conditioning.

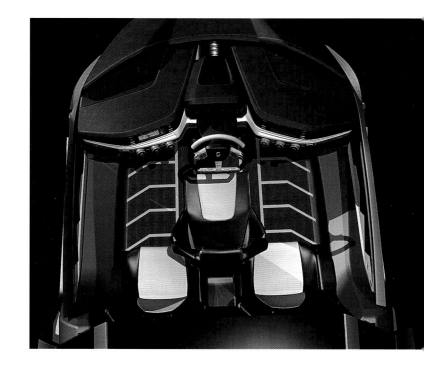

PININFARINA SINTESI

During the show, Pininfarina's management announced the opening up of its capital, with the family thus losing its majority stake in the business. By January 2008, Electric Vehicles Pininfarina Bolloré, owned in equal parts by the two founding entities and dedicated to the production of an electric car with effect from 2009, had already seen the light of day. Aside from its restructuring, Pininfarina has kept the dream alive with the Sintesi, whose lowered silhouette conceals a technology known as 'liquid', comprising four fuel cells delivering 20 kW of power to each wheel. Thanks to this technology spreading the mechanical elements around the passengers, it was possible to re-think the architecture and provide generous interior space in an overall length of less than 4.80 m. The Sintesi marks the official entry onto the scene of Lowie Vermeersch, who was appointed Head of Design in August 2007.

RENAULT MÉGANE COUPÉ

The Mégane Coupé Concept announces the arrival of a product that's already planned. The definitive car will retain the general silhouette of the concept, but some of its individual features will be toned down. On the prototype, produced at G-Studio in Turin, the doors take the form of large wings which fold and spread. The colours and materials play upon the car's sporting character, on the contrasts between scarlet and anthracite, and between the warmth of leather and the cold modernity of carbon. The turbocharged 2-litre engine delivers 200 hp at 5800 rpm and 280 Nm of torque at 2600 rpm.

SAAB 9-X BIO-HYBRID

Prior to the extension of its range, Saab is pursuing its long-term explorations under the leadership of Anthony Lo, Director of Advanced Design for GM Europe. The 9-X Bio-Hybrid project is the outcome of a new crossing of diverse species, in this case, the estate car, coupé and two-door saloon. The front end picks up on the theme introduced with the Aero-X, but the volumes are more conventional and very compact (length restricted to 4.42 m). The rear set-up is highly functional and is equipped with a modular opening system. The hybrid drive comes in the shape of a 1.4-litre 4-cylinder engine (200 hp), which runs on biofuel, paired up with an electric motor powered by a lithium-ion battery.

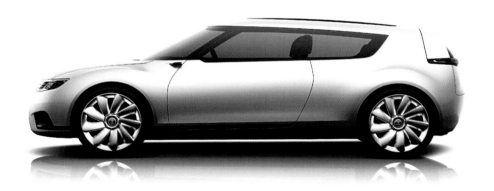

FIORAVANTI HIDRA

Leonardo Fioravanti, a former Head of Styling at Pininfarina, has been independent since 1991 and is a loyal follower of the Geneva Motor Show. He is now flanked by his son, Matteo, who is in charge of design at his company. The Hidra project is a kind of grand touring estate car, which remains very classic in style, but Leonardo Fioravanti has not forgotten his roots as an engineer and always sets great store by coming up with carefully conceived technical solutions. The car is thus equipped with an ingenious system of air-jets in place of conventional windscreen wipers, and in theory could accommodate either conventional batteries for an electric power-plant, or a fuel cell for running on hydrogen. It all depends on which way the environmental winds blow…

HYUNDAI HED-5 i–MODE

It is increasingly inappropriate to attempt to classify the new products of world design according to existing systems of categorisation. Hyundai's latest offering subscribes to the growing tendency to mix genres. The vast and airy volume of the interior has something of the compact MPV, while the exterior profile is more closely aligned with that of a saloon. The overall treatment is resolutely Baroque and reveals an elaborate complexity in the ornamentation and the shape of the windows. The front and rear doors open in opposite directions onto an interior that's dispensed with the central pillar. The Hyundai is powered by a 2.2-litre 4-cylinder turbodiesel (212 hp), which will be inherited by a production model as of 2009.

MAGNA STEYR MILA ALPIN

Established in Austria and inheritor of the great Steyr-Puch marque, Magna Steyr is a major original equipment manufacturer, supplying numerous carmakers with mechanical and body parts, and whose activity also extends to small-series assembly. Aston Martin has thus announced that its future Rapide saloon is to be built by Magna Steyr in Graz. The company also has a Research & Development department, which created this compact (3.54 m long) all-terrain vehicle boasting impeccable environmental credentials. Magna Steyr recommends compressed natural gas (CNG) to power its three-cylinder engine. With its unusual proportions, the Mila Alpin can accommodate three people, plus a fourth in extremis.

ESPACE DÉVELOPPEMENT X80

At 73 years of age, Philippe Guédon, the former chief executive of Matra Automobile, remains an indefatigable unveiler of new dawns for the motor car. He's now tackling the dilemma of the urban car, with his company Espace Développement. The X80 accommodates three people despite its exceptionally small size (2.55 m long). The front bumpers, which telescope as soon as the vehicle starts moving, have been patented. A 750 cc two-cylinder engine is in the pipeline, but for the time being it's no more than a model produced by the Italian coachbuilder Cecomp.

45

The growth goes on

The big news in Beijing was still the growth of the Chinese market; during 2007 car sales increased 20% to exceed five million and make China the second largest market in the world. With income levels rising at over 10% year-on-year, and with the number of car models available doubling every two years, the growth and diversification of the Chinese car market is clearly continuing apace.

This development rate was particularly evident at the Beijing Auto Show in April with a large number of new production car debuts from domestic Chinese car brands, as **Sam Livinstone** witnessed. Whilst many of these were designed by Italian consultancies, there were also more locally developed designs than before. There is now a number of capable automotive design facilities in China and some brands, such as SAIC and JAC, even have European design centres despite having no short-term plans to sell in western markets.

IAT WUFENG CROSS

IAT was established in 2002 in cooperation with the Japanese company International Application Technology, and is the largest independent Chinese automotive design house. As well as capabilities in design and prototype build, it also has power-train and body development facilities to provide a 'one-stop-shop' service for car manufacturers. The Wufeng, which means 'Strong Sharp', is a V6-powered compact four-wheel drive coupé with some SUV genes evident in its details and in its height, which makes for a unique and appealing 'coupé crossover' type of car. Other notable elements of its design are its sweeping side feature line and rear aspect, its dramatic electric-powered butterfly doors, and its marked tumblehome – the way the car tapers upwards when viewed from the front or rear.

GUANGZHOU HONDA LI NIAN

Li Nian is the first car developed by Guangzhou Honda, a manufacturing joint venture between the Chinese Guangzhou and the Japanese Honda. The exterior of Li Nian is in the form of the fashionable and now widespread concept of crossover. With its concise and solid front and smooth side lines, it presents a dynamic and vigorous style. This concept car is supported by Honda technology but no technical details were provided.

FAW HONGQI SUV

The HongQi SUV is the name of this Range Rover-sized SUV concept from First Auto Works' Red Flag brand. The show car is a concept preview of a similar production design expected in 2010 that would feature a range of multi-cylinder engines including the in-house developed V12 engine of the concept. HongQi takes cues from Chinese culture, but several observers felt that there was also a marked similarity in its grille design with the Lincoln Navigator and Mazda style front fenders. A rakish side window shape, sporty front and rear air inlet and outlet grilles, and the distinctive 'boomerang' rear light shapes define the exterior, whilst the interior is modern with an airy and premium feel.

BEIJING 700R

The 700R Concept Coupe is one of the three own-branded concept cars Beijing Automobile has produced. It is the result of in-house research and has a gorgeous appearance with a simplified '北' (Bei) as the logo of '北京' (Beijing). Though no precise announcement was made, production could start as early as 2010, with engines ranging from 1.8 to 3.0 litres. A hybrid version may be developed as well. The interior is equipped with advanced features like Bluetooth and Car Safety View Video System.

SIVAX IZANA

Named after the Japanese god Izanaginomikoto, the Izana is a concept from the Chinese studio of the Japanese automotive design consultancy Sivax. The design is characterised by its classical rear-drive coupé proportions, pronounced fender lines, domed roof to accommodate 2+2 seating, and the clean and modern detail design.

The scissor doors open dramatically to reveal a simple, but premium-feel interior which features innovative amber ambient back-lighting. This is set within unusual, but elegant, copper-finished elements that float above the main door surface, centre console and centre tunnel.

Riding high on the wave of new technology

The Paris Motor Show got under way just days after the opening salvos of the financial crisis, thus casting further shadows over a French car industry already hit by tax penalties on cars that exceed stringent pollution limits. The effect of this backdrop was to encourage all manufacturers to place even more emphasis on ecological considerations. **Serge Bellu** gives us a guided tour of the most interesting concepts.

VENTURI VOLAGE

Gildo Pallanca Pastor has brought Venturi a Leitmotif in the form of electricity. The Volage is the fruit of close collaboration with Michelin, and uses the latter's Active Wheel technology for its drive and suspension. Each wheel develops 55 kW (78 hp), propelling the car from 0 to 100 km/h in less than 5 seconds! Using a touch-screen, the driver can select the setting he wants, to make the car handle like a front or rear-wheel drive, with an over-steering, under-steering or neutral feel, while favouring range over power, or comfort over sporting dynamics. The Volage has the same carbon chassis as the Fétish, thus keeping weight down to 1075 kg. The styling is by Sacha Lakic, a designer with a quirky talent, free of all influences.

GT BY CITROËN

Light-years from the everyday concerns of Citroën, this project was brought to fruition in conjunction with Polyphony, for the latter's Gran Turismo 5 video game. Drafted under the authority of designer Gilles Vidal, with Takumi Yamamoto in charge of exterior design and Pascal Grappey of interior design, the sports coupé exalts the most outrageous styling cues with expressive delight. The prototype was elaborated by Estech, who borrowed the chassis and suspension components from a replica Ford GT 40, and the car will be powered by a fuel cell. The cockpit is stunning, thanks to the use of a stereo-lithographic technique capable of producing complex shapes with a nickel or copper-effect finish. In these forbidding times, it's reassuring to see Citroën turning its hand to an exercise of this type.

LAMBORGHINI ESTOQUE

Lamborghini's spokesmen insist that this is a show car, but developments at Porsche and Aston-Martin have forced the company to put together some ideas for a grand tourer. The design remains faithful to the marque's identity, through its front end and lowered profile, and was produced by the studio of Manfred Fitzgerald, under the watchful eye of Walter de' Silva, Volkswagen Group's Head of Design. The logical solution to the power-plant problem would be to borrow the V10 from the Gallardo LP 560-4 (a 5.2-litre unit developing 560 hp), but there's also talk of using a turbocharged V8, a hybrid and even a diesel! For the record-book, the only four-door Lamborghini ever previously built was the Faena, the sole creation of Pietro Frua, made in 1978.

PEUGEOT RC HY-MOTION 4

Peugeot kicked off the Paris Motor Show under a cloud of inner turmoil. Jérôme Gallix, who succeeded Gérard Welter at the head of the company's Style Centre in 2007, resigned a few days before the show, in the wake of a management re-shuffle at ADN, PSA Peugeot Citroën's research and development centre. Jean-Pierre Ploué, Citroën's Head of Design since 1999, was promoted to Head of Design for both the Group's brands, Peugeot and Citroën. The RC HY-Motion 4 saloon, measuring 4.71 m in length, was conceived, however, under the direction of Jérôme Gallix, and evokes the style that he stamped on the future direction of the brand. The hybrid power-plant combines a mid-mounted 218 hp 1.6-litre petrol engine with a six-speed gearbox and a 95 hp front-mounted electric motor. Peugeot has also set ambitious targets for the car in terms of CO_2 emissions (109 g/km) and aerodynamics (Cx 0.24).

SAAB 9-X AIR

Despite adverse winds and tides, Anthony Lo has perfected a new style for a brand whose identity had faded into the mists of General Motors. Elegant and discreet, the 9-X Air is made in the image of its creator. This cabriolet benefits from the original, patented Canopy Top system, which uses fabric instead of metal, to save weight and space. The canopy folds away naturally and automatically in three parts in the rear compartment. The 9-X Air is powered by a 1.4-litre BioPower engine, which combines a turbocharger with bio-fuel and hybrid technology. With 200 hp under the bonnet, it accelerates from 0 to 100 km/h in 8.1 seconds, while keeping CO_2 emissions down to just 107 g/km on the mixed cycle.

RENAULT ONDELIOS

Renault has never lost its image as the inventor of the MPV. Almost a quarter of a century after the launch of the first Espace, therefore, the one-box cruiser could take its styling cues from the Ondelios, a comfortable, fluid, streamlined monolith with space on-board for six, and an interior inspired by the latest 1st class aircraft cabins. measuring 4.80 m in length, the Ondelios has a drag coefficient of 0.29. Patrick le Quément, Renault's Director of Design, wanted its volume to be treated as a "single-material object, in which bodywork and glazed surfaces blend into one". Stéphane Janin oversaw the work of the Technocentre, while the car was built by G-Studio in Turin. The hybrid power-plant is based on a 2-litre diesel beefed up to give 205 hp and 450 Nm of torque.

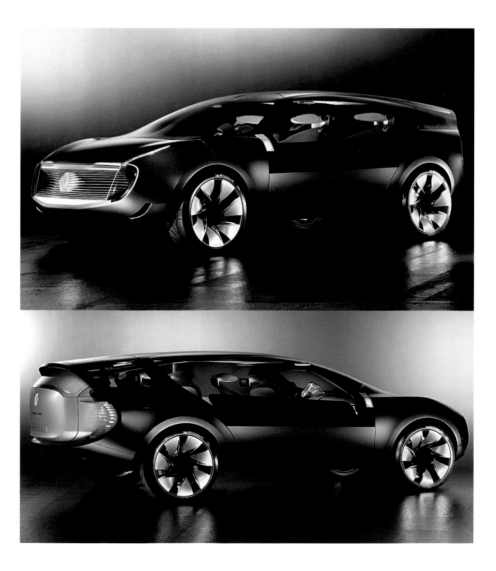

CITROËN HYPNOS

Just as the rigorously rational C3 Picasso was making its appearance, Citroën unveiled a project that impresses first and foremost for sheer size: 4.90 m long by 2.17 m wide! The mechanicals are more modest, with a hybrid power-plant that mates a 200 hp 2-litre diesel with an electric motor housed in the rear axle. Pitched mid-way between a saloon and a 4x4, the Hypnos plays on the ambiguity of the crossover. The styling, which was overseen by Carlo Bonzanigo, oozes virility, with sculpted flanks and interior colour gradations. The low relief on the leather upholstery evokes the architecture of the building that houses the Citroën showroom on the Champs-Élysées in Paris. As for the traditional chevrons, they curve slightly, no doubt announcing the dawn of a new era…

MAZDA KIYORA

After a series of highly futuristic projects, Mazda has toned things down a bit with this creation, by the European team led by Peter Birtwhistle. The work of two French designers – Mickael Loyer on the exterior and Grégory Vera on the interior – this compact, urban saloon (3.77 m long), is the forerunner of a future family model destined for the European market. The accent is on the lightness of the package, courtesy of a visible structure in carbon fibre. The styling is built around the idea of transparency and the flow of water, in keeping with the car's name – Kiyora – which means 'purity' in Japanese. The Kiyora gets an MZR 1.3-litre 4-cylinder direct injection engine, with CO_2 emissions of less than 90 g/km and a Smart Idle Stop System.

HEULIEZ WILL

The French-based based car-body builder, now 60% owned by Argentum Motors, an Indian group, is riding high on the wave of new technology. Visually, the Will has much in common with the Opel Agila, which in turn resembles the Suzuki Splash, but beyond this familiar exterior, everything is new. The project was developed in close collaboration with Michelin, and uses the latter's Active Wheel technology, which includes an electric motor, suspension and braking device in each front wheel, and the same electric suspension in the rear wheels. The Will has two boots, one at the back and one at the front, in the space freed up by the engine. The aim is to bring the Will into production as of late 2009, with a view to manufacturing 5000 units in the first full year.

NISSAN NUVU

According to François Bancon, the man in charge of the project, "the Nuvu is a new take on the city car of tomorrow". Despite its length of less than three metres, it accommodates three seats: a comfortable chair for the driver, and two rather Spartan seats, one next to and one behind him, for passengers. The Nuvu avails itself of electrical energy, the latest weapon in the armoury of Carlos Ghosn, Chairman of Nissan and Renault. A series of small solar collectors in sheet-form are fitted in the glazed roof, and power the lithium-ion batteries via a 'trunk' located behind the driver. As well as offering electronic controls, the Nuvu is expected to have a range of 125 kilometres and a maximum speed of 120 km/h.

BERTONE BAT 11

Geneva. For the first time for aeons, there was no Bertone stand at the Geneva Motor show this year. As the result of an economic crisis that turned into a family quarrel, the BAT 11 was unveiled at a private evening presentation in the city. It shares the same platform as the Alfa Romeo 8C Competizione. Its extrovert style is a homage to the BAT trilogy (the 5, 7 and 9) built between 1953 and 1955, and is the work of the team headed by the faithful David Wilkie, against the most inauspicious backdrop imaginable. The project was commissioned by Gary Kaberle, owner of the 1955 BAT 9 for 45 years!

BMW GINA

Munich. On video, in person, Chris Bangle, BMW Group's Head of Design, explains the philosophy encapsulated in the acronym GINA (Geometry and Functions in 'N' Adaptations, where 'N' means infinite). On a prototype reminiscent of the Z4, a textile 'skin' envelops a structure combining metal and carbon fibre. Certain parts of the structure are mobile, so the bodywork adapts to the needs or wishes of the driver, thus generating a unique sensation of freedom and individuality. Much like the supple bodywork invented by the coachbuilder and aviator, Charles Weymann, in the 1920s… And it is no coincidence that the video is being shown at the new museum belonging to BMW Welt, which has recently been celebrating the marque's future and culture.

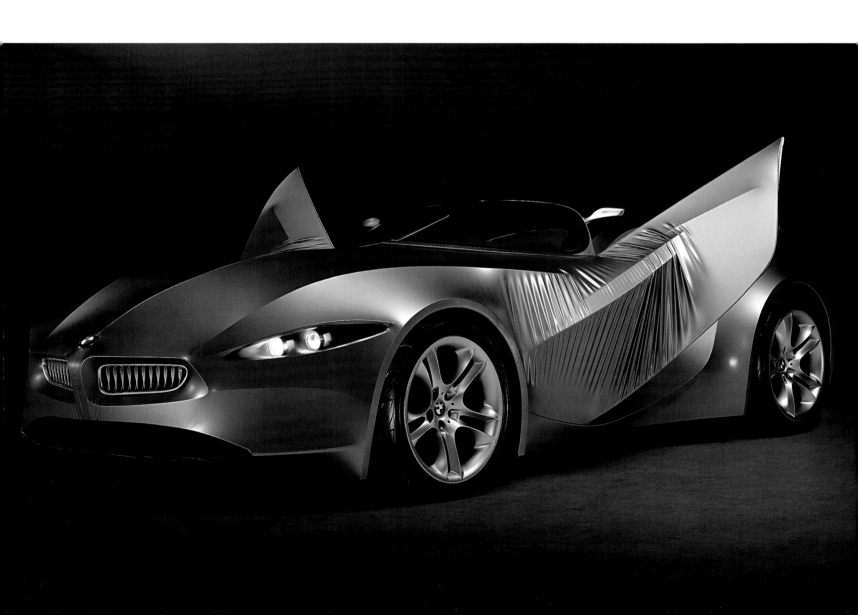

BMW M1 HOMMAGE

Concorso d'Eleganza Villa d'Este. BMW is marking the 30th birthday of its M1 by displaying a contemporary interpretation of the only mid-engined coupé the company has ever produced. But the M1 Hommage is not just loyal to its roots. It's also… orange. The same orange as the 1972 Turbo designed by the Frenchman Paul Bracq, which provided the inspiration for the M1 created six years later by Giugiaro. The M1 Hommage is just a design exercise for the time being and has no engine under the bonnet.

TOURING MASERATI A8GCS BERLINETTA

Concorso d'Eleganza Villa d'Este. Founded in 1926, Carrozzeria Touring closed its gates in 1966. Roland d'Ieteren, the Belgian Volkswagen importer and much more, has decided to revive the Touring name and brings us the A8 GCS Berlinetta, based on the Maserati GranSport whose 4.2-litre V8 it is expected to inherit. Its all-new chassis features a lightweight tubular structure that's a direct descendant of the system used on the Superleggera, which was the pride of Touring. The styling is the work of Louis de Fabribeckers, a 31-year old designer who trained at the ISD in Valenciennes.

PININFARINA ROLLS-ROYCE HYPERION

Pebble Beach Concours d'Elegance. Andrea Pininfarina, Chairman of Pininfarina SpA, died in a road accident on 7th August 2008, a few days before the Pebble Beach Concours d'Elegance. He was due to attend the event to hand over the keys of his latest creation to Roland Hall, for whom it was built. The Hyperion is based on a Rolls-Royce Phantom Drophead Coupe, converted into a 2-seater cabriolet by moving the driving position backwards, which also creates space for hunting guns behind the engine. The body is made of carbon fibre and aluminium, and the clock, supplied by Girard-Perregaux, can be removed from the dashboard and worn as a wrist-watch.

GUANGZHOU A-HEV

Despite being a more regional affair than its Beijing and Shanghai counterparts, the Guangzhou Motor Show still saw the launch of several models new to the Chinese market and the unveiling of an Italian-designed concept car. Two pillars of Bertone – Roberto Piatti, the former managing director of Stile Bertone, and Giuliano Biasio, the company's head of exterior style from 1999 to 2006 – set up Torino Design in March 2006, with a specific view to targeting the Chinese market. The duo had already presented projects for Chery at Beijing in 2006 and Shanghai in 2007, before unveiling this one-box four-door model, designed for use with a hybrid power-plant, at Guangzhou. The car is 4.55 m long, 1.90 m wide and a lofty 1.49 m high, and has rear-hinged rear passenger doors and no central pillar, to maximise ease of access. Guangzhou Automobile Group (GAG) currently builds cars for Honda and Toyota, but will be rolling out its own products as of 2010.

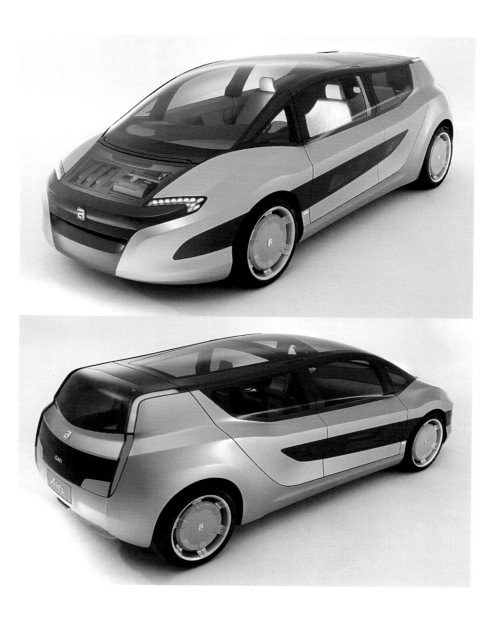

MAZDA KAZAMAI

Moscow. Russia's motor show has become a must for western and Asian car manufacturers, as they rush to stake an early claim in this vast potential market… Mazda has a habit of creating concept cars specially adapted to suit the local public. As such, Moscow saw the unveiling of the Kazamai, a sporting 4x4 with fluid styling characterised by sensual, organic lines, that follows in the footsteps of the Nagare. Relatively compact (4.52 m long by 1.93 m wide), the Kazamai is powered by a latest-generation 2-litre DISI (direct injection spark ignition) petrol engine. Mated with a six-speed gearbox, it promises moderate thirst and low CO_2 emissions.

The story in detail

2008 will be viewed by many as a landmark year for the automotive industry. Against a background of increasingly difficult market conditions, this was the year that the severity of the climate crisis came home to roost with manufacturers.
The message, however, is not all doom and gloom. The team at **CarMen GmbH** has analysed the significant show cars of 2008 and has found a wealth of inventive responses, not only to environmental issues, but also to the questions of the integration of advanced Human Machine Interface (HMI) technologies and the use of strong colour to develop automotive interior design.

ECOFORM

Does "Eco" have its own form language? With the ever-increasing importance of environmental sustainability in the automotive industry, it is clear that designers are trying to find new ways to communicate environmental values. Consequently, two main themes appear to be developing in the latest show cars.
The first theme encompasses the use of more expressive forms taken from nature, as epitomised by Mazda's Furai and Nissan's Forum, to create sexy, sculptural products and details, backed up with sensual, eco-sensitive materials.
The key idea seems to be to communicate a oneness between the vehicle and the natural environment from which it came. It's an approach that allows brands to express sensitivity to environmental issues while maintaining the strong emotional pull that attracts consumers. The second theme is a revisiting of 'form-follows- function'. In this case, clearly demonstrated by the Saab 9-X Bio-Hybrid, eco-credentials are being expressed primarily through a more pragmatic, consumer-product oriented take on aesthetics and materials. This highly rational approach also makes more obvious uses of technology to communicate advanced and efficient operation. The emergence of this pressing need for environmental sustainability presents a fantastic possibility for designers to deeply question current design solutions. This is a real opportunity to redefine interior and exterior automotive architecture and materials and give a new, deeper meaning to "eco-design".

BMW GINA

MAZDA FURAI

NISSAN FORUM

SAAB 9-X

KIA SOUL

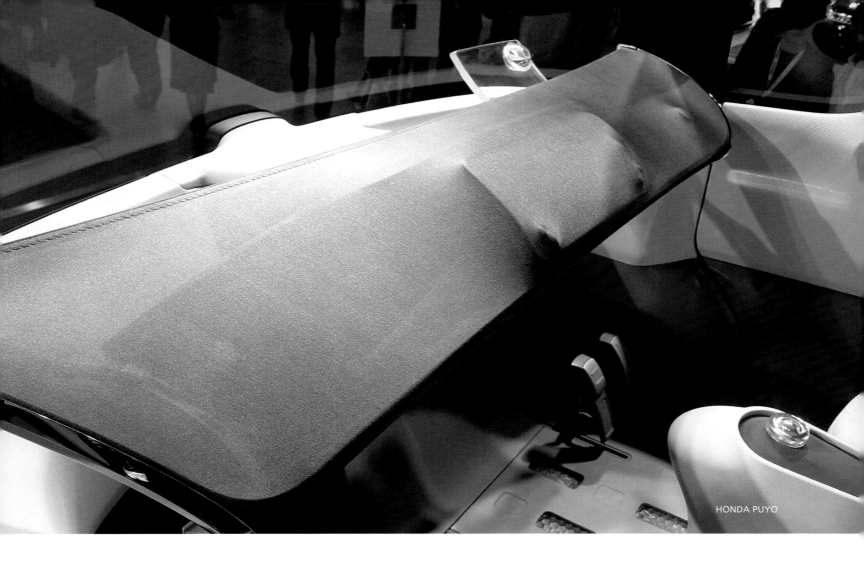

HONDA PUYO

HUMAN MACHINE INTERFACE

Digital technology is revolutionizing the way
we will interface and control our vehicles in the
future. The car will become much more integrated
into our daily life, providing sophisticated
communications systems in addition to mobility.
Brands like BMW and Volkswagen are working
hard to integrate internet services and new interface
technologies into their vehicle systems, often through
strategic alliances with the giants of the tech sector
such as Google and Apple. Our interface with mobile
phones and computers is affecting the functional
expectations we have of our vehicle interiors and the
influence of Apple's advances in interface design is clear
to see. Automotive designers are now looking to employ
touch-screen technology and new "smart materials" to
redefine the architecture and functionality of control areas.
This is a challenging area for the design teams and one
which is bringing some new and exciting solutions. New,
fresh interpretations of form and material are a designer's
everyday work, but true innovation is something special.

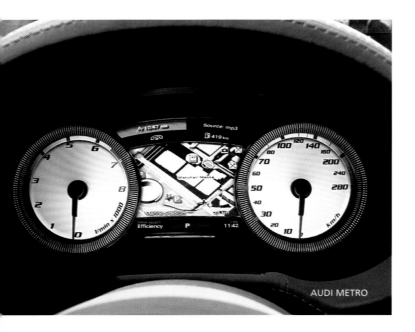

AUDI METRO

PININFARINA SINTESI

LAND ROVER LRX

RENAULT MÉGANE COUPÈ

COLOURS

Over the last decade designers have revitalised automotive interiors with a whole range of new materials, both synthetic and natural. Now, at long last, they've discovered colour! Reflecting the increasing use of strong colours in furniture and product design, automotive interiors are set to follow as designers use colour as another avenue to express individuality. However, rather than being broadly applied, colour is being used for contrast, often in a playful way, against the increasingly 'naked' structural components of automotive interiors. By their very nature, these underlying structures continue to be rendered in a more traditional, technical pallet of greys, blacks and metal finishes but often with innovative new surface textures. Interestingly, the form language of these elements is continuing to shift in a more organic direction, following a trend that has been championed for some time in the architectural realm by Zaha Hadid and Santiago Calatrava.

FORD EXPLORER AMERICA

LAND ROVER LRX

TOYOTA IQ

HYUNDAI iMODE

TOYOTA A-BAT

2008, a year without equal

Under intense pressures both external and internal, the world motor industry underwent historic change in 2008, observes respected author **Karl Ludvigsen**. Both Old and New Worlds showed great vitality as they coped creatively with seismic shifts in tastes and demands.

Two thousand and eight marked a decisive turning point in the history of the motor vehicle. Superficially the driving forces for change were the sharp increase in the price of crude oil, which peaked at more than $140 during July, and the resulting rise in the cost of petrol at the pump. American average price for a gallon of self-serve regular petrol reached $4.00 on 6 June while comparable prices for Europeans neared a tax-burdened $10.00. Even inflation-adjusted these were the highest prices on record for automotive petrol. Yet the real impact in America, the change that had the world's largest car market facing a dramatic upheaval, was more personal. It was the dawn of the $100 tank of petrol. With a 31-gallon tank, a big sport-utility like Chevrolet's Avalanche easily swallowed far more than $100 for a fill-up. Said one Avalanche owner, "Usually I don't let it get real empty so I don't have to see that $100 on the pump." Trauma was even greater for owners of the GMC Yukon with its 38.5-gallon tank. Consequences were striking and immediate. Ford and Chevrolet pickups that led American car sales in the first third of 2008 plummeted from their perches while the comparable Dodge dropped out of the top ten best-sellers altogether. While pickups dropped by one-third in popularity Honda's evergreen Civic soared by one-third to take over as American market leader, followed by Toyota's Corolla. Such was the demand for Civics that year-old cars were attracting higher prices than new ones. The market shift, said a Ford spokesperson, was "totally unprecedented and faster than anything we've ever seen. We recognize that this market is changing dramatically." "All the factors are working against the truck market," commented an analyst. Only those who needed them for work, like building contracts, were still buying pickups, said a dealer: "You aren't going to have the guys who get them as a macho thing any more." And with a housing market hard-hit by the mortgage crisis, even contractors were questioning their need for new pickups. Although Europe had never taken to heart the American passion for pickups, events there were similar – if less

dramatic – in 2008. While big sport-utilities, MPVs and large luxury cars suffered, compact models enjoyed rapid growth. Market leaders were European-style compacts: Volkswagen's Golf, Peugeot's 207 and Ford's Focus in that order. The future outlook was similar, driven by Europe's firm plans to impose limits on the CO_2 emissions of automobiles. While European cars sizes weren't expected to change greatly—they have been under pressure from high petrol costs for a long time—their motivation was set to be drastically and permanently altered. A clear sign of trends in the market was that Volkswagen's special three-litre Lupo, a flop on the market nine years ago, was one of Germany's most-demanded used models.

FUEL AVAILABILITY AND GLOBAL WARMING

These profound changes were driven both by concerns about global warming and by the relentless rise in the cost of auto fuels. While the debate about global warming was vigorous, the scientific consensus was that it was a real phenomenon that demanded reduced production of greenhouse-gas CO2. Public policy throughout the developed world demanded a response from the auto industry. The issue of fuel availability and cost was different. The world had been down that road in the wake of the energy crises of the 1970s, prompting dramatic new initiatives including GM's V8 diesels introduced in 1977. When America was coming out of its early-1980s recession, however, OPEC opened its spigots. Seizing the moment, unenlightened authorities slapped more taxes on diesel fuel that extinguished demand for fuel-saving diesels in America. Quick to forget the years of queuing for fuel, Americans went back to their petrol-hungry cars and trucks. Was this likely to happen again after the crisis year of 2008? It was extremely unlikely. Demands on the petroleum supply were intense and growing. In China alone the rise in energy demand from 2000 to 2007 was 65%, contributing 12% to increased global oil demand. In 2008 China accounted for half the continuing rise in global oil consumption. This was set against supply that was struggling to keep pace.

A compensating factor was that by mid-year of 2008 higher petrol prices were bringing the classic economic result of reduced demand, especially in North America. Americans were driving less. "The U.S. is always quicker to react to changes in international prices," said a Swiss oil analyst. "In Europe the reaction at the pump is a bit less direct." Nevertheless motor-fuel demand was in retreat in France and Germany from mid-year of 2008. Speculation that had driven the oil price to its peak of more than $140 a barrel subsided during 2008. A consensus among experts was that a longer-term price of $120 was likely. This, plus mandated pressure on carbon dioxide emissions, was ample to cause a sea change in the actions of the auto companies and their customers.

That car buyers were changing their desires, said former American Motors CEO Gerald Meyers, "sure looks like it's going to be lasting." Even more importantly, he added, "The auto companies are behaving like it's going to be permanent." The head of one of them, GM's Rick Wagoner, observed that "these higher gasoline prices are changing customer behaviour, and rapidly. We at GM don't believe that this is a spike or temporary shift. We believe that it is, by and large, permanent." The historic change in his industry was welcomed as a challenge by Mike Jackson, head of AutoNation, America's largest retail-dealer organisation. "We are going to have to convince consumers why they should pay more for a smaller engine...or some new technology that is going to give them a tremendous fuel-efficiency benefit. If I have high gas prices and an open-minded consumer, it's very do-able. If we have cheap gasoline, it's impossible." Such was the seismic shift in 2008 that Jackson – and his global retail colleagues – were pushing at an open door.

Biofuels, a palliative that many had hoped would ease pressure on both fuel supply and CO_2 generation, suffered significant setbacks in 2008 that curtailed their future prospects. The year saw the long-expected collision between the demands of fuel production, on the one hand, and the need for food, on the other. The world's peoples and their governments were not about to trade food for motor fuels.

Pointing out that the economic viability of biofuels in the developed world depended heavily on various forms of government subsidies, the respected Organisation for Economic Co-operation and Development (OECD) said that this support "has a limited impact on reducing greenhouse gases and improving energy security, and has a significant impact on world crop prices"—namely an impact upward rather than downward. The OECD was critical of biofuels made from wheat, sugar beets, vegetable oils and corn because their net effect is only a small reduction in greenhouse gases. The OECD was happier with the South American use of sugar cane to make ethanol fuel, a process giving an 80% reduction in greenhouse emissions. Having led since the energy crisis years in the growth and use of ethanol fuel, Brazil was being joined by Argentina, Colombia and Peru as biofuels producers, some making biodiesel from soy beans. In the United States which – perhaps surprisingly – led the world in biofuels production, controversy reigned in 2008 over the crops' impact on conventional agriculture. Some, sensibly, urged a reduction in the U.S.'s 51-cent duty per gallon of imported Brazilian ethanol. Biofuels' impact on food production wasn't hypothetical. Researchers reported price rises of 8% for grains and 17% for oils as a result of government biofuels policies. Mirroring these increases in 2008 were continued sharp rises in the cost of raw materials critical to the motor industry. Auto makers like Audi and Jaguar who had bet heavily on aluminium to reduce weight were penalised by record high prices for that metal. "For some classes of vehicles aluminium-intensive bodies will work," said Jim Queen, GM's Vice President of Global Engineering; "for many others they just won't pay." In the near term the increase in demand from the developing world, especially China and India, is pushing up materials costs, including a 63% rise in steel prices from 2007. "Since 2004 we have additional costs amounting to €800 million for raw materials," said BMW purchasing chief Herbert Diess. He was fighting the efforts – successful so far – of component suppliers to pass on the added cost to auto makers.

DOWNSIZING

Even the maker of the world's cheapest car, the Tata Nano, feared that its plan to offer a fully fledged motor vehicle for the equivalent of only $2500 was placed in jeopardy by rising materials costs. India's Tata rebooted the agenda for the world's car makers in January of 2008 when it introduced its four-door, rear-engined Nano as a step up from the nation's swarms of scooters and motorcycles, forecasting eventual sales of one million units. Its sensationally low price was half that of the world's next least costly car, China's Chery QQ. In May India's Bajaj Auto announced its response. Jointly with closely linked Renault and Nissan, each of which owned one-quarter of the venture, Bajaj would launch its $2500 contender, code-named ULC for 'Ultra-Low Cost', in 2011. To the effort Renault brought the expertise of

its Romania-based Dacia Logan project, which shocked its European contemporaries in 2004 with a base price of only €5,000. Impressively profitable, the Logan has been joined on the market by its hatchback sister the Sandero, costing €7,500. Profitability comes from an option list that prices real-world Sanderos as high as €11,600. EFC for 'Entry Family Car' is Toyota's code name for its new challenger at the bottom of the market to be made both in India and Brazil. Its original plan to base the EFC on its Yaris was rejected in favour of a ground-up approach. Only that way could Toyota match the Nano, on which "Tata's engineers really, really scrutinised the car's design to provide the most value possible for the customer," according to GM's Jim Queen. "They went right down to the gnat's ass on some of this stuff." Low-cost cars from both East Europe and the Third

World, rising petrol and material prices and pressure to reduce greenhouse gases presented auto makers in the OECD nations with a radically new paradigm in 2008. They also had to accommodate the whims and knee-jerk reactions of their national governments. Spain, for example, was cutting speed limits to 50 mph as part of a 31-point package to reduce its oil imports. Britain framed its car taxes to penalise high CO_2 emissions while China graduated taxes according to engine size from 1% for the smallest to 20% for the largest. Governments also played roles in efforts to increase the use of electric cars. Although their role in greenhouse-gas reduction was debated, depending on the cleanliness of their power source, electrics at least had the merit of reducing emissions in the urban areas to which they were best suited. Most aggressive in forging relationships with governments was Nissan, whose Carlos Ghosn committed it to electric-car production in 2010. Shared with its partner Renault, Nissan's initiative depended heavily on the help of governments like that of Israel, which cut the normal purchase tax of 72% to only 10% for electric cars. Oil-poor and compact, with 90% of its residents driving less than 50 kilometres daily, Israel was seen as ideal for electric-car exploitation. "Whoever puts the most incentive on the table is going to get the technology first," said Renault-Nissan's Ghosn. Other countries joining his club were Denmark and Portugal. Pure electrics still stuttered in America, where a reliable 100 miles was seen as the minimum daily range for a battery-powered car. Learning from the fiasco of its two-passenger EV-1, General Motors was readying its series-hybrid Chevrolet Volt for a 2010 launch. It will have a small engine to top up its batteries for ranges beyond an electric-only 40 miles. In Britain GM was proffering the incentive of production of a European version of the Volt in a Vauxhall plant to encourage the government to support its idea of 'super credits' for low-emissions vehicles to balance the rest of its models to attain the fleet average of 130 grams per kilometre of CO_2 that the E.U. was expected to mandate. The Holy Grail of electric and hybrid vehicles, successful use of the energy-packed lithium-ion batteries that power laptops, was realised in 2008 by California's Tesla Motors for its $100,000 sports car and Fisker for its $80,000 Karma saloon. Tesla also announced plans for a $60,000 saloon model. Mainstream use of lithium-ion batteries was initiated by Mercedes-Benz with the 2009 launch of the hybrid version of its S-Class model. Supplied by Continental, using cells made in Japan by its business ally Enax, its batteries are kept cool by the car's air-conditioning system. BMW concentrated on a pure electric car to be launched in 2012 while Volkswagen's lithium-ion partner for a 2010 hybrid is Sanyo. Well aware that not even 'super credits' from electric cars would adequately reduce their fleet CO_2 emissions, auto makers began making radical changes in their engines in 2008. Though their buzzword was 'downsizing', it dawned on several of them that this wasn't a concept likely to appeal to customers, so 'rightsizing' became the mantra. Be that as it may, the result will be sixes in place of eights, fours in place of sixes and triples replacing fours—all in aid of lower petrol consumption and reduced CO_2 emissions. How are these smaller engines expected to cope? Much as had been the case in America under similar circumstances in the early 1980s, the answer was turbo-supercharging. Reducing engine displacement while restoring power with an exhaust-driven turbocharger offered the potential of a 15 to 20% fuel-economy improvement for comparable performance, even 25% with direct fuel injection. Poster child for the process is Volkswagen's 1.4-litre TSI engine, which combines turbocharging with supercharging to mimic the power and torque of a large unit. "Customers are gradually getting used to the idea that a bigger displacement isn't necessarily good," said GM Europe chief executive Carl-Peter Forster, an exponent of 'rightsizing'. The new trend was flagged at the end of 2006 by Burkhard Göschel of BMW, which had always been adamantly opposed to turbocharged engines. "What we are doing in the car industry," Göschel said, "and you can see this at BMW, is that we are shifting over to turbocharged engines with a high point of efficiency. In the future we will have downsized engines with turbochargers." This marked a tectonic shift that gained momentum in 2008. So dramatic is the transformation that two companies that had never previously built turbos, Bosch and Mahle, formed a joint venture in mid-2008 to start producing them in 2011 for both diesels – on which they were already virtually standard – and petrol engines. Honeywell, inheritor of the long turbo tradition of AlliedSignal and Garrett AiResearch, was chosen by Ford as its supplier for a new 2010 V6 engine, while BorgWarner aims to double its European turbo capacity. Others making new turbo investments are Continental and a joint venture between Daimler AG and Japan's IHI Group. Needless to say, turbocharged and direct-injected petrol engines are more expensive. Volkswagen's twin-blower TSI four is thought to rival the added cost of a diesel.

ALLIANCES

Combined with the pressure from raw-material prices, retail costs of cars are expected to rise by an estimated €2000. Small wonder then that there's intense interest in the cost-reduction strategies shown by the Logan and Nano. As well, car makers are seeking new alliances to gain the economies of scale they need to keep costs under control. Strikingly revived under the no-nonsense stewardship of Sergio Marchionne, Fiat was at the nexus of several alliances in 2008. Ford unveiled its new Ka, replacing the original whose cheeky style, dating from the Jac Nasser era, endured for 12 years. Sharing a platform with Fiat's 500, it is built in a joint-venture factory in Poland. Fiat was also in talks with BMW about a product-sharing alliance centred on their respective Alfa Romeo and MINI brands. Assembly in North America was on many boardroom agendas in view of the dollar's continuing weakness against the euro. Reflecting the sharp shift in the U.S. market, Toyota announced its plan to start producing its Prius there in 2010 while reducing its local assembly of sport-utilities. A major mid-year announcement was Volkswagen's decision to invest $1 billion in a plant in Chattanooga, Tennessee to produce a

new mid-sized saloon from 2011. GM supported its struggling Saab arm with a plan to produce a model in the United States. Speaking of struggling, in March of 2008 Ford and Tata announced their agreement to shift the beleaguered Jaguar and Land Rover operations to the Indian company's account. In its dowry Ford provided the new Jaguar XF saloon, fortunately for fans of the leaping cat an impressive model. Relishing its new global role, Tata was in talks with Chrysler about distributing some Jeep models in India. The two companies are already co-operating on development of an electric car. Meanwhile Ford CEO Alan Mulally left open the issue of whether he was also prepared to consider spinning off Volvo. Straining under an eye-watering $67 billion of losses over the past three years, General Motors announced plans to recoup $15 billion. Two-thirds were to come from internal measures while one-third was to flow from asset sales. For the latter GM was looking to Chinese sources as well as to India, where Mahindra & Mahindra – edged out by Tata in the race for Ford's luxury brands – was a candidate to take over Hummer to assist a planned 2009 launch of its vehicles in America. All auto makers were strategising in 2008 to expand their market reach. Nissan was implementing a long-nurtured plan to bring its Infiniti marque to Europe, with first deliveries planned for 2009. In June Ford strengthened its East European reach by taking over a former Daewoo plant in Romania that was originally established by Citroën. From 2009 it would make light commercials and then cars. Emerging nations were targeted by the Japanese auto makers, who realised that they'd been too cautious in their efforts in China. They didn't want to miss the Third World's next boom country. One such was clearly Russia, which roared past Germany in 2008 to become Europe's largest national car market. There Mitsubishi allied with PSA Peugeot Citroën to set up a car and SUV plant for all three marques. Russia's largest domestic producer, AvtoVAZ, gained an important new partner in 2008 when Renault spent $1 billion to acquire a 25% share in the Volga-based company. By far the most popular domestic brand, its Lada range will be enhanced in 2010 by the addition of two new models on Renault platforms.

BEST SELLERS IN THE USA

	Make	Sales*	Variation	Market share
1	General Motors	2,412,666	-17.77%	22.40 %
2	Toyota (with Lexus, Scion)	1,793,302	-10.41%	16.65 %
3	Ford Motor Co**	1,587,670	-17.98%	14.74 %
4	Chrysler	1,183,519	-25.04%	10.99 %
5	Honda (with Acura)	1,180,583	-1.08%	10.96 %
6	Nissan (with Infiniti)	785,699	-3.36%	7.29 %
7	Hyundai (with Kia)	565,752	-4.18%	5.25 %
8	Volkswagen Group	243,371	-1.28%	2.26 %
9	BMW Group	236,660	-4.80%	2.19 %
10	Mazda	215,408	-5.69%	2.00 %
11	Daimler	195,629	+8.40%	1.81 %
12	Subaru	143,789	+3.73%	1.33 %
13	Mitsubishi	80,105	-24.30%	0.74 %
14	Suzuki	74,517	-9.13%	0.69 %
15	Jaguar + Land Rover***	35,102	-27.01%	0.32 %
16	Porsche	21,076	-19.80%	0.19 %
17	Isuzu	4,189	-24.30%	0.04 %
	Total USA	**10,766,177**		**- 12.84%**

*Sales January through September 2008
** Without Jaguar and Land Rover
*** Ford Motor Company until March 2008, then Tata Group

BEST SELLERS IN EUROPE

	Make	Sales*	Variation	Market share
1	Volkswagen	1,211,549	-2.1%	10.3%
2	Ford	975,087	-3.7%	8.3%
3	Opel/Vauxhall	935,464	-10.7%	7.9%
4	Renault	883,662	-3.7%	7.5%
5	Peugeot	810,484	-5.8%	6.9%
6	Fiat	765,277	+2.1%	6.5%
7	Citroën	678,516	+3.7%	5.8%
8	Toyota	608,529	-12.2%	5.2%
9	Mercedes	547,654	-4.6%	4.7%
10	BMW	529,189	+1.1%	4.5%
11	Audi	507,169	-0.1%	4.3%
12	Skoda	359,738	-1.2%	3.0%
13	Nissan	277,081	+16.7%	2.3%
14	Seat	268,335	-9.8%	2.3%
15	Honda	215,738	-13.4%	1.8%
16	Hyundai	214,304	-6.8%	1.8%
17	Suzuki	202,374	-7.6%	1.7%
18	Mazda	202,287	+8.1%	1.7%
19	Kia	188,047	+0.1%	1.6%
20	Volvo	176,569	-11.0%	1.5%
21	Chevrolet	147,268	-4.3%	1.3%
22	Dacia	138,452	+11.1%	1.2%
23	MINI	118,541	+8.8%	1.0%
24	Mitsubishi	96,706	-12.9%	0.8%
25	Lancia	89,487	-7.8%	0.7%
26	Alfa Romeo	78,619	-30.6%	0.7%
27	Chrysler	77,117	-15.3%	0.7%
28	Smart	76,811	+15.7%	0.7%
29	Land Rover	58,327	-28.1%	0.5%
30	Saab	52,410	-17.8%	0.5%
31	Jaguar	30,958	+15.8%	0.3%
32	Lexus	23,232	-26.1%	0.2%
	Total Europe	**11,710,521**		**- 4.44%**

* Private cars registered from January through September 2008 in the 27 countries members of the European community, Norway and Switzerland

BEST SELLERS IN JAPAN

	Make	Sales*	Variation	Market share
1	Toyota	1,026,669	-0.98%	30.51%
2	Nissan	480,708	-2.35%	14.28%
3	Honda	456,433	+4.82%	13.56%
4	Suzuki	420,975	+0.73%	12.51%
5	Daihatsu	395,141	+2.54%	11.74%
6	Mazda	173,787	+2.02%	5.16%
7	Subaru	117,970	-3.11%	3.50%
8	Mitsubishi	114,615	-14.15%	3.40%
9	Lexus	20,168	-24.98%	0.59%
	Total Japan	**3,364,489**		**- 0.89%**

* Private cars registered from January through September 2008

Source: Automotive News Data Center

AvtoVaz aims to be making 1.5 million cars yearly by 2015. At the industry's macro level, Ford, which lost its number two spot in world sales five years ago, slipped to fourth when the Volkswagen Group edged past. With efficiency-conscious Porsche having taken a majority holding in Volkswagen, the Group's outlook improved further during 2008. Korea's Hyundai-Kia Automotive Group took fifth place, moving past both Honda and Nissan thanks to strong sales both at home and abroad. In this historic year the 77-year reign of General Motors as the global sales leader came to an end, the coup de grâce administered by Toyota. Calling industry leadership "a badge of honour" in 2007, GM chief executive Rick Wagoner said, "We're going to fight to keep the position, and if one day we lose it, we'll fight to get it back." After 2007, when GM led by only 3100 vehicles, Toyota advanced on a wide front to take the laurels in 2008. Wounded giant GM will indeed fight to regain the title. But it has more rivals than ever and in more parts of the world. From 2008, a year without equal in the industry's history, the clock is restarting – now.

There's electricity in the air

Brooding skies loom heavy over Europe's car industry, reports **Xavier Chimits**. Dragged down by lacklustre performance in southern Europe, sales had already started falling before the first waves of the financial crisis broke. Against this backdrop, the pomp of the Paris Motor Show could easily have resembled the orchestra on the Titanic playing on, as the look-out finally spotted the iceberg. But manufacturers managed to avoid this trap, by keeping ahead of the game. Admittedly, centre stage in Paris was taken by the Mk 6 Volkswagen Golf, the Mk 5 BMW 7 Series (both omitted from this review because they're so similar to the models they replace) and the Renault Mégane. Beyond this thread of continuity, there was a palpable new passion for electric and hybrid vehicles. Almost every manufacturer had some on show. Carlos Ghosn sung the praises of the Mégane in his speech, before promptly posing for photographs in front of the prototype of Renault's electric car. Never mind the Mégane, the mainstay of the Renault range… On the first day of the show, Carlos Ghosn wanted to associate himself and Renault with electric cars. But the electric Renault won't be out until 2011, and the Chevrolet Volt – expected to be re-badged as an Opel in Europe – until 2010. The only European electric car to hit the road in the meantime, will be the Pininfarina financed by the Bolloré group. The Paris show pointed to a parting of the ways. The capacity of batteries still limits the use of electric vehicles for out-of-town use. But as hybrids need two motors, they don't come cheap. So electric vehicles and hybrids are set to carve out their own space in a market that will still be dominated by combustion-engined models for the next two to three decades – and it's the latter that will bring the biggest energy savings in the future. BMW has been quick to grasp this. The Bavarian manufacturer's stand was encircled by white BMWs, their flanks marked with their respective CO_2 emissions and the simple statement: Best in Class.

PININFARINA B°

The French industrialist Vincent Bolloré has been working on a lithium-metal-polymer battery for 15 years, and is now venturing into the world of electric cars in partnership with Pininfarina. Lithium-metal-polymer batteries are designed to operate at 80° C and, unlike lithium-ion batteries, they don't need cooling. The B° (its provisional name) will hit the road at the end of 2009, but orders will be taken as of the car's definitive presentation at the next Geneva motor show. Its appearance, in the meantime, is likely to remain broadly unchanged. Equipped with an electric motor between the front wheels, 300 kg of batteries under the seats and a series of photo-electric cells on the bonnet and roof, the car will have a range of 250 km.

THINK CITY

The Norwegian company, Think, has been betting on electric cars since 1991. And it's not had a smooth ride: divorced from Ford in 2003, it went bankrupt in 2005, before being reborn thanks to an injection of Norwegian capital. Think is now selling the latest incarnation of the City, a three-door, four-seater city car measuring 3.12 m in length. Capable of 100 km/h, it has a range of 200 km and recharges in four hours. But you still need a private garage to recharge the batteries – a rare luxury in town – which is one of several limitations of all-electric vehicles.

FORD KA

New Ka, new style! While the first Ka, launched in 1996, derived from the New Edge Design prevailing at Ford at the time, its successor, built on the same platform as the Fiat 500, embraces the cheeky, rounded shape of the latest city cars, while adopting a raked belt-line to point up its dynamic character. Measuring 3.55 m in length, the Ka offers a choice of two engines: a 69 hp 1.2-litre petrol and a 75 hp 1.3-litre diesel. But since this three-door hatchback is aimed at young, urban buyers, it offers three individual trims based on the three special editions: Digital Art, Grand Prix and Tattoo. So just pick the Ka for the way you are!

DACIA SANDERO

The Dacia family is growing. After its seven-seat estate and before its pick-up, Dacia is proud to present the Sandero, manufactured for the moment in Brazil and Romania. In shape and size (4.02 m), the Sandero clearly draws inspiration from the Mk 3 Renault Clio, and true to Dacia tradition, it comes with a big boot (320 l) and a small price tag (€7800). But at this price, equipment levels are Spartan and there's no power steering. The Sandero will make its debut with two petrol engines – a 75 hp 1.4 and a 90 hp 1.6 – soon to be beefed up with an 85 hp 1.5 diesel.

FORD FIESTA

The Fiesta had faded more and more anonymously into the urban landscape. So Ford decided to give its star model a complete makeover. The latest generation Fiesta thus swaps the bland features of its predecessors for the ultra-taut lines of Ford's new house-style, complete with low side windows, ridged waistline and streamlined headlamps stretching way back along the wings. But it's not just the styling that's original: unlike its rivals, the Fiesta (3.95 m) has chosen not to grow in size, as part of a strict weight-watching regime. The new Fiesta is available with four petrol engines, ranging from 60 to 120 hp, and two diesels, delivering 68 and 90 hp.

CITROËN C3 PICASSO

Citroën is due to launch its small MPV (4.08 m) before the new C3 on which it's based. A shade longer than its Opel Meriva and Renault Grand Modus rivals, and featuring two-box architecture, the C3 Picasso offers class-leading load capacity of 385 litres, or 500 litres with the sliding rear seat fully forward, and 1506 litres with the rear seat folded. Four engines are on the menu: two petrols, delivering 95 and 120 hp, and two HDi units, offering 90 and 110 hp.

ALFA ROMEO MITO

The name is an amalgam of 'Mi' for 'Milano', where it was designed, and 'To' for 'Torino', where it is made. Positioned, by virtue of size (4.06 m) and spirit, mid-way between the MINI and the Audi A3, the smallest Alfa is Italian to the tips of its toes, with a purebred, sensual, dynamic look and a front end inspired by the 8C Competizione. Available in three-door guise only, it can be well-mannered around town, feline on the open road and limpet-like on wet tarmac, thanks to a button for selecting three driving modes: sport, normal or all weather. The MiTo starts its career with two petrol engines (a 1.4 delivering 120 or 155 hp) and two diesels (a 90 hp 1.3 and a 120 hp 1.6), but you don't need a crystal ball to predict that the range will soon see the addition of some hotter versions.

RENAULT MÉGANE

Unlike the Volkswagen Golf, the Mégane is still in search of itself, so here's a third generation and a third new style! But at least the new Mégane escapes the fault of recent Renaults, which were not consensual enough, and its front end expresses true personality, with a ridge emerging from the windscreen pillars and sweeping round the bonnet. With a length of 4.30 m, the Mégane has one of the largest boots in its class, at 405 litres. The tailgate on the coupé version, meanwhile, extends the slope of the roof, to underscore the car's sporting look. The range includes three petrol engines (110, 140 and 180 hp) and six diesels (from 85 to 160 hp).

OPEL INSIGNIA

In the wake of declining demand for family saloons, Opel has pensioned off the Vectra. Much longer (4.83 m) than its predecessor, the Insignia makes a break with the past with its fluid four-door coupé styling, accentuated with a comma carved into the front doors. The four-door will be complemented with other versions, including hatchback, estate and AWD variants. Designed to replace the Signum too, the Insignia offers a choice of seven engines, topping out at 260 hp (2.8 V6 petrol) and 160 hp (2.0 diesel).

LANCIA DELTA

Lancia is staking nothing less than its survival on the Delta. Although built to a low budget, on a platform shared with the Fiat Bravo, which in turn came from the old Stilo, the car is aiming high, firstly in terms of its size (4.52 m) and racy silhouette; secondly in terms of its refinement, complete with two-tone paint, sliding and reclining rear seats and Alcantara or full-grain leather upholstery; and lastly in terms of its flagship engines (a 190 hp 1.9 JTD and a 200 hp turbocharged direct injection petrol unit) and range of high-tech equipment, including piloted suspension and active steering. The Delta thus joins the exclusive club of premium compact cars.

CITROËN C5

Let's face it, the old C5 had no character. Its replacement, by contrast, features taut, elegant lines, which bear witness to Citroën's stylistic renaissance. The interior, meanwhile, is futuristic, and it even takes a bit of time for your fingers to get used to where all the switchgear is on the fixed-hub steering wheel. But the long C5 (4.78 m) represents a departure from the Citroën tradition of Hydractive suspension on its large cruisers, because entry-level models come with standard steel springs instead! The C5 has the same chink in its armour as other French flagship saloons, though, with power output peaking at 210 hp on the petrol versions, and 173 hp on the diesels.

RENAULT KOLEOS

Renault finally goes 4x4. As a child of the
Alliance, the Koleos owes much to Nissan (it's
based on the X-Trail platform) and shares its
bodywork with the Samsung QM5. This compact
4x4 (4.52 m) subscribes to the latest trend, by
offering a 4x2 version for €2000 less. Its styling
is consensual, but despite being a bit stodgy
on the road, because of its comfort-orientated
dynamics, the Koleos is surprisingly alert off it,
with its differential lock and hill descent control.
There's even a screen to show the driver the
vehicle's angle of inclination and steering angle.

AUDI Q5

After starting at the top with the Q7, Audi
is now working its way down the SUV ladder
with the Q5 (4.63 m), designed to take on
the BMW X3 and Mercedes GLK. With a low
roof (1.63 m), flowing lines and raked tailgate,
it looks more like a raised estate car than an
off-roader, and will be hard put to stake out
different territory from the A4 Allroad due for
release in mid-2009. Whether straight-four
or V6, all of the Q5's engines are mounted
longitudinally, leaving room lower down
the ladder for the future Q3 with transverse
power-plant, due out at the end of 2009,
which will complete Audi's SUV line-up!

FORD KUGA

As is often the case (Focus CC, C-Max),
Ford was the last of the major players to enter
a new market segment. The advantage? It
gave them time to see how tastes evolved
and then respond accordingly. The Kuga
thus subscribes to the latest trend in compact
SUVs, which now resemble raised estate
cars more than true off-roaders. Its fluid
lines are enhanced with some nice – though
artificial – design touches, such as false side
air intakes and a double scoop on the bonnet,
and the Kuga's on-road agility is almost
saloon-like. It also comes in a 4x2 version that
costs €2000 less, but the car's boot is small
(410 l) for an SUV of this size (4.44 m).

MERCEDES GLK

While SUVs are generally losing their rough edges and coming to resemble high-riding estate cars, the GLK is going against the trend. With its jutting angles, straight roof and compact size (4.53 m), it takes its styling cues from the Mercedes G. Just to let you know that of all the well-bred SUVs, this is the one that's least afraid of the rough stuff. The GLK (K stands for *Kurz*, meaning short in German) also comes in two different configurations, namely Sport pack and Off-Road pack, which changes its driving dynamics for off-road use. The GLK is available with four engines: the 280 (231 hp), 350 (272 hp), 220 CDI (170 hp) and 320 CDI (224 hp).

VOLVO XC60

The immense XC90 puts the emphasis on comfort. The XC60 (4.63 m) embraces two other values: agility and safety. Available with three engines (a 285 hp 3.0-litre and a 2.4D in 163 or 185 hp versions), it features fluid lines, a lowish roof (1.69 m), muscular flanks and slender light clusters mounted high on the wings. The XC60 thus sends out a message of dynamism, in keeping with the qualities of its Ford Mondeo chassis. What's more, standard equipment includes an unprecedented system for preventing low-speed collisions: at speeds of up to 30 km/h, a laser sweeps the road ahead and applies the brakes if it detects the risk of a collision and the driver fails to react!

BMW X6

The concept is peculiar. What, after all, is the point of an off-road four-door coupé? The X6 is basically an X5 with the bodywork re-designed from the central pillar back. It has the same weight (2100 kg), length (4.85 m) and on-road manners as the X5, and the same off-road capability, with ground clearance of 20 cm. The same engines too: 3.5i 306 hp, 5.0i 407 hp, 3.0d 235 hp, 3.5d 286 hp. But it costs about €4000 more, despite accommodating just four people as against the X5's seven, thanks to the latter's third row of two fold-away seats… So who's the X6 aimed at? Presumably, empty-nesters keen to carry on enjoying the pleasures of SUV motoring without the kids in tow…

ROLLS-ROYCE PHANTOM COUPÉ

After the Phantom cabriolet with teak
decking, it's now the turn of the coupé.
The doors are still rear-hinged, but the
suspension and steering have been stiffened,
while a Sport setting makes the auto
gearbox more responsive. Rolls-Royce thus
describes this Phantom as "dynamic", which
is hardly the first adjective that springs
to mind when describing a coupé that's
5.61 m long and weighs in at 2590 kg.
Having said that, armed with a 460 hp
6.75-litre V12 , the Phantom Coupé does get
from 0-100 km/h in less than six seconds.

VOLKSWAGEN SCIROCCO

Bringing nostalgia in its wake, the Scirocco is blowing once again on the coupé segment. Based on the Iroc concept car unveiled in 2006, it has lost the green paint and trapezoidal grille, which was too close to the Audi house-style. But the essence has remained, including the car's compact size (4.26 m), curving flanks and fastback silhouette. The Scirocco inherits its platform from the Mk V Golf, as well as the latter's best-performing engines, namely the 1.4 TSI (122 or 160 hp) and 2.0 TSI (200 hp). Pending a 170 hp version, the TDI 140 is keeping a lower profile by adopting a common rail system. And as befits a coupé, the Scirocco has two separate seats in the back.

ARTEGA GT

Founded by Paragon, an original equipment manufacturer, and based in Westphalia in Germany, Artega, advised by Karl-Heinz Kalbfell (formerly of BMW, Rolls-Royce and Maserati), has just brought its first model into production. Designed by Henrik Fisker and equipped with a mid-mounted 300 hp 3.6-litre V6 of Volkswagen origin and a 6-speed DSG gearbox, the GT is currently available in two-seater coupé form, pending the arrival of a roadster version. Its compact size (4.01 m) and carbon-aluminium structure help the Artega keep its weight down to 1100 kilos. According to its creators, it has a top speed of 272 km/h and does 0 to 100 km/h in less than five seconds.

LOTUS EVORA

At last, something really new from Lotus, and not just an umpteenth variation on the Elise theme! Measuring 4.34 m, the Evora is a mid-engined 2+2 coupé, with a 276 hp 3.5-litre V6 of Toyota origin. With a 0 to 100 km/h time of less than five seconds, the Evora goes head to head with the Porsche Cayman S and BMW Z4 Coupé. But while its contours and low roof (1.22 m) make it very much a Lotus, the Evora doesn't share the Spartan spirit of its siblings, and comes with a refined interior, air conditioning and Isofix fittings for the rear seats! All this takes its toll on the car's weight, which amounts to 1350 kilos. The range should soon see the addition of some leaner, meaner versions.

FERRARI CALIFORNIA

The success of the Bentley Continental – a GT that's suitable for everyday use – riles Ferrari. Maranello's response, therefore, is called the California and is Ferrari's first ever model with a front-mounted V8. Slightly longer (4.56 m) than an F430, the California puts the emphasis on user-friendliness, with a fold-away hard top, 2+2 layout, 360-litre boot and even a folding rear seat! The fourth Ferrari line has not, however, taken its manufacturer into a new pastures. With its 460 hp direct injection 4.3-litre V8 engine, aluminium body, 0 to 100 km/h time of four seconds, optional F1 Trac traction control system and carbon-ceramic brakes, it remains true to its eminently sporting values. But opinion is already divided between the purists, who find it too much of a GT for a Ferrari, and a more accommodating clientele, who will no doubt give it a warm welcome.

A smaller market with more competitors

Vehicle sales in the North American market have fallen from previous heights of 17 to 18 million units to less than 13 million as the economy cools down. Among the domestic makers, General Motors' revitalized car line-up, including the launch of the highly praised Cadillac CTS and Chevrolet Malibu, have the maker optimistic. Ford is still struggling, counting on a remake of its F-150 truck and the Flex to turn its fortunes around. Chrysler, now privately held, is hoping its new Ram pick-up will give it a boost, although it will be difficult with gasoline well above $3 per gallon. The company has embarked on a crash program to upgrade interiors and develop a replacement for its mid-market Sebring, which has failed to live up to expectation. Even imports are feeling the pinch. Toyota's full-size pick-up Tundra has not generated significant new sales. Honda's all-new Accord is off to a slow start and Nissan, having moved its headquarters from California to Nashville, has seen major turnover in its executive ranks and tough sales. Meanwhile, small players like Hyundai and Volkswagen are making big plans to expand in North America, the Korean automaker with its first full-size V8 rear-drive sedan and VW looking for a U.S. assembly plant to counter the skyrocketing euro and to develop mid-priced sedans specifically for this market. More competitors fighting for a smaller overall market spells difficult times ahead for all. **Matt DeLorenzo** presents the most significant new entries.

CHEVROLET VOLT

Heir to Chevrolet's electric and hybrid
EV1, of which 1,000 units were built ten
years ago, the Volt four-seater saloon,
measuring 4.50 m, is powered by an
electric motor that drives the front wheels.
Its lithium-ion batteries give it a range
of 60 km. But a petrol engine generates
the necessary energy to run the electric
motor, so the Volt can go a further 500 km
before stopping at a pump or power socket.
Presented in its definitive version, it will
go on sale in the United States at the end
of 2010, and then in Europe in 2011.

CHEVROLET CRUZE

Chevrolet's European line-up was short of a family saloon that was not just a re-badged Daewoo. So the Cruze, which at 4.61 m is 20 cm shorter than the Evanda, will now fill that gap. With its arching roof, raked windscreen and short rear overhang, the Cruze joins the pack of four-door coupés. Rather than innovating, the car takes its cues from other saloons of character and features sculpted flanks, headlights tapering back along the bonnet and a two-stage grille. But its engines are sober, with a 150 hp 2.0-litre diesel for now, pending the arrival of a 120 hp version, and 1.6-litre and 1.8-litre petrol units, delivering 112 hp and 140 hp respectively.

LINCOLN MKS

Lincoln's new flagship sedan departs from the orthodoxy of a rear-drive drive V8 in favor of V6 power with a choice of front- or all-wheel drive. The car will first be powered by a 3.7-litre engine rated 270 hp. A year after launch, a direct injection twin-turbo 3.5-litre V6 with more than 300 hp will be an option. All MKS models are equipped with 6-speed automatic transmissions. The MKS will be one of the first Ford products to utilize the company's capless fuel filler technology which eliminates the inconvenience of forgetting to put the gas cap back on after fueling, and also saves time during refueling by doing away with unscrewing and replacing a fuel filler cap. The car is built on Ford's global D platform with a 112.9-inch (2.88 m) wheelbase and overall length of 204.1 inches (5.20 m). The MKS sports a new split waterfall grille design that will become a signature cue on all future Lincoln models.

FISKER KARMA

The Karma is the first ground-up new design from Fisker, a car company run by designer Henrik Fisker – late of Aston Martin and BMW. Current Fisker designs are coach built and based extensively on modified BMW and Mercedes production designs, but the Karma is a totally different act. Karma previews a production model announced to have 'plug-in' lithium-ion batteries powering a rear electric motor, with a range-extending small petrol engine. This is then unusually combined with a four-door coupé body in the mould of the BMW CS that was shown at Shanghai last year. The similarities with the BMW continue with the twin-aperture grille graphic, and this is a seductive design. The interior extends the exterior's classical theme with chocolate and cream leather, circular air vents and three-spoke steering wheel.

Karma is 195 inches long (4.97 m) and is given for a top speed of over 125 mph (200 km/h), with an acceleration of 0-60 mph (96 km/h) in less than six seconds. Orders are being taken at an estimated price of $80,000 for delivery in 2010.

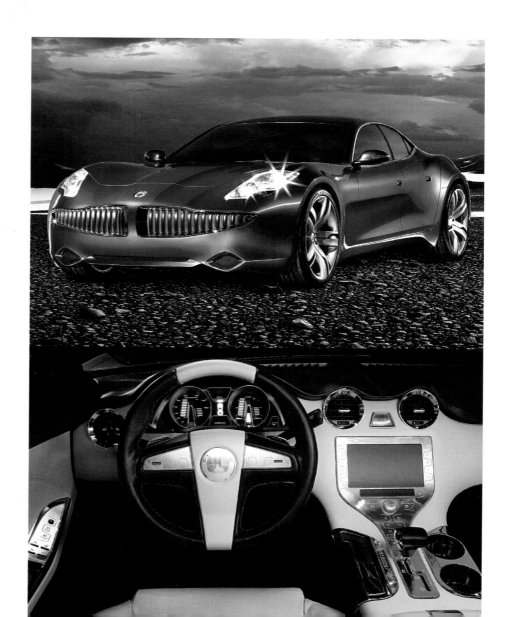

2010 CHEVROLET CAMARO

The long-awaited return of Chevrolet's pony car answer to the Mustang bows in early 2009. The Camaro's design, inspired by the 1969 model, remains true to that of the concept that showed at the 2006 North American International Auto Show in Detroit. The greenhouse is slightly taller and the pillarless hardtop design has been abandoned in favor of a traditional B-pillar hidden behind a fixed rear quarter window, which allows the car to retain its hardtop look. However, the basic shape and dimensions of the concept have been retained. The top model in the range is the Camaro SS, which features a 6.2-litre V8 making 400 hp. Buyers are offered a choice of six-speed manual or automatic transmissions. A direct injection 3.6-litre V-6 making 300 hp will also be available, with the same choice of gearboxes. A convertible is expected to follow within a year and then will be followed by a more powerful Z28.

DODGE CHALLENGER

While the Challenger SRT-8 was introduced
as a 2008 model, only 6000 were built, all
with a 425-hp 6.1-litre V8 and five-speed
automatic transmission. After the six-month
production run, the rest of the Challenger
line bowed as '09 models, which included
the 250-hp 3.5-litre V6 SE and the
370-hp 5.7-litre V8 R/T. The SE has a
four-speed automatic, while the R/T
is equipped with a five-speed auto.
A six-speed manual is available in all
models, including the SRT-8 for '09 and
includes a standard hill-start-assist feature
that prevents the car from rolling backwards
on an incline. The Challenger is built
off a shortened Dodge Charger platform
with a 116.0-inch (2.95 m) wheelbase
and 197.7-inch (5.03 m) overall length.

TOYOTA VENZA

This new addition to Toyota's expanding line of crossovers is designed to be much more car-like in execution that the Highlander, which looks more like a traditional SUV. Based on Camry running gear, the Venza offers a choice of a base 2.7-litre four-cylinder engine and an optional 268-hp 3.5-litre V6. Available in front- or all-wheel drive, the Venza comes with a six-speed automatic transmission as standard equipment. Riding on a 109.3-inch (2.78 m) wheelbase, the Venza has an overall length of 189.0 inches (4.81 m). The vehicle will be built at Toyota's Georgetown, Kentucky plant in the USA.

DODGE JOURNEY

Based on the front-drive Avenger mid-size car platform, the Dodge Journey is a five-door crossover aimed at capitalizing on the popularity of vehicles with SUV styling. Available in either front- or all-wheel drive, the Journey is designed to replace the discontinued short-wheelbase version of the Dodge Caravan minivan. Power comes from a base 173-hp 2.4-litre inline four equipped with a four-speed automatic transmission or an optional 235-hp 3.5-litre V6 with a six-speed automatic. The Journey rides on a 113.8-inch (2.90 m) wheelbase and measures 192.4 inches (4.90 m) in overall length. It offers optional third row seating for up to seven passengers.

FORD FLEX

Instead of building a new minivan to replace the Freestar, Ford is looking to redefine the people-hauling segment with the Flex, a boxy crossover vehicle that combines the look of a station wagon with an SUV. Instead of a minivan's sliding doors, the Flex has traditional front and rear doors. The vehicle rides on a 117.9-inch (3 m) wheelbase and is 202.3 inches (5.15 m) in overall length. Buyers will have a choice of front or all-wheel drive. When equipped with optional three-row seating, the Flex can carry up to seven passengers. The Flex is powered by a 3.5-litre V6 producing 260 hp and a six-speed automatic transmission.

VOLKSWAGEN ROUTAN

American consumers who expected Volkswagen to enter the minivan market with something that looked like the retro-inspired Microbus concept will be disappointed by the Routan, which is essentially a reworked Chrysler minivan built in Windsor, Canada. Still, the Routan gives Volkswagen quick access to a large market. Although the basic architecture of the vehicle is the same as the Chrysler entries, the Routan has a distinct Volkswagen family look to the front of the vehicle, a one-inch lower ride height and an interior that has higher quality materials. Two V6 engines are offered, a 3.8-litre making 197 hp and a 4.0-litre rated at 253 hp.

Booming markets!

Matt DeLorenzo observes that a sign in the shifting balance in Asia is reflected in auto shows. The Tokyo Motor Show used to be the must see, and be seen at, show for the Pacific Rim. Now it's Beijing or Shanghai. Japan's tightly controlled access to its market (a contracting one at that) makes it less attractive to global players who enjoy greater access to China and its promise of double digit growth in vehicle sales.

As a result, both foreign joint ventures and China's indigenous makers are booming. But China is only half the story in Asia. India is also on the cusp of putting millions on wheels. While the Tata Nano has generated global headlines for its low price and promise of allowing more than a quarter million Indians a year a chance at owning a car, other makers have been moving into the Asian subcontinent to beef up their own manufacturing capabilities and take advantage of the country's low wage base and highly educated workforce. India also offers something that China does not: because of its British-based common law, there is a healthy respect for intellectual property rights, which helps established makers fend off cheap knock-offs. India's standing in the global industry will only be further enhanced by Tata's acquisition of Jaguar and Land Rover from Ford.

TATA NANO

Ratan Tata wants to be the Henry Ford of India and may just achieve that with the Nano, an inexpensive car developed specifically for this Asian subcontinent. Tata, which was formerly known as Tata Engineering and Locomotive Co. (Telco) is India's largest producer of cars and commercial vehicles. The company began building locomotives in 1945 and produced its first commercial vehicle in 1954. The Nano has an eye-popping low 100,000 rupee (approximately $2500) retail price tag for the Base version (there is also a Luxury variant), and beneath its futuristic egg-shape body is a rather rudimentary automobile. Power comes from a rear-mounted inline 623 cc two-cylinder engine producing 38 hp, mated to a four-speed manual transmission. The four-door hatchback has an 87.8-inch (2.24 m) wheelbase and measures 122 inches (3.10 m) in overall length. Fuel economy is said to be 4.5-litres per 100 kilometres or about 47 miles per gallon. The Nano accelerates to 45 mph (72 km/h) in 14 seconds and has a top speed of 65 mph (105 km/h). Tata plans to build 250,000 of them annually for domestic consumption and has no immediate plans for export.

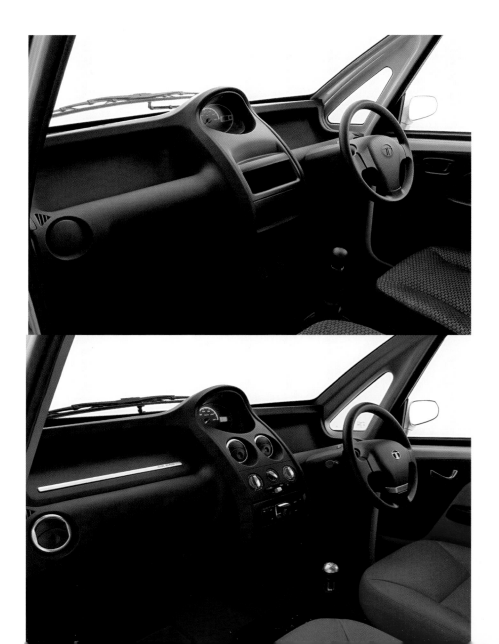

TOYOTA IQ

Looking to offer Europeans an alternative to the Smart, Toyota introduced the iQ city car at the Geneva Motor Show. This two-door hatchback features seating for three adults and one child and rides on a diminutive 78.7-inch wheelbase (2 m). The car itself isn't much longer at 117.5 inches overall (3 m). The front-engine, front-drive iQ will offer a choice of two petrol (1.0 and 1.3-litre) and one diesel (1.4 litre) power-plants. Several innovations, including a new differential design, a flat fuel tank beneath the rear seat and a unique dash design contribute to the spaciousness of the cabin. Despite its small size, the iQ is said to have a five-star rating in European crash tests. Toyota has set a sales target of about 100,000 units per year.

GEELY PANDA

In honour of the 2008 Beijing Olympics, Geely introduced a small city car with headlamps and a grille that look like the face of a Panda. Naturally, Fiat, which has sold a Panda for years, is not amused, but can do little to stop the sale of the car in the Chinese market. While the front of the car is unique, the rest of the sheetmetal, including the rear glass hatch, is similar to that of the Toyota Aygo, a Panda competitor. The new Geely model is powered by a choice of a 1.1 or 1.3-litre four-cylinder engine.

SUZUKI ALTO

Looking to lower manufacturing costs and boost sales at the same time, Suzuki plans to build the Alto micro car in India, where it is called A-star. The five-door hatchback is powered by a 1.0-liter three-cylinder engine mated to a five-speed manual transmission. It rides on a 92.9-inch (2.36 m) wheelbase and has an overall length of 141.0 inches (4 m). The interior features a floating, wing-shaped dashboard with a drop-down centre console. Unlike the bare-bones Tata Nano, the right-hand drive Alto boasts such features as four-wheel disc brakes, traction control and dual front and side airbags.

KIA SOUL

With its cubic volumes, raised bonnet, flared wheel-arches and high, flat roof (1.61 m), the Soul subscribes to the small off-roader school of styling. Despite its military looks, the new Kia is a peaceful urban car with front-wheel drive. Measuring 4.11 m in length, this rival to the Citroën Picasso C3 and Renault Modus takes advantage of its vertical tailgate to offer the same 340-litre load space (in five-seat configuration) as the Kia Cee'd in the next class up. The Soul offers a choice of two 1.6-litre engines – one petrol and one diesel – each delivering 126 hp.

ROEWE 550

Shanghai Automotive Industry Corporation, which continues to build the Rover 75 under the Roewe 750 nameplate in China, has added a second model to its range with the 550, a slightly smaller and much more contemporary looking sedan powered by a turbocharged 1.8-litre gasoline inline four. The 550 rides on a 106.4-inch (2.70 m) wheelbase and measures 182.0 inches (4.63 m) in overall length. This front-drive sedan is apparently based on an all-new platform developed by SAIC.

NISSAN MAXIMA

Built on an all-new platform, the Maxima four-door sedan features a 1.9-inch (5 cm) shorter wheelbase than the previous model, but is 1.5 inches wider to improve cabin comfort and handling. It is powered by an updated version of Nissan's VQ V6 engine family. The revised engine produces 290 hp and 261 lb ft of torque. All Maximas are equipped with the Xtronic continuously variable transmission (CVT) with a manual mode that provides stepped operation similar to gear shifts in a conventional transmission. The exterior design embodies a philosophy of 'liquid motion' with crisp character lines and muscular body contours. The new V-shaped headlamp treatment will expand to other Nissan models.

HYUNDAI GENESIS

The Korean automaker is looking to move beyond offering inexpensive, front-drive models by introducing the more substantial rear-drive Genesis in coupé and sedan form. The full-size four-door has a 115.6-inch (2.94 m) wheelbase and an overall length of 195.9 inches (4.99 m) and will be the first V8 model offered by the company in the U.S., its engine rated at 375 hp and coming with a six-speed automatic transmission. Two V6 engines will also be offered, a base 3.3-litre producing 266 hp and an optional 306-hp 3.8-litre.

TOYOTA AVENSIS

Admittedly, the job of the Avensis is more about convincing than seducing, but European buyers found the first two generations too dull, and gave them a widespread thumbs-down. The new Avensis thus comes in a version designed for the European market at Toyota's design centre in Sophia-Antipolis. With more flattering, athletic lines, it has balanced proportions, scooped out sills and streamlined headlights. Available in saloon and estate variants (4.70 m and 4.77 m respectively), it offers a choice of three petrol engines (132, 147 and 152 hp) and three diesels (126, 150, and 177 hp).

HONDA FCX CLARITY

One of the first fuel cell vehicles to go into public hands is the Honda FCX Clarity, of which several hundred are being leased in Southern California to consumers as part of a test programme. The vehicles are being leased for three years at $600 per month. The customers will be chosen on their proximity to three refuelling stations located in Santa Monica, Torrance and Irvine, California. The Torrance facility is a prototype of a home fuelling rig that converts natural gas into compressed hydrogen. The Clarity combines a 100 kW fuel cell stack with a small lithium-ion battery pack to deliver a vehicle range of about 270 miles (430 km). The Clarity's fuel cell is supplied with compressed hydrogen from a single 5,000 psi (350 bar) tank. The four-door four-passenger Clarity rides on a dedicated platform with unique styling that incorporates a cab-forward design to maximize the passenger space. The vehicle's size puts it between the Civic and Accord in Honda's line.

TOYOTA URBAN CRUISER

If you thought the Urban Cruiser was going to step straight into the shoes of the old three-door RAV4, you're in for a surprise: measuring 3.93 m in length, it takes none of the styling cues of a conventional 4x4! With its high belt-line, wide track, moderately raised roof (1.54 m) and stocky appearance, it looks more like a tough all-purpose brawler, equipped with four-wheel drive but also available in a 4x2 version. Is this a foretaste of the future direction of leisure 4x4s? Featuring a sliding and folding rear bench in 4x2 guise, the Urban Cruiser comes with just two engines: a 100 hp 1.3-litre petrol and a 90 hp 1.4-litre diesel.

MAZDA BIANTE

The Biante is a tall minivan positioned between the Premacy (with which it shares a platform) and the larger Mazda MPV. The most striking design elements are the headlamp lenses which flow into the front quarter glass. Built exclusively for the Japanese market, the Biante boasts twin sliding doors as well as the longest and widest dimensions in its class. Offered in both front- and all-wheel drive, the Biante is equipped with 2.0-litre direct injection petrol four-cylinder or a front-drive only model with a petrol 2.3-litre four. Projected volume is approximately 3000 units per year.

OKUYAMA K.O 7/8

Former Pininfarina design chief Ken Okuyama has struck out on his own to produce a limited production sports car in Japan. The K.O 7 is a two-passenger open sports car powered by a mid-mounted 250 hp 2.0-litre inline four. Okuyama drew his inspiration from Colin Chapman's legendary Lotus 7. Designed for use primarily as a track car, the K.O 7 measures 141 inches (3.60 m) in overall length and stands just 43.3 inches (1.10 m) tall. The companion car, which uses the same chassis, is the K.O 8, a closed coupé. Instead of the roadster's conventional power-plant, the coupé will be a pure electric with a lithium-ion battery pack driving a 100 kW electric motor. Okuyama expects a range of about 100 miles (160 km).

Active Wheel: Michelin reinvents the wheel

In 1996, Michelin launched a research team to look into electric power-trains. What major changes could we expect from their inevitable development? Both as regards the tyres, of course, but also the cars themselves? Because it was obvious that the traditional car, reliant solely on oil, could not be sustained. In 2004, the fruits of this research were christened 'Active Wheel'. The wheel was presented at the Paris Motor Show and also tested at the Shanghai Challenge Bibendum on the first Michelin concept car to be fitted out with the technology. Four years later, mass production is becoming a possibility. No-one is in a better position to talk about it than **Patrick Oliva**, the French manufacturer's Director of Future and Sustainable Development.

Venturi Volage, Heuliez Will: the car's transformation is happening at last! The two vehicles (unveiled in the preceding pages of Automobile Year), which were first shown at the Paris Motor Show and are ostensibly so different, in fact have more in common than it first appears: electric motors in the wheels, electronic suspension, complete chassis overhaul, new attitude to what performance means and, to top it off, both have a certain something beyond the zero emissions, silence and total innovation which you can't ignore. The Venturi, the sports car of your dreams, has stunning acceleration and road-holding. The Heuliez, a small five-seater city sedan, is a paragon of energy efficiency and thanks to a smart replaceable battery system, can offer an adaptable range of between 150 and 400 km. Once the batteries are empty, they can be recharged or changed very quickly. The secret behind these technological gems is a minor revolution: Michelin's Active Wheel. The automotive industry has dreamt of something similar for years. Michelin spent twelve years working on it. The aim, which has been reached, was to get as many functions as possible into the wheel without damaging the vehicle's dynamics, taking special care not to increase the unsprung mass. Active Wheel covers the tyre, the rim, the brake disks and shoes, an electric traction engine and active electric suspension. Systematic work on making the traction engine smaller has helped the manufacturers achieve 30 kW (41 hp) of power when in continuous use, with peaks of 60 kW, for a mass of just 7 kg.

The synchronous engine with permanent magnets – its nominal speed is 12,000 rpm and it is liquid-cooled – has a cog on its output shaft which engages with an interdependent cogwheel on the wheel's rotation axis. It couldn't be more simple! But they still had to make it happen. A motor can be placed in either two or four of a vehicle's wheels. Each motor is controlled electronically and, as they are reversible, can, functioning as a generator, play an active part in the vehicle's braking, allowing for the traditional mechanical brakes to be made smaller. The suspension is also integrated into the wheel. In contrast to a regular shock-absorber, it has the advantage of a number of function modes thanks to its electronic controls. In parallel with a coil spring bearing the static load of the vehicle, an electric jack consisting of an electric motor coupled to a cog/rack acts to correct the state of the spring. The suspension's response time is lower than three thousandths of a second and makes for unrivalled comfort. As for road-holding, driving pleasure and passenger comfort, you can forget about shuddering along; the chassis is always kept parallel to the road-surface. A central control unit transmits the necessary adjustments in real time to the four suspension units so that, whatever the driving conditions, and regardless of whether the vehicle is accelerating, braking or turning, it sticks to the road without rolling or pitching. By eliminating the need for a central engine, transmission, differential, half shaft, anti-roll bar and, of course, the exhaust system, Active Wheel makes the car much lighter and its design very simple: four wheels attached

The Active Wheel works equally well on both electric vehicles which use batteries and those using fuel cells. The Michelin Hy-Light 2 concept car was demonstrated during the Challenge Bibendum in Shanghai.

to a chassis carrying only electronics and batteries for which bodywork has to be designed to create a living space quite unlike what we are currently used to. Michelin's Active Wheel is undoubtedly the dawn of a new automotive era because this unprecedented design, very hi-tech but simple to make, proves how adaptable it is to the full range of a car's uses with the Volage and the Will: from the nippy city car (two-wheel drive) to the racing beast (four-wheel drive with impressive torque). Active Wheel can be designed for hybrid vehicles too. By obviating the need for the heavy central engine/transmission block, the use of Active Wheel also means that the design of the front of a car can be rethought to improve energy absorption in case of impact. Furthermore, at a time when energy diversity and efficiency and a reduction in CO_2 emissions have become urgent necessities, the Volage and Will are right on the ball: the Will uses less than 15 kWh/100 km! In France, that would mean fuel costs of well under two euros per 100 km and as regards CO_2 emissions, they stand at less than 15 g/km when batteries are recharged on the national grid. Emissions would stand at approximately 70 g of CO_2/km in Germany and under 7 g of CO_2/km in Sweden, the extent of the difference dependent, of course, on the source of the electricity. In the worst case scenarios, where electricity is generated in coal-fired power stations (China, Greece, …), it remains under 140 g of CO_2/km (whilst the current average is 160 g of CO_2/km for Europe and 240 g in North America). The Volage is not to be outdone. It is a paragon of cleanliness in its class, consuming almost ten times less

energy than most of its competitors. The passion for cars reconciles with the environment and society's demands.

In 1895, the Michelin brothers were fitting the first car – of their own design, the Eclair – with tyres. In 2008, Venturi and Heuliez might well be inspired pioneers of a major automotive development thanks to Michelin's Active Wheel.

The Active Wheel from every angle. On the inside to the left you can see the suspension spring with its electric motor, and on the right the electric traction engine generating 30 kW (41 hp) and weighing 7 kg, with the brake caliper underneath.

Modern diesel engine technology

Paul Frère contributed to Automobile Year from its first issue, in 1953. At the time, he was already a confirmed journalist and a racing driver on the rise who, a few years later, would win the South African Grand Prix with a Cooper and the 24 Hours of Le Mans with a Ferrari. His writings, mostly technically oriented – he was also an engineer – were always extensively researched. This combination of knowledge and experience made him a perfect candidate for the jury of the Challenge Bibendum, the Michelin-organised event dedicated to sustainable mobility, in which he participated enthusiastically. Paul left us last February at the age of 91. A few days before passing away, true to his commitment, he delivered the following article. Whilst there is indeed much talk today about the future of electric vehicles, one should not discard the development potential left in the Otto cycle and in the diesel engines.

The first patents taken by Rudolf Diesel date back to 1892 and 1893 but it was not before 1923 that diesel engines had been developed to be sufficiently compact to power a heavy truck, and 1936 before it could be used for a passenger car, the Mercedes-Benz 260 D. The engine had a capacity of 2.6-litres and its Bosch four-piston pump injected the fuel into a pre-combustion chamber, patented in 1909 by Prosper l'Orange working at the Benz company as a development engineer. Its power was 45 hp and it weighed more than 4 kg/hp. Its advantage was that its specific consumption was notably lower than contemporary gasoline engines. Direct injection diesels were even more economical (about 15%), but were only used in trucks because of their excessive combustion noise.

A first step towards changing the 'trusty workhorse' character of the diesel was turbocharging (Mercedes-Benz in 1978) and the first acceptable direct injection passenger car came in 1989: the turbocharged, 2.46-litre Audi 100 TDI which, helped by an intercooler, developed 120 hp (48.8 hp/litre). Its acceptably quiet operation was obtained by the use of two-stage injectors that in the first stage made a 'pilot' injection to start the combustion just before the piston reached top dead centre, followed by the main injection of which it ensured an instant combustion. The two-stage injection was made possible by two springs in series controlling the opening stroke of the injector needle, the first comparatively soft for the pilot, the stronger one for the main injection. The injector needle was still passive, its up and down movements being obtained by the pressure of the fuel delivered by the pump which was also responsible for the injection's timing, controlled by the electronic engine management system.

The next important step was the introduction of the 'common rail' direct injection system, originally developed by Fiat who sold all the rights to Bosch for its final development and production. It was first seen on the JTD engine of the Alfa Romeo 156 that was also the first European car using a variable geometry turbocharger.

In the common rail system, almost universally used today, the injectors are active, their needle being activated by a solenoid (later also by piezo-electric actuators), monitored by the engine management adapting the timing and duration of the injection to the engine's load and rpm as well as other data such as temperature, atmospheric pressure, etc. The simplified high pressure pump now took care only of providing the common rail (in reality a big and strong tube usually running along the cylinder head) and the injectors with highly pressurized fuel. In first generation systems the maximum pressure was 1350 bar, but in the latest, third generation, it is up to 2000 bar with the fuel penetrating into the combustion chamber (usually carved in the piston) through a number of holes (six to eight) of less than 0.2 mm diameter. The higher the injection pressure, the finer is the pulverization of the fuel and the more complete is the combustion, resulting in improved fuel economy and reduced CO and HC (hydrocarbon) emissions. The injection process and timing is monitored electronically and gets an almost instant response from the solenoids and the very light needle, or quicker still from the piezo-actuators, the latter making up to five injections per power stroke possible.

This in turns allows an accurate control of the pressure rise in the cylinder, important not only for the reduction of the combustion noise, but also because the formation of poisonous nitrogen oxides (NOx) is decreased as the peak pressure and temperature of the burning gases is lowered. But this reduction can only be a compromise as lower pressures and temperatures increase the formation of the also legally limited soot particulates. This is a big problem as the NOx cannot be reduced by a conventional three-way catalyst because the diesel operates with excess air. New solutions will be discussed at the end of this article.

In 1999 the extreme injection pressure of 2000 bar has already been achieved in four-cylinder engines of the Volkswagen Group using one pump-injector per cylinder. In this system the pump and the injector are a single unit operated by the exhaust camshaft. But correctly controlling the multiple injections seems to have been a serious problem with this system, causing undesirable noise and harshness. It is progressively being abandoned in favour of the also less costly common rail.

Turbocharging and combustion noise have led to a reduction of the compression ratio of modern diesel engines from around 22:1 in indirect injection units down to 16-17:1, without any serious loss of efficiency, as the lower thermal efficiency is approximately compensated by the lower friction losses, while modern glow plugs have solved the cold starting problem that otherwise the lowered compression would have caused.

Though the comparatively slow combustion of the diesel fuel limits their crankshaft speed to less than 5000 rpm, most engines now have four valves per cylinder. One important reason is that in direct injection engines the turbulence required for a fast and complete combustion must, at low engine speeds, be created by a curved intake port delivering the air charge tangentially into the combustion chamber, which is detrimental to good breathing and limits the power obtainable at higher revolutions. For this reason a second port with easy breathing capacity must be added. In some cases it is controlled by a throttle valve that remains closed at low revolutions in the interest of a high turbulence. A second reason for the four valves is that they allow the injector to be placed vertically in the cylinder axis for a perfectly symmetrical distribution of the injected fuel in the combustion chamber.

POWER, WEIGHT AND EMISSIONS

Turbocharging is essential to obtain a good specific power and weight from a diesel engine, but fixed geometry turbos create another compromise: a small turbo provides a useful boost at low crankshaft revolutions together with minimum 'turbo lag', but limits the top-end power; a larger turbo is less low-speed efficient, creates more 'turbo lag', but ensures good top-end power. This is the reason for using turbochargers with variable geometry, obtained by mobile exhaust gas guide blades. Instead of a variable geometry turbo, some

manufacturers use two small turbos of which only one is fed by the exhaust gases of all cylinders at low revolutions; as revolutions increase, a system of flap valves direct the gases of half the number of cylinders to the second turbo.

diesels are heavier than petrol engines of similar power (but much lower torque) not only because of the extra weight of their high pressure injection system, their turbocharger and the intercooler. Their higher combustion pressure also requires a stronger structural stiffness. But the progress of design and metallurgy has considerably contributed to reducing the weight of such large components as the cylinder block and head, thanks to thin wall cast iron technology and of the widespread replacement of iron with aluminium and magnesium, while the 'bedplate' technology has notably increased the rigidity of the crankcase. The specific weight of modern 1.5 to 2.0-litre turbodiesels is now down to around 1 kg/hp, less for larger units and down to an estimated 0.4 kg/hp for the V12 racing engines of Audi and Peugeot, in spite of the air intake restrictors required by the Le Mans regulations.

Several modern diesel cars pass the Euro 4 emission regulations without requiring a particulate filter, but the Euro 6 (2012) emission laws require a drastic reduction of the soot particulates as well as of the nitrogene oxides (NOx) contained in the exhaust gases to be reduced from 0.25 to 0.08 g/km. The problem is that the formation of NOx is reduced when the peak temperature in the combustion chamber is lowered while simultaneously the particulate formation increases. To meet future requirements, the problem must be solved by treating NOx and soot particulates separately as, for example, by the Continuous Regenerating Trap (CRT) system. The NOx hurdle being the stiffer one, whenever the engine is not operated at full load, a considerable amount of cooled exhaust gas is recirculated (EGR) to replace some of the air which would otherwise reach the combustion chamber. It can amount to up to 60% of the charge and as it does not participate in the combustion, it acts as a cooling medium. The soot particulates are then treated in the particulate filter, as described below.

Particulate filters must be periodically cleaned by burning the soot and avoid an excessive exhaust back pressure causing a loss of power and increased fuel consumption. If the filter is just a trap made of chicanes, the temperature of the exhaust gases reaching the trap must be at least 600° C, which normally happens only when the engine operates a full load. If this does not happen often enough, several technologies can solve the problem. They are used whenever sensors detect an excessive exhaust back pressure. One is the post injection (injecting a small quantity of fuel after the main injection) which burns the post-injected fuel in the exhaust system, raising the particulate filter's temperature to 600° C; the other (as pioneered by PSA Peugeot Citroën in 2000) is to inject for a short time an urea-like additive upstream of the filter, which reduces the ignition temperature of the soot to around 300° C. A third system is the catalytic trap (CRT = Continuously Regenerating Trap) that continuously regenerates the filter from 300° C on and also has the merit of further reducing the NOx emissions, but can only be used in countries where Diesel fuel with a very small sulphur content is available.

The latest CAFE (USA) regulations can be met with the combination of an oxidation catalyst followed by a NOx retaining (de-NOx) catalyst and a particulate trap located downstream of it. When the de-NOx catalyst is saturated, the electronic engine management makes the engine operate for a short period in the Lambda = 1 or lower mode by increasing the EGR. This reduces the NOx to harmless nitrogen and water, at the cost of a slight increase of fuel consumption. The number of these cleaning processes can be reduced by replacing the purely mechanical filter by a catalytic filter that helps partly burning the particulates at temperatures lower than 600° C. This is the technology called Bluetec by Mercedes-Benz, but also adopted by Volkswagen-Audi and BMW. It meets the current U.S. emissions regulations, except in five states.

An even more effective reduction of the NOx is achieved with an SCR (Selective Catalytic Reaction) catalyst in combination with the electronically controlled injection, upstream of the SCR catalyst, of an additive called Ad-Blue, a mixture of a urea-like fluid and water. This technology, developed by Mercedes-Benz for heavy trucks, can eliminate up to 80% of the NOx output and is adaptable to passenger cars. The Ad-Blue is contained in a separate small tank that, in a passenger car, does not require topping up between normal inspection intervals. This system meets all U.S. regulations and has been introduced in 2008. It will probably be required to meet the Euro 6 regulations in 2012 as well.

On the 2007 Geneva salon Honda exhibited an experimental version of its 2.2-litre diesel engine fitted with an exhaust system achieving similar results, by using ammonia to lower the burning point of the soot particulars and eliminate 80-85% of the NOx contained in the raw (before treatment) emissions. The main difference from the Bluetec system using Ad-Blue is that it does not require any liquid additive, the ammonia being produced in the system itself. As long as the engine operates in the normal excess air mode, the exhaust gases, of which part of the NOx have been reduced in the oxidation catalyst, reach the combined particulate filter and NOx trap catalyst. Of these gases, the NOx are eliminated and the residual emissions are harmless IDO (water), CO_2 (carbon dioxide) and O_2 (oxygen). When the NOx trap is saturated, the engine management selects for

a short time the rich mode that adds carbon monoxide (CO) to the gases fed into the NOx trap and combine to form $2 NH_3 + O_2$, NH_3 being ammonia which has a very aggressive smell, but combines with NO and O_2, so that in the end only harmless N_2 (Natrium) and H_2O (water) leave the tail pipes. Compared to the current Euro 4 emission limits, the NOx emissions are reduced by a further 85% and those of particulates by 80%, meeting the requirements of even the proposed Euro 6 and U.S. Bin5 limits. Honda hopes to have this new system ready for production in 2009.

THE NEXT STEP

While diesel technology made enormous progress in the last two decades, Otto engine technology also had to adapt to ever more severe poisonous emission legislations and to the worldwide measures taken to reduce the carbon dioxide emissions. Basically Otto cycle engines emit less poisonous emissions than diesels, specially NOx and soot particulates of which the reduction requires a more complicated exhaust gas treatment, while Otto cycle engines emit more CO_2 because of their higher fuel consumption. But the technology of the two systems has progressively come closer. Electronic management, common rail direct fuel injection with piezo-electric injectors metering the fuel injected, and improved combustion chamber design have made compression ratios of as high as 12.0-12.5:1 possible in Otto cycle gasoline engines. Since in diesel engines the control of the injected fuel mass has been transferred from the high pressure pump to piezo-electric injectors together with a fuel distribution system very similar to the common rail system of gasoline engines, but with much higher (up to 2000 bar) pressures, the compression ratio of diesels has come down from around 22:1 to anything between 16:1 and 17:1 in the interest of less harshness and lower NOx formations. In both types of engines, increased internal and external exhaust gas recirculation (EGR) help further reduce combustion temperatures and NOx emissions and – in Otto cycle engines – pumping losses when the engine operates at part load.

Such similarities suggest that it might be possible to develop an engine combining the advantages of Otto and diesel cycle engines in a single type of engine, while improving their overall efficiency, reducing their critical NOx emissions and further reducing their fuel consumption and CO_2 emissions. That may be the next step in the development of internal combustion engines and one such engine was disclosed, still at an early development stage, by Mercedes-Benz in the Frankfurt IAA of 2007 under the name of DiesOtto engine. The main aim of these new generation HCCI (Homogeneous Charge Compression Ignition) or CAI (Controlled Auto Ignition) engines is to more completely burn the fuel/air mixture in the combustion chamber by instantaneous auto ignition of the entire charge at the right moment. Even with the best current fuel injection system, this is not the case, resulting

MERCEDEZ-BENZ DIESOTTO

in a loss of efficiency and being the cause of the formation of carbon particulates in diesel engines. It is known that other manufacturers, among them General Motors and Volkswagen Group, have similar developments running.

The Mercedes engine uses current commercial gasoline. It features a variable compression ratio and both a high pressure (200 bar) gasoline injection system plus conventional spark plug ignition, is turbocharged and operates in three phases, all in the Lambda mode (air/fuel weight ratio 14.6:1), which greatly simplifies meeting the strictest emission legislations with a conventional three-way catalyst. Except at very low rpm and very low load, the correct Lambda ratio is obtained entirely by EGR, thanks to variable intake and exhaust valve timing and lift (possibly with camless, solenoid operated valve gear when the engine reaches the production stage), in order to avoid pumping losses. The operating ranges of the three stages are as follows:

– Stage 1 (cold start, very low load and rpm). The engine operates on the Otto cycle with spark ignition and a stratified charge.

– Stage 2 (increasing load and rpm). The engine is switched from the Otto to the diesel cycle. This involves raising the compression ratio, adapting it to the level required for the self-ignition to happen at the right moment under varying operating conditions (load and rpm) and adapting the exhaust gas recirculation as required to retain the Lambda ratio under all conditions. With spark plug ignition, reliable firing is obtained for a charge containing a maximum of 20-25% recirculated gas; with the homogeneous charge

diesel cycle, the compression generated heat fires the entire charge simultaneously, even at low loads with an exhaust gas proportion of up to 75%, making it possible to lower the switch point from Stage 1 to Stage 2. A further requirement is that the switch from Otto cycle to diesel cycle takes place seamlessly and must not be felt by the driver and his passengers. Needless to say, all this necessitates sophisticated electronics, including a combustion chamber temperature sensor on which the exact ignition point of the homogenous charge depends, and a long development. This diesel cycle stage is the one in which the HCCI engine operates most efficiently, most economically and produces least NOx and soot particulates. Unfortunately this stage extends over a comparatively small span of loads and revolutions and a large amount of the development effort is currently dedicated to its extension.

– Stage 3. If higher power and torque is required than obtainable in the diesel mode, a seamless switch back to the Otto cycle, again involving high performance electronics, is required. HCCI engines in no way exclude high specific power or torque: the Mercedes-Benz experimental 1.8-litre DiesOtto engine develops 238 hp and a maximum torque of 400 Nm!

These are the main lines of a promising development which, if backed by the introduction of less pollutant fuels than those of fossil origin – for example synthetic fuels, ethanol, E85, etc. – could result in almost zero pollution in the broadest terms from engines based on universally known and reliable technologies. HCCI engines would not require any drastic modifications of the current car architecture or any modification of the existing refuelling infrastructure.

My journey of some 15 years with the T.25

It was during the summer of 1993, writes **Professor Gordon Murray**, and I was about midway through my morning journey to McLaren Cars in Woking when the seed of the idea that was to become the T.25 City Car – 'T' for 'Type' and '25' for it is the 25th chassis I design – was planted. A short section of my 18-mile drive to Woking was on the A3 dual carriageway which runs from Portsmouth to London, a 5-mile reminder of the automobile madness which is London commuting. On this particular day the traffic was actually stationary and I had plenty of time to contemplate the drivers and vehicles around me. Most of the cars had only one occupant and they were largely heavy, expensive models occupying much more road space than they actually needed to. As I completed my journey I reflected about the situation and quickly came to the conclusion that this could not be sustainable and I began to consider what sort of vehicle would be required to protect our mobility and our much cherished personal freedom.

In 1993 we, at McLaren Cars, were building the first few F1 road cars. I had been lucky enough to have been given the opportunity to design the ultimate sports car from a complete clean sheet of paper so I was well aware of what a powerful tool that could be. What if I applied the same total re-think approach to a personal transport vehicle? This too could be a car designed to solve a problem rather than an idea for a vehicle design which in production could be aimed towards a particular market segment. So my City Car idea was born not to be low consumption and low emissions but to protect our mobility – the low emissions and consumption targets would be added to the design brief many years later as world pressure began to build and centre more around the fossil fuel issue. Up until this point in 1993 my working life had been about performance vehicles – 20 years in Formula One and many sports car designs – but the driving force had always been lightweight and innovative packaging, something that absolutely applies to Formula One design. This coupled with the fact that I have always liked small, light cars was all I needed to begin a 15-year study and design for a completely new approach to personal transport vehicles.

THE iSTREAM PROCESS

The approach we have used in designing our manufacturing process and in particular the T.25 City Car is to analyse the role of each part of the car and to select a material to suit its usage, whilst keeping in mind low capital investment and full lifecycle CO_2 damage. We call this process iStream (stabilised tube exo-frame automotive manufacture). As ultra lightweight is the target, steel is used to directly carry all the main load paths in the vehicle both for everyday usage and for crash. The steel surrounds the occupants in a complete

safety cage and is stabilised with a composite monocoque which gives further occupant protection and adds greatly to the torsional rigidity of the chassis. Further structural composites are used for interior cabin panels to complete the structure and the body is lightweight, up-cycled plastic panels whose only job it is to keep the rain out. The result of this new approach to material selection is that the car is extremely rigid and strong. We have also targeted a very low full lifecycle carbon footprint including everything from the moment the ore is dug out of the ground, the factory building and running energy costs. Our initial studies show a 40% reduction in overall CO_2 footprint with our process and our vehicle. The manufacturing process has at its heart a separate body/chassis system which can dramatically reduce capital investment in factory kit out and tooling whilst also reducing development costs. Many different body styles and vehicle types can be built on the same chassis. The T.25 itself is the first of many vehicles planned to use the iStream manufacturing process and this particular vehicle is designed to target six different market segments in the UK/Europe/Japan market. Initially the vehicle is being developed with a highly efficient petrol engine but the construction and design concept will support any number of new power-trains and fuels. The T.25 internal design is a mini MPV offering six different layouts in one vehicle in order to meet the selected market segment usage requirements. The Design Team have taken a fresh look at every component on the car with weight and cost saving as our targets: nothing has escaped our attention even details such as door latches and heater unit have been scrutinised for weight reduction. Our current weight target for the base model T.25 is just 550 kg. The Gordon Murray Design team have exercised the process before, during the design of the McLaren F1, but never with such low cost targets! As the car employs our iStream manufacturing process and is designed to assemble in just a few hours, the only opportunities to save costs are with the design of components and sub assemblies and by reducing parts count – our target is to reduce the overall parts counts of a conventional three-door mini hatch by at least 20%. The huge advantage of having an engineering team with an innovative approach and the depth of experience we have (some 1800 man years of working together in the automotive industry) is that it is possible to rethink almost everything on the motor car which results in most areas of the vehicle being very practical and very unconventional. For example access for occupants is different for an average car, the seating configuration offers six different layouts, even the way the child seats and luggage are loaded is unconventional.

THE SAME PRIORITIES AS THE MCLAREN F1

Designing a car with such small proportions brings many problems to the design team. The T.25 is just 2.4 metres long and 1.3 metre wide! Firstly the car's styling needs to be fresh, classless and timeless if it is to have any chance of being the next iconic small car after the1957 Fiat 500 and the 1959 Mini. Secondly, it must be graphically proven to potential customers that the car is as safe as a typical small hatchback. Thirdly it cannot be daunting to drive in traffic so the eye line of the driver must be at least at the same level as a full-sized car and most of all it must be fun to drive. Our vehicle dynamics department has concentrated on this last point and we have developed a low cost but sophisticated rear suspension for the T.25 which will become a powerful tool in overcoming the inherent problems in small, short wheelbase vehicle dynamics. We are also placing the same priorities as we did on the F1 road car on areas such as primary control positions, steering feel, ergonomics and visibility

as these design targets go a long way to making the vehicle fun and safe to drive. The T.25 is rear engine because from a crash and packaging perspective, a front engine car has huge limitations once in the sub three-metre length category. My journey of some 15 years with the T.25 City Car may have started that day back in the traffic jam in the summer of 1993 with the goal in mind to reduce congestion but now the programme has developed into a more complex solution to nearly all our future automobile problems – congestion, and also parking, running CO_2 emissions, low speed urban accident damage, localised vehicle manufacture, low investment and flexible product to market system, multi-bodied vehicle opportunities, reduced product to market times, reduced shipping and distribution costs, low sales price, low running costs, reduced accident repair costs and putting the fun back in to small car motoring. One fact I'm sure of is that our automotive world is changing and evolving as it always has but the rate of change right now in 2008 is far greater than we have seen in the past. The sales figures for cars in the first six months of 2008 show such a dramatic swing away from large, powerful cars towards smaller, more efficient cars that the inertia in the automotive industry and in particular the product planning has no hope of keeping up with the change. Weight and size are two powerful tools that car designers have right now to use in the short and medium term. Our iStream process can certainly deliver a product to customer by around 2012 but if I have a dream, it would be to create a new class of 'world vehicle' for personal transport to protect our freedom and mobility for another two or three decades as work continues on new power-train and fuel technology and also to prove once and for all that small cars can be safe and fun to drive!

T.25 CITY CAR - ADVANTAGES *Jan. 2008*

CONVENTIONAL PARKING   T.25 PARKING

DIRECT LOAD PATH FRAME
TECHNOLOGY PROVIDES A
RACING TYPE SAFETY CELL
FOR OCCUPANTS

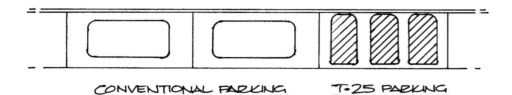

SEPERATE CHASSIS AND BODY LINES
DELIVERS FASTER ASSEMBLY TIMES,
EARLY CHASSIS-ENGINE MARRIAGE
AND FEWER END OF LINE RE-WORKS.

ULTRA-LOW CAPITAL INVESTMENT
- FACTORY SIZE
- FACTORY COST
- TOOLING / FIXTURES
- VEHICLE UPDATES

LARGE REDUCTION IN FULL LIFECYCLE CO_2 FOOTPRINT

M. P. V. CONCEPT
6 DIFFERENT LAYOUTS
IN ONE VEHICLE

2 x T.25 VEHICLES IN ONE
MOTORWAY LANE

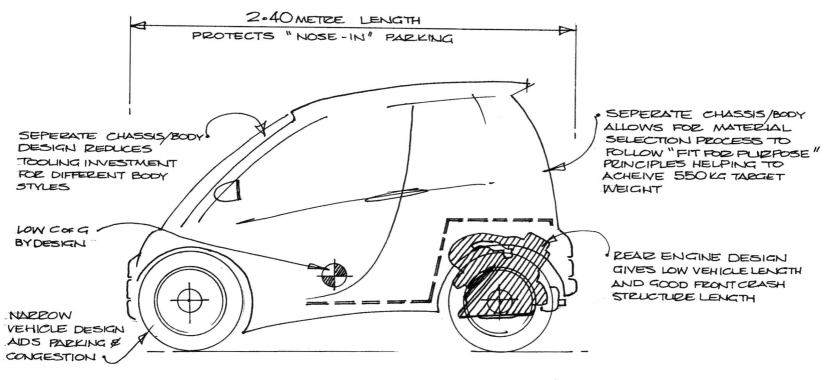

2.40 METRE LENGTH
PROTECTS "NOSE-IN" PARKING

SEPERATE CHASSIS/BODY
DESIGN REDUCES
TOOLING INVESTMENT
FOR DIFFERENT BODY
STYLES

LOW C of G
BY DESIGN

NARROW
VEHICLE DESIGN
AIDS PARKING &
CONGESTION

SEPERATE CHASSIS/BODY
ALLOWS FOR MATERIAL
SELECTION PROCESS TO
FOLLOW "FIT FOR PURPOSE"
PRINCIPLES HELPING TO
ACHEIVE 550 KG TARGET
WEIGHT

REAR ENGINE DESIGN
GIVES LOW VEHICLE LENGTH
AND GOOD FRONT CRASH
STRUCTURE LENGTH

PROTECTING PERSONAL MOBILITY   T.25 GRW. 2008

119

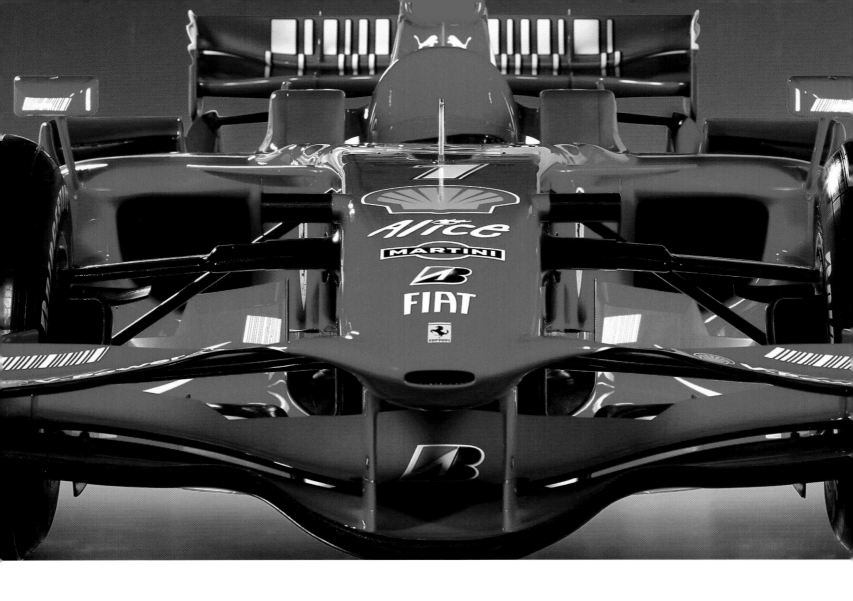

Motor Sports

A perfect thriller!

The 2008 championship went down to the wire, ultimately being settled in the last few yards of the final Grand Prix of the season. On the Interlagos circuit, Felipe Massa virtually led from start to finish. Once he crossed the line, he thought he had become World champion in front of his crowd and on his home circuit (which would have been the first time since the very beginnings in 1950 when Farina won the title in Monza) but thirty seconds behind the winning Ferrari, the race for the championship tilted decisively in favour of Lewis Hamilton as, in extremis, he clawed his way back to the 5th place! This decisive Grand Prix had a story worthy of Alfred Hitchcock with two bursts of rain interrupting the race's smooth running, first at the start and then when the chequered flag was almost in sight. Lewis Hamilton's success was rightly celebrated. The British driver didn't steal this title at the end of his second season in F1 aged just 23, making him the youngest ever champion. No, in the finale to a season which he had dominated so skilfully, Hamilton managed to resist the pressure which had harmed him a year earlier, when he lost the championship to Kimi Räikkönen by a single point on the very same circuit. Massa's victory at least guaranteed the constructors' championship for the Scuderia Ferrari which is now run by a new generation of managers and engineers who are just as worthy as their illustrious predecessors. Lewis Hamilton's triumph means McLaren-Mercedes secured another drivers' championship title after Mika Häkkinen won them the same honour nine years ago… And Ron Dennis secured his revenge for having been dragged through the mud due to the spying affair that poisoned the paddock for so many months in 2007. This season, the FIA hardly made McLaren's job any easier by penalising Hamilton any time they got the chance (such as in Spa where the Englishman still went on to beat his Brazilian rival) or sometimes favouring Massa and the Scuderia for no reason (by imposing a penalty on Bourdais in Japan when he seemed to be more the victim than the guilty party) and the stewards will not have gone up in people's estimations in a year which, behind the scenes, has been rocked by the scandal surrounding Max Mosley's private life. But just when you thought he had been weakened by the press's sensational revelations, the president of the FIA dug in his heels and restarted the debate on far-reaching reforms – of both a technical and economic nature – to Formula 1 with the teams which have now come together under the FOTA (Formula One Teams Association) banner. A new era in the history of Grand Prix could be about to begin. Narration by **Pierre van Vliet**.

Well done Lewis! The first Grand Prix of the season is dominated by Lewis Hamilton who drives an impressive race at Albert Park in Melbourne. A start to the 2008 championship to cheer the hearts of the McLaren team after a 2007 season blotted by the spying affair and the well-publicised heavy fine they had to pay. By taking the lead in the championship right from the off, the young Englishman puts himself in a good position in the race for the title.

With a rare position on the front of the grid, Fernando
Alonso does his best, in his home Grand Prix, to
stay up there by slipping in between the Ferraris and
the McLaren but his Renault engine gives up the
ghost on the 34th lap, making way for Hamilton
to join Räikkönen and Massa on the Barcelona
podium. A perfect 1-2 for the Scuderia which
also gives them the lead in the championship.

Lewis Hamilton plays a risky game in Turkey; to try to get past the seemingly untouchable Ferraris, McLaren goes for a three-stop strategy. The Brit manages to get past Massa by braking repeatedly late after the second pit-stop but another stop sees him pushed down into 2nd by the time he reaches the chequered flag… behind the Brazilian and ahead of Räikkönen.

A spot of luck was needed to win at Monaco and all the more so in view of the sporadic rain that meant race conditions were even more treacherous than usual; trapped in the wet after a shunt at the Bureau de Tabac turn, Hamilton (who has a damaged wheel rim from hitting the barrier) gets back to the pits unscathed. He sets back off with the bit between his teeth and manages to avoid all the obstacles, and this Grand Prix had plenty, to take the race and go back into the lead in the drivers' championship.

A year after the terrible accident which emblazoned itself in people's minds, Robert Kubica becomes a legend by winning the Canadian Grand Prix. The Pole drives magnificently; starting from the front row of the grid, he makes the most of a collision between Hamilton and Räikkönen as they came out of the pits with the safety-car on the track to secure BMW Sauber's first win with a valiant Nick Heidfeld making it a one-two thanks to a cunning one-stop strategy. Historic stuff!

No luck for Kimi! Just as he is dominating the French Grand Prix, having secured pole position, he sees his lead over his team-mate Massa fade away, rather like the bodywork around the exhaust on his V8 Ferrari. This means the Brazilian wins at Magny-Cours but 'Iceman' holds on to second to make it a Scuderia one-two. That just shows the advantage the Reds had in France. It should be remembered that Hamilton was severely punished for his blunder in Canada by being pushed 10 places down the grid and was then given a drive through penalty for a strong-arm passing move shortcutting a chicane. Which meant that the third step on the podium went, unexpectedly, to Jarno Trulli in an improving Toyota.

Nico Rosberg, driving flat out in the streets of the
principality he knows so well for having lived there
since childhood, throws all caution to the wind to get
the Williams to the front before coming off violently
at La Piscine; with debris from the shattered car strewn
all over the track, Massa, Webber and Hamilton forge
a path that avoids their tyres coming into contact
with bits of carbon as sharp as a Swiss army knife…

Lewis Hamilton gives a master class in the rain at the British Grand Prix by winning with over a minute to spare from his nearest rival, a surprising Nick Heidfeld, with a return to form in the BMW. Right from the off, the British prodigy sets about cancelling out the handicap he's had in qualifying by diving for a tight line at Copse Corner behind his team-mate Heikki Kovalainen (who had secured his first pole position) to the surprise of Mark Webber (who was on the front row of the grid) and Felipe Massa. Incredible!

131

Timo Glock, Toyota's young German driver, was
not blessed with luck in his own country; a broken
suspension on the 35th lap sent his car crashing into
the pit-wall at Hockenheim. Yet Glock still managed
to notch up the 7th-fastest race-lap, faster than
team-mate Jarno Trulli who was brilliant in qualifying
and was on the second row of the grid, confirming the
Japanese team's constant progress. The current GP2
champion went on to notch up his best ever result two
weeks later by managing second place in Hungary.

Lewis Hamilton's attempt to get by Kimi Räikkönen in the new chicane three laps from the finish at the Belgian Grand Prix was what started the trouble; did the McLaren gain an advantage by going straight through the exit to avoid hitting the Ferrari as the stewards claimed? The British driver was still able to mount a successful passing manoeuvre on the Finn on the very next turn, braking at the Source corner, and there is nothing to suggest that this move was made easier by what had just happened. Lewis was given a 25" penalty and pushed back down to 3rd; Kimi lost control of his Ferrari on the penultimate, rain-sodden lap, handing victory to Felipe Massa, now just two points off Hamilton in the drivers' championship.

The early pecking order at Spa, with the majestic backdrop of the Eau Rouge valley, was somewhat unexpected: Hamilton led from pole, then came the two Ferraris ahead of the surprise package of Sebastien Bourdais in the Toro Rosso who managed a fairytale start from 9th on the grid, as did Jarno Trulli (11th after qualifying) who worked his way up to 6th behind Alonso's Renault. The French driver drove an attacking race before getting trapped in the rain on the last of the 44 laps and saw himself go from 4th down to 7th within a couple of corners. Bourdais was inconsolable and livid at having lost ground so close to the finish while still battling for his place in 2009.

The 2008 season has made for a nice variety of winners with seven different men victorious in races. At Monza, three young drivers who had all experienced the joy of a first win came together on the podium: Heikki Kovalainen still seemed incredulous at finishing 2nd without ever troubling the tremendous Sebastian Vettel, who, to everyone's surprise, led his Toro Rosso to victory by making the most of his Ferrari engine on a track which was soaking wet one minute and dry the next in quite magnificent fashion. As for the third opportunist, Robert Kubica, it was a repeat appearance on the Monza podium as he had also come in third on his debut in 2007; in doing so, the Pole kept himself in the running for the drivers' championship by taking full advantage of the misadventures which befell his rivals for the world crown on the Milan track.

This world-first Grand Prix raced under the floodlights was a roaring success and its progress, interrupted by two safety-car interventions, saw Fernando Alonso (thanks to an aggressive strategy) leave the Ferraris and McLarens in his wake. By winning in the streets of Singapore and then backing that up with another win in Japan (where Hamilton and Massa were both penalised) two weeks later, the Spanish former champion reminded us that he is at the top of his game and put Renault back into 4th place in the constructors' championship ahead of Toyota.

Sport, technology and showbiz

Pierre Dupasquier, engineer and formerly in charge of competition at Michelin, analyses the delicate balancing act between private and factory teams in Formula 1 this year as well as the energy considerations that the showcase motorsport needs to take into account. But he starts with a few comments on the season thus far.

Before I start on the two subjects I'd like to deal with here, let me make an honest observation. This season, one team has surprised me, or should I say, disappointed me, right from the off and that's Red Bull-Renault. Of course I didn't think that Red-Bull would regularly be battling it out for top spot with the two leaders, Ferrari and McLaren. But the young team had much of what they needed to be able to produce performances that would have grabbed our attention. I met the team owner, Dietrich Mateschitz, several times in 2004 and 2005. I found his personality and charisma very attractive. And his professional achievements speak for themselves. The experience the team and Christian Horner had, plus Adrian Newey's involvement, and Geoff Willis's, were all trump cards. Considerable financial backing, solid skills, a reliable, top-quality engine, two quick drivers who were up to making the most of a good lot… yet we haven't seen any such thing. Gerhard Berger, who's been managing the satellite team, Toro Rosso, hasn't had the chance to put his talents to good use by helping the mother ship, despite Vettel's sensational win at Monza. I'm too far removed from the paddock to provide an answer but their results remain a mystery to me.

The duo of Ferrari and McLaren have served us up the duel we expected. As long as their people and resources were as they should be, it was hard to see who could get close to them. It was obvious that Renault wasn't up to compete with the big guys, regardless of Fernando Alonso's talent and determination. As for Toyota, not yet, not until they co-ordinate their strategy and their drivers. BMW could potentially compete but Mario Theissen's team hasn't got experienced drivers who've won titles which is what they need. The same goes for Frank Williams' team; they've got a good engine but the resources they have mean they can't keep up with the leading pack.

THE POSITION OF PRIVATE TEAMS

Formula 1 is a flamboyant, seductive public institution right at the heart of our showbiz society. Bernie Ecclestone has got it up there as one of the top must-see events. He's managed to increase its audience so much that it's become a talking point in the same way the World Cup has for football or a Grand Slam tournament has for tennis lovers. This worldwide passion could almost make you forget F1 is a technical sport. The importance of that aspect depends on the times and the promoters. It appears that in the battle between sport, technology and showbiz, the latter is increasingly dominating which has serious consequences for the structural relationship between the large car manufacturers and private teams; I was going to say amateur technicians, who have always been the basis of competition ever since the sport was founded. There are skills and the personal and economic interests which both are going to factor into their involvement with the sport.

It might be useful to remember where this passion, which those involved in the sport and those who follow it are still hooked on, sprang from. Right from the outset, it became clear that by working on the car, you could improve its performance which was, of course, hard-wired into the genes of the people making the cars at the time. At the same time, two drivers wouldn't get the same results even when using the same tools and, to top it all, some industrialists were beginning to use these early contests as proof that their technological designs were well-founded. The Michelin brothers, for example, chose the sport to demonstrate that the sometimes radical changes they made to tyres were a step forward for cars as a whole; they began as early as 1895 at the Paris-Bordeaux-Paris Rally.

It's a good way of showing the complexity of the factors which, at any given time, are going to affect sporting categories: the show, the rivalry between technical teams or the pleasure of performing and competing and all

Anna-Louise Felstead '08

supported by advertisers or car professionals. What can even experienced, passionate craftsmen do when their resources are in no way comparable to those of the large constructors if they decide to get involved to show off their technical skills and, at the same time, their ability to offer high-performance and global quality models to the world?

I've discussed it all several times with Bernie Ecclestone, the man who 'conceived' modern F1, and I can safely say that his overriding attitude is one of realism. Bernie might be sentimental in areas of his life which I know nothing about but as far as he's concerned F1, his F1, is a business; you can't kill off the wonderful teams which started the whole sport, such as Lotus, Tyrrell, Brabham, Lola, Ligier or even Williams, nor reject support from the likes of Mercedes, Toyota, BMW, Honda or Renault who lend the sport credibility. I didn't mention the scuderia from Maranello because they're a case apart; they're such an exclusive constructor that they live from racing alone.

You've already heard me say I regret that Mr. Aguri Suzuki's team disappeared in the middle of the season. Of course you can't say that Aguri was what we tend to call a modest craftsman because his initiative had the moral backing of all Japan who knew the talented driver well and loved him. And Michelin had worked with him on several occasions. Fukui-san, Honda's dynamic president, gave him considerable help, both financial and technical. But Honda revised its F1 strategy and the support they gave was insufficient in view of the competition in 2008. Who knows what the future holds for Williams, Force India or Toro Rosso?

We are also given food for thought by looking at the budgets the teams have at their disposal; they range from 50 million euros for the humbler teams to some 400 million for the best-off. The figures need to be adjusted for the engine; the costs are indeed very different depending on whether

it's designed and produced in-house or simply bought. I'm sure Bernie Ecclestone is sad Aguri Suzuki is gone and he needs to make sure that private teams survive. You know that the boards of large industries can't be emotional when they're accountable to their shareholders and Bernie understands all too well that it'd be suicide if F1 depended on the good will of the large constructors alone. In the same way that the sport-showbiz balance has to be struck, the constructor/independent team balance will remain a real challenge.

The same goes for researching a formula which wouldn't be a black hole for our precious petrol creating enough pollution to make even our most tolerant environmentalists pale with horror.

FUEL AND THE ENVIRONMENT

Of course Formula 1 and motorsports in general don't account for huge fuel consumption or significant pollution when viewed in the context of the risks the planet faces. Yet the FIA heads have asked F1, the mother of all motorsports, to come up with a device which could recover the significant energy expended when cars travelling at 300 km/h have to reduce their speed to 80 km/h as they approach a corner. That means a whole load of kilojoules being pumped into the atmosphere which could be reused during acceleration. There are two workable principles: directly storing the energy by accelerating a rotating mass, such as a flywheel, or using a generator which would store the energy as electricity in a battery or capacitors. The idea is interesting but not new and several vehicles already function on the same principle, including all electric vehicles, especially underground trains. Michelin even built some very spectacular test tracks which are still to be found in Clermont-Ferrand where carts moved by electric engines would climb a slope and then come back down again, transforming their engines into generators and thus recovering some of the energy they'd used on the way up. A few teams have started testing some developments. We have heard that a technician from a German team was recently injured in an 'electric incident,' the details of which have been slow to come to light.

Isn't the FIA lacking in ambition? Partial energy recovery using an old principle doesn't quite seem up to F1's skill-level. Although the delicate balance between showbiz, costs and technological investment we were talking about is leaning ever closer to glitz and glamour, the men and women of the scientific and technological communities who are presiding over the developments in current cars are amongst the most brilliant of their generation; they are young and, incidentally, well-paid. So we can expect top ideas and developments from them.

We also know that there are several attempts under way to liberate the ways we move around from the oil dictatorship. Some of them are already up and running, in a limited but nonetheless satisfying way. BMW, for example, has made some hydrogen-fuelled 7 Series available to diplomats in Brussels to demonstrate that the system can work large-scale even if production, stocks, transport and all sorts of other problems linked to the fuel are still a long way from being solved.

If you analyse what it is that characterises F1, a number of problems are solved by the fact that time, place and action all come together in the perfectly secure paddock environment. Getting the hundreds of F1 manufacturing engineers, who've been bored stiff since the federal authorities froze maximum engine revolutions at 19,000 rpm, to talk on that type of subject should bring rapid results. A positive thing would be to get F1 to make a useful contribution to the development of individual mobility. In that way, we wouldn't be getting away from the traditional definition of racing cars altogether and nor would we be fundamentally changing the track environment.

Electricity is another powerful and mobile source of energy. Some vehicles powered by the 'good fairy' do exist but here it's really a case of removal far from the traditional car: electricity doesn't make any noise! As long ago as the 1960s I initiated tests in the Paris area on cars which ran on an electric engine with their inventor, the engineer Grégoire. I was trying to reduce tyre resistance and he was trying to improve overall performance but he was cautious about short-term progress in energy storage in the battery. He was right to the extent that that is always the delicate point – but serious progress is being made quickly and electricity can come from elsewhere. Fuel cells are a reality.

Solar energy too. In Australia, a car powered exclusively by solar energy covered the 3000 km between Darwin and Adelaide at an average speed of almost 100 km/h…

But even taking into account the time-frame and the urgency, the enormous amount of work and the resources that have been put into the ongoing operation don't seem to be equal to the very minor technical effects the development will have on our daily mobility.

My words aren't meant to be exhaustive and are only aimed at encouraging the FIA to be more ambitious. Be brave, people. Be brave!

Scuderia Ferrari Marlboro

The Ferrari F2008 retained all the aerodynamic excellence of the F2007 which had been crowned champion the season before and improved its performance on slow corners, meaning it did better on winding circuits like Monaco or Budapest where the previous model had rarely done well. The new technical team run by Aldo Costa did a good job. However, the Ferrari suffered from the same problem the BMW had, namely tyre temperature during qualifying, and reigning champion Kimi Räikkönen found it very hard to get on the front row of the grid – unlike his team-mate Felipe Massa. The Brazilian was in the ascendancy over the summer and scored some impressive wins, such as in Valencia, but plummeting reliability, as an agonising retirement in Hungary (three laps from

the finish with him well in the lead) and a refuelling incident in Singapore are testament to, dented his title hopes. Massa also saw ups and downs in his driving: he was impressive on tracks he likes (Bahrain and Turkey) but less so on others (Monaco or Silverstone in the rain). The new Scuderia, under the leadership of the ever-smiling Stefano Domenicali, made operational mistakes due to an occasional lack of rigour or discipline which led to incidents unheard of during Ross Brawn's reign. And Kimi Räikkönen committed a number of errors, such as embarrassing crashes at Valencia and Singapore, by attacking excessively to make up for his shortfalls in qualifying. Ferrari have the option of maintaining the Finn's services until 2010 but the questions about his motivation remain.

Kimi Räikkönen

Felipe Massa

Stefano Domenicali

Vodafone McLaren Mercedes

The MP4-23 got off to a flying start in Melbourne but was outclassed by the Ferrari in the early part of the season. Lewis Hamilton got the best out of his tyres in qualifying yet their more rapid wear in the races themselves sometimes saw him go for a new strategy, such as the three stops at the Turkish Grand Prix. The aerodynamic developments brought in at Silverstone clearly improved braking and traction which saw the British driver regularly fight it out for top spot and team-mate Heikki Kovalainen record his first win in Hungary. Lewis was untouchable in England in the rain and in Germany in spite of a risky strategy and went on to drive the rest of the championship with the experience of an old veteran rather than crack under the pressure, always managing to score good points if victory itself eluded him. Hamilton's brilliance and the thirst for revenge which has spurred Ron Dennis's team on since the all-too-publicised affair in 2007 fuelled McLaren and Mercedes's ambitions all season. Faced with a Scuderia undergoing change after Jean Todt's fading into the background and Ross Brawn's departure, the fighting spirit coming out of Woking was perhaps what made the difference. Relatively unknown engineers such as designer Tim Goss and aerodynamicist Simon Lacey were very responsive under the overall management of Martin Whitmarsh and the success of their work was no doubt the key to the championship.

Lewis Hamilton

Heikki Kovalainen

Ron Dennis

145

BMW Sauber F1 Team

After unpromising early tests, the F1.08 with pretty radical aerodynamics finally lived up to all the hopes and proved it had got closer to the top cars, the McLarens and the Ferraris; the average gap was about three tenths per lap whereas it was five tenths a year earlier. However, like a number of other cars in the 2008 line-up, the BMW struggled to get the Bridgestone tyres' temperature up, especially at the front. The drivers had to go rough on the car, especially in qualifying, and Robert Kubica turned out to be a lot better at doing so than team-mate Nick Heidfeld. The pair managed a resounding double at the Canadian Grand Prix by taking full advantage of the incident which saw Räikkönen and Hamilton knocked out of the race at the exit to the Montreal pit-lane but they never got anywhere close to repeating that thereafter.

The Pole was very consistent and even led the drivers' championship mid-season thanks to his car's unfailing reliability yet he never seemed a likely candidate for overall victory. In the latter half of the championship, he complained more often of the BMW's lack of development compared to its rivals. Nick Heidfeld could rely on his experience in certain circumstances, such as when he secured 2nd place in the rain at Silverstone, but was made to look second rate by his formidable team-mate. Mario Theissen's leadership of the team was consolidated; he was well supported by technical director Willy Rampf and engineer Walter Riedl, a BMW man through and through, who was in charge of working on the F1.09 and the new regulations (such as the introduction of KERS) from early summer.

Robert Kubica　　　　*Nick Heidfeld*　　　　　　*Mario Theissen*

ING Renault F1 Team

The return of the prodigal son may not have had the desired effect but Fernando Alonso has done all he can to pull the team up by making the most of what he's been given and driving aggressively and opportunistically when given half a chance, as he demonstrated with the historic win in Singapore. But the R28 chassis was basically lacking aerodynamic support and dynamism (no doubt to do with aerodynamic engineer Dino Toso's death), while the French V8 ('frozen' in every sense of the word) fell down the engine hierarchy due to its lack of power and torque. So the Spanish two-time world champion had to settle for the odd success here and there (like qualifying on the front row in Barcelona and coming fourth in Australia and Hungary)

before his night-time triumph, and sacrificing the honour of the first podium finish to new-boy Nelson 'Nelsinho' Piquet who finished 2nd at Hockenheim thanks to a string of events in his favour. This saw the young Brazilian keep his drive after a disastrous start to the season. But it was Renault Sport in Viry-Châtillon who took the freeze in engine development literally which obviously wasn't what the competition had done. With the regulations in place for five years, at least in theory, you've got to wonder how Renault can get out of this funk. The ever-pragmatic Flavio Briatore has asked his technical right-hand man Pat Symonds to concentrate on a faultless R29 for next season, thus making a very early break with the current car.

Giancarlo Fisichella

Nelson Piquet

Flavio Briatore

Panasonic Toyota Racing

The Toyota TF108 is a real step up from its predecessor, cutting the gap separating it from the front of the grid by about half a second compared to 2007. But the chassis was still very sensitive to the track surface; it far preferred the flatness of Magny-Cours (as Jarno Trulli's podium finish in France demonstrates) to bumpy or high-camber circuits. A very specific front suspension design which made for hardly any variation in geometry gave an aerodynamic advantage but also explained the erratic performance over bumps. The jointly managed technical team, with Pascal Vasselon in charge of the chassis and Luca Marmorini in charge of the engines, brought the car a long way forward. It

doesn't yet perform like the top teams' cars but it is still a success for a team with, admittedly, unlimited resources but little experience. Thanks to that 34-year-old head on his shoulders, Jarno Trulli drove like a true number 1, excellent in qualifying and often doing well in the races (which wasn't always seen as his strong point in the past) and was well supported by Timo Glock, one of the season's revelations, who hit the headlines in Budapest with a remarkable 2nd place. Toyota would seem, then, to be on the right track even if we might ask ourselves whether their current structure hasn't reached its limits; we'll know for sure in a few months' time.

Jarno Trulli

Timo Glock

Tadashi Yamashina

Scuderia Toro Rosso

The success late in the season of a small team like Toro Rosso has relaunched the debate on independent teams benefiting from a chassis made by another constructor. With a budget of under $100 million, STR has managed to succeed where giants like Toyota and Honda have been failing for years in spite of massive investment. Sebastian Vettel's win at Monza was rightly seen as a breath of fresh air for F1 insofar as it uncovered a true champion in difficult conditions but also in that it brought the question of 'client' chassis back into the arena. According to the agreements currently in place, the FIA has granted Toro Rosso a waiver until the end of 2009 on the condition that they design and produce their own chassis for 2010. Suddenly, Dietrich Mateschitz, co-owner with Gerhard Berger of the Faenza outfit (originally Minardi), announced

he would be selling his shares. The energy drink magnate had actually created a specific set-up called Red Bull Technologies aimed at supplying both the teams he controls. So Scuderia Toro Rosso has a chassis identical to Red Bull Racing's but with Ferrari engines and the associated components (transmission, electronics, cooling). The STR03 is a cut and paste of the RB4... with an extra 30 hp which is generally viewed as the power surplus the Ferrari V8 has over the Renault! All of a sudden the STRs could be set for more downforce and came up with the sort of performances we're now familiar with. Furthermore, the engineer Giorgio Ascanelli (formerly of McLaren and Ferrari), wisely taken on by Berger to succeed Gabriele Tredozi, has done a remarkably good job.

Sebastian Vettel

Sebastien Bourdais

Gerhard Berger

Red Bull Racing

The top team of the mighty Red Bull, probably F1's biggest commercial sponsor, have been a disappointment in 2008. Mark Webber's performances in qualifying and the races themselves (the Australian has notched up more than 20 points), supported by improved reliability, and veteran David Coulthard's sole success (finishing on the podium in Canada before announcing his retirement) mask the very average competitiveness level of the RB4 chassis with the Renault RS28 V8 engine. Adrian Newey had to contend with limited resources, though there was consistent progress thanks to the installation of a second wind-tunnel, and Red Bull Technologies' unwieldy structure, with it also having to look after sister team

Toro Rosso. Yet it is the Renault engine's obvious lack of power, cruelly highlighted when compared to the Ferrari V8 engine the Toro Rossos are equipped with, which has seen the RB4 flounder this season. Aerodynamics improved constantly, yet it was ultimately the STR03s which benefited more than anyone. As his reputation would suggest, Adrian Newey was innovative in instigating a fashion for shark-fin wings on the engine cover (ensuring better rear stability) which would soon be copied by the majority of other teams. The engine problem remains real for 2009 as the development freeze will no doubt prevent Renault from completely making up lost ground.

David Coulthard

Mark Webber

Christian Horner

AT&T Williams

Sir Frank's valiant team continued its slow decline, which, given the current climate, you can't help wondering how they'll stop. With limited resources compared to the large constructors but in all likelihood comparable to those of Red Bull Racing thanks to a very dynamic commercial department, Williams had a failed season. The FW30 got off to a pretty good start with Nico Rosberg scoring big points straight off (a podium finish in Australia), but then went wrong with its design philosophy which prevented weight being shifted forwards to make more of the Bridgestone tyres. Sam Michael and his team did try to remedy the problem but without success; yet the drivers couldn't capitalise on the only circuits where

the phenomenon wasn't too evident, such as Monaco or Montreal. Rosberg didn't drive badly, often making it to Q3 and also scoring some points (8th in Bahrain, Turkey and at Valencia) before grabbing another podium finish thanks to taking his chances in Singapore, and the same goes for Kazuki Nakajima whose top speed speaks for itself. In comparison to the Toyotas, whom they inherited their engines from, the Williams did demonstrate their limits with development reduced to the minimum in the second half of the championship. The explanation is simple: Patrick Head decided in summer that all the team's efforts would be put into the 2009 FW31 given the upheaval in the technical regulations.

Nico Rosberg

Kazuki Nakajima

Frank Williams

Honda Racing F1 Team

The Japanese team (based in Great Britain, naturally) sort of withdrew to be able to make a better go of things in 2008. The results have hardly been spectacular. The RA108 got off to not a bad start in comparison to the disastrous RA107 thanks to better co-ordination (at long last) between the wind-tunnels and the track; is this the Ross Brawn effect already? Recruited at considerable expense, the British engineer demanded full powers and the post of team principal, relegating the more obscure Nick Fry to administrative duties. The car was developed until mid-season which helped Jenson Button and Rubens Barrichello secure some decent results (6th place in Spain for the Englishman and in Canada for the Brazilian, who

finished also an excellent 3rd in the rain at Silverstone). But once the summer break was over, the Hondas went backwards, never making Q3, and a decision was made to devote the team's funds to 2009 to better capitalise on the radical regulation changes. It is noteworthy that engineer Jacky Eeckelaert, formerly in charge of running operations, now provides a link to Honda's R&D centre in Japan to make the best use of resources. Ross Brawn needs to raise the competitiveness level to maintain his reputation and leadership at a constructor which has competition in its blood, with all the expectations that that presupposes, especially if Toyota continue to make progress…

Rubens Barrichello

Jenson Button

Ross Brown

Kingfisher Force India

The Little Thumb in the line-up is hoping to get a lot bigger thanks to the considerable investments being made by its new owner, the Indian entrepreneur Vijay Mallya, after a number of chaotic seasons where the management changed hands more than once, from Jordan to Force India via Midland and Spyker. The team is still housed next to Silverstone; its factories have been modernised and Mike Gascoyne's technical crew (which has been strengthened by Mark Smith's arrival from Red Bull Racing) came up with a chassis which is essentially based on the car they finished the 2007 season with, plus some aerodynamic developments. On the track, the Force India cars reduced the gap separating them from pole by about two seconds on average but that still wasn't enough to move them away from the back of the grid. The odd but all too rare flash of brilliance from Giancarlo Fisichella, who qualified in 12th in Monza in the rain, for example, and Adrian Sutil's sadly unrewarded exploits in Monaco (he was hit by Räikkönen's Ferrari when he had made his way into the points) remain the highlights of a year where not a single championship point was notched up. The appearance of the seamless shift gearbox mid-season also helped them get nearer the best cars – without them really being able to worry the other client teams Williams or Toro Rosso. It should be remembered that Toro Rosso paid Force India a $4 million penalty to avoid being taken to court over the rather vague case of the 'client chassis'. Tensions between manager Colin Kolles and technical director Mike Gascoyne rather poisoned the atmosphere within the team but Vijay Mallya remains upbeat, convinced that India can shine in F1 with a Grand Prix in New Delhi on a new track built by the ubiquitous Hermann Tilke on the cards for 2010.

Adrian Sutil

Giancarlo Fisichella

Colin Kolles

Super Aguri F1 Team

After a fairly successful 2007 season thanks to the SA07, which had formerly been the Honda RA106 (the car in which Button won in Hungary in 2006), Super Aguri sadly gave up at the start of the European season when asked to remove the team trucks from the Istanbul paddock shortly before the Turkish Grand Prix. Honda had already had to pay so that Aguri Suzuki and Takuma Sato could pursue their adventure but the lack of a real

sponsor ended up disheartening the Japanese manufacturer. As the SA08 (which was really the disastrous Honda RA107) appeared to have limited potential at best, candidates weren't exactly barging each other out of the way in their rush to invest; first the Magma Group and then the German Weigl decided to throw in the towel, forcing the F1 minnows into humiliating liquidation.

Takuma Sato

Anthony Davidson

Aguri Suzuki

Australian Grand Prix

KEY

◁ Start Location
5 Gear
251 Speed (km/h)
156 Speed (mph)
2.4 Lateral G-force
16 Turn number
T3 *Timing Sector
33.7 *Sector Time
1:24.4 **Target Lap Time
🏁 Finish Location

*The circuit is split into three timed sectors which, when added together, make up the lap time.
**A lap time that drivers aim for based on pole position 2004.

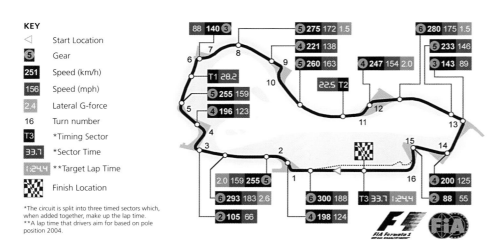

Albert Park, Melbourne, Australia – March 16
Length of the circuit: 5.303 km/3.295 miles
Race: 58 laps
Distance: 307.574 km/191.110 miles
Weather: sunny and hot

QUALIFYING

	Driver	Car	Chassis	Time
1	Lewis Hamilton	McLaren	MP4-23 04	1'26"714
2	Robert Kubica	BMW	F1.08-03	1'26"869
3	Heikki Kovalainen	McLaren	MP4-23 03	1'27"079
4	Felipe Massa	Ferrari	F2008-267	1'27"178
5	Nick Heidfeld	BMW	F1.08-03	1'27"236
6	Jarno Trulli	Toyota	TF108-02	1'28"527
7	Nico Rosberg	Williams	FW30-03	1'28"687
8	David Coulthard	Red Bull	RB4-04	1'29"041
9	Timo Glock	Toyota	TF108-04	1'29"593
10	Sebastian Vettel	Toro Rosso	STR02B-04	no time
11	Rubens Barrichello	Honda	RA 108-04	1'26"173
12	Fernando Alonso	Renault	R28-03	1'26"188
13	Jenson Button	Honda	RA 108-02	1'26"259
14	Kazuki Nakajima	Williams	FW30-04	1'26"413
15	Mark Webber	Red Bull	RB4-03	no time
16	Kimi Räikkönen	Ferrari	F2008-268	no time
17	Giancarlo Fisichella	Force India	VJM01/05	1'27"207
18	Sebastien Bourdais	Toro Rosso	STR02B-03	1'27"207
19	Adrian Sutil	Force India	VJM01/03	1'27"859
20	Takuma Sato	Super Aguri	SA08-06	1'28"208
21	Nelson Piquet	Renault	R28-01	1'28"330
22	Anthony Davidson	Super Aguri	SA08-05	1'29"059

MELBOURNE

Starting on pole, Hamilton is untroubled throughout. Kovalainen and Massa collide on the first corner; Vettel stalls and his car is smashed up by Button's; Nakajima gets in the way of Davidson who, in turn, sends Webber's car flying into the air; Glock and Piquet fight it out… and almost make Fisichella flip right over. The safety car comes out. Kubica, brilliant in qualifying with a lighter car, is the first to pit; the Pole slips down the field and isn't helped by the repeated appearances of the safety car. He is eventually knocked out of the race by Nakajima. Räikkönen, who was 15th on the grid due to a problem with his fuel pump, manages to claw his way up to 3rd but finds the gravel twice. Midway through the race, Massa (who has just rejoined the track) retires with engine trouble. This sees the McLarens heading for a one-two finish but Glock comes off the track spectacularly just as Kovalainen is due to pit and this costs the Finn his place on the podium. Heidfeld and Rosberg, who have driven steadily throughout, take full advantage. Heikki battles it out fiercely with Alonso, who's in a fighting mood. He gets past him but hits the rev limiter and the Renault gets past him in turn. They are handed 4th and 5th places on a plate by the retirement due to engine failure, three laps from the end of the race, of the… Toro Rosso, driven superbly by Bourdais. Räikkönen can't take advantage, due to the same problem. Barrichello is 6th on the track but is disqualified for jumping a red light. Nakajima, the last driver to cross the finishing line, ends up with three points. What an extraordinary Grand Prix (15 retirements!), which gives Lewis Hamilton his fifth victory.

RESULT

	Driver	Car	Time	Laps	Stops
1	Lewis Hamilton	McLaren	1h34'50"616	58	2
2	Nick Heidfeld	BMW	+5"478	58	2
3	Nico Rosberg	Williams	+8"166	58	2
4	Fernando Alonso	Renault	+17"181	58	2
5	Heikki Kovalainen	McLaren	+18"014	58	2
DQ	Rubens Barichello	Honda	+52"453	58	3
6	Kazuki Nakajima	Williams	+1 lap	57	3

RETIREMENTS

Sebastien Bourdais	Toro Rosso	transmission	55	2
Kimi Räikkönen	Ferrari	engine	53	1
Robert Kubica	BMW	collision	47	2
Timo Glock	Toyota	accident	43	1
Takuma Sato	Super Aguri	transmission	32	1
Nelson Piquet	Renault	collision	30	1
Felipe Massa	Ferrari	engine	29	2
David Coulthard	Red Bull	collision	25	1
Jarno Trulli	Toyota	battery	19	0
Adrian Sutil	Force India	hydraulics	8	0
Sebastian Vettel	Toro Rosso	accident	0	0
Jenson Button	Honda	accident	0	0
Mark Webber	Red Bull	accident	0	0
Giancarlo Fisichella	Force India	accident	0	0
Anthony Davidson	Super Aguri	accident	0	0

FASTEST LAP

Heikki Kovalainen	McLaren	1'27"418	43

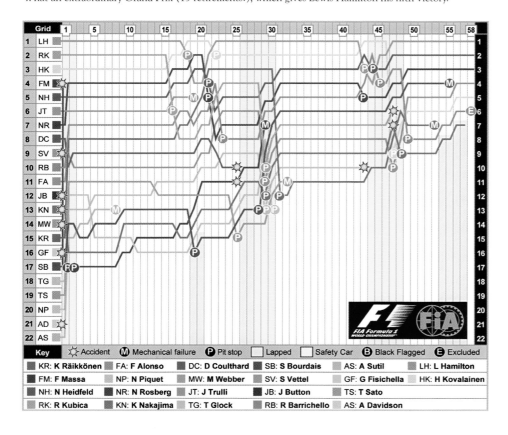

Key ☆ Accident Ⓜ Mechanical failure Ⓟ Pit stop ▢ Lapped ▢ Safety Car Ⓑ Black Flagged Ⓔ Excluded

KR: **K Räikkönen** | FA: **F Alonso** | DC: **D Coulthard** | SB: **S Bourdais** | AS: **A Sutil** | LH: **L Hamilton**
FM: **F Massa** | NP: **N Piquet** | MW: **M Webber** | SV: **S Vettel** | GF: **G Fisichella** | HK: **H Kovalainen**
NH: **N Heidfeld** | NR: **N Rosberg** | JT: **J Trulli** | JB: **J Button** | TS: **T Sato**
RK: **R Kubica** | KN: **K Nakajima** | TG: **T Glock** | RB: **R Barrichello** | AS: **A Davidson**

Malaysian Grand Prix

◁ Start Location
5 Gear
251 Speed (km/h)
156 Speed (mph)
2.4 Lateral G-force
16 Turn number
T3 *Timing Sector
33.7 *Sector Time
1:24.4 **Target Lap Time
▨ Finish Location

*The circuit is split into three timed sectors which, when added together, make up the lap time.
**A lap time that drivers aim for based on pole position 2004.

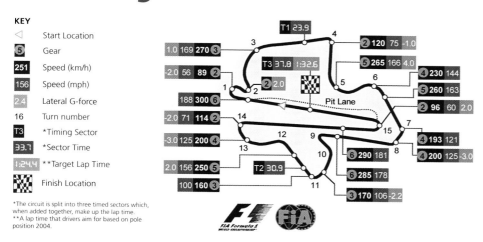

Sepang, Kuala Lumpur, Malaysia – March 23
Length of the circuit: 5.543 km/3.444 miles
Race: 56 laps
Distance: 310.408 km/192.887 miles
Weather: dry and overcast

QUALIFYING

	Driver	Car	Chassis	Time
1	Felipe Massa	Ferrari	F2008-267	1'35"748
2	Kimi Räikkönen	Ferrari	F2008-268	1'36"230
3	Heikki Kovalainen	McLaren	MP4-23 03	1'36"613
4	Lewis Hamilton	McLaren	MP4-23 04	1'36"709
5	Jarno Trulli	Toyota	TF108-02	1'36"711
6	Robert Kubica	BMW	F1.08-03	1'36"727
7	Nick Heidfeld	BMW	F1.08-04	1'36"753
8	Mark Webber	Red Bull	RB4-04	1'37"009
9	Fernando Alonso	Renault	R28-03	1'38"450
10	Timo Glock	Toyota	TF108-01	1'39"656
11	Jenson Button	Honda	RA108-02	1'35"208
12	David Coulthard	Red Bull	RB4-02	1'35"408
13	Nelson Piquet	Renault	R28-01	1'35"562
14	Rubens Barrichello	Honda	RA108-04	1'35"622
15	Sebastian Vettel	Toro Rosso	STR2B-04	1'35"648
16	Nico Rosberg	Williams	FW30-03	1'35"670
17	Giancarlo Fisichella	Force India	VJM01/05	1'36"240
18	Kazuki Nakajima	Williams	FW30-04	1'36"388
19	Sebastien Bourdais	Toro Rosso	STR2B-03	1'36"677
20	Takuma Sato	Super Aguri	SA08-06	1'37"087
21	Adrian Sutil	Force India	VJM01/02	1'37"101
22	Anthony Davidson	Super Aguri	SA08-05	1'37"481

SEPANG

Ferrari's revenge. The two F2008s monopolise the front row of the grid with Massa ahead of Räikkönen. The McLarens should have been on the second row but Kovalainen and Hamilton are relegated to 8th and 9th place (i.e. penalised by being demoted five places) for impeding Heidfeld and Alonso in testing. Kimi's start is better than Felipe's but the Brazilian manages to crowd him out and keep his lead. Trulli, Heidfeld and Alonso knock each other about further back and all lose places as a result. Massa is in control until he pits for the first time. Räikkönen comes in two laps later and comes back out onto the track ahead of his rival; that's the race won. The McLarens are out in front but Hamilton's progress through the field is held up by a stubborn right-hand front wheel during one of his stops. There's a moment of drama on the 31st lap as Massa loses control of his car and ends up stuck in the gravel. Kubica makes the most of it and ends up 2nd on the podium ahead of Kovalainen. Trulli, who has driven a great race, manages to contain Lewis's final assault and holds on to 4th place. Heidfeld, who ends up 6th after becoming the main casualty of the collisions on the first corner, has to content himself with driving the fastest lap. The two points left up for grabs are fought over to the last between two Renault engines with Webber in the Red Bull holding Alonso off right up to the finish line. It's the reigning world champion's first victory of the 2008 season but Hamilton still leads the championship overall.

RESULT

	Driver	Car	Time	Laps	Stops
1	Kimi Räikkönen	Ferrari	1h31'18"555	56	2
2	Robert Kubica	BMW	+19"570	56	2
3	Heikki Kovalainen	McLaren	+38"450	56	2
4	Jarno Trulli	Toyota	+45"832	56	2
5	Lewis Hamilton	McLaren	+46"548	56	2
6	Nick Heidfeld	BMW	+49"833	56	2
7	Mark Webber	Red Bull	+1'08"130	56	2
8	Fernando Alonso	Renault	+1'10"041	56	2
9	David Coulthard	Red Bull	+1'16"220	56	2
10	Jenson Button	Honda	+1'26"214	56	2
11	Nelson Piquet	Renault	+1'32"202	56	2
12	Giancarlo Fisichella	Force India	+1 lap	55	2
13	Rubens Barrichello	Honda	+1 lap	55	3
14	Nico Rosberg	Williams	+1 lap	55	2
15	Anthony Davidson	Super Aguri	+1 lap	55	2
16	Takuma Sato	Super Aguri	+2 laps	54	2
17	Kazuki Nakajima	Williams	+2 laps	54	2

RETIREMENTS

Sebastian Vettel	Toro Rosso	engine	39	1
Felipe Massa	Ferrari	spin	30	1
Adrian Sutil	Force India	engine	5	0
Timo Glock	Toyota	accident	1	0
Sebastien Bourdais	Toro Rosso	spin	0	0

FASTEST LAP

Nick Heidfeld	BMW	1'35"366	55

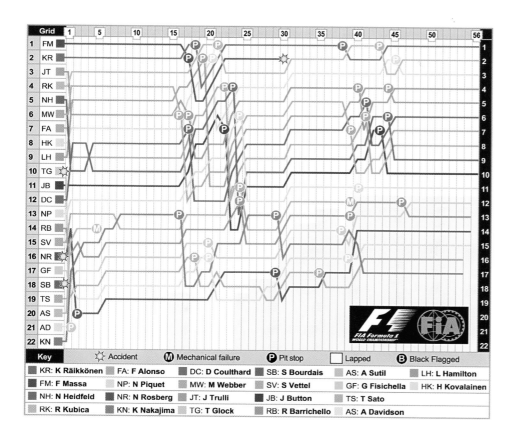

Key				
KR: K Räikkönen	FA: F Alonso	DC: D Coulthard	SB: S Bourdais	AS: A Sutil	LH: L Hamilton
FM: F Massa	NP: N Piquet	MW: M Webber	SV: S Vettel	GF: G Fisichella	HK: H Kovalainen
NH: N Heidfeld	NR: N Rosberg	JT: J Trulli	JB: J Button	TS: T Sato	
RK: R Kubica	KN: K Nakajima	TG: T Glock	RB: R Barrichello	AS: A Davidson	

Bahrain Grand Prix

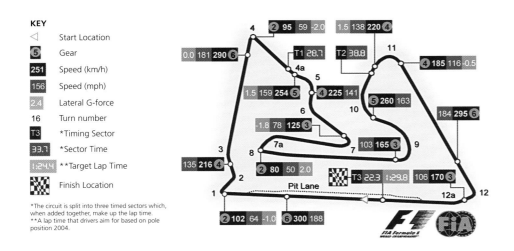

Manama, Bahrain – April 6
Length of the circuit: 5.412 km/3.363 miles
Race: 57 laps
Distance: 308.238 km/191.539 miles
Weather: sunny and dry

QUALIFYING

	Driver	Car	Chassis	Time
1	Robert Kubica	BMW	F1.08-03	1'33"096
2	Felipe Massa	Ferrari	F2008-267	1'33"123
3	Lewis Hamilton	McLaren	MP4-23 04	1'33"292
4	Kimi Räikkönen	Ferrari	F2008-268	1'33"418
5	Heikki Kovalainen	McLaren	MP4-23 03	1'33"488
6	Nick Heidfeld	BMW	F1.08-04	1'33"737
7	Jarno Trulli	Toyota	TF108-02	1'33"994
8	Nico Rosberg	Williams	FW30-03	1'34"015
9	Jenson Button	Honda	RA108-02	1'35"057
10	Fernando Alonso	Renault	R28-03	1'35"115
11	Mark Webber	Red Bull	RB4-04	1'32"371
12	Rubens Barrichello	Honda	RA108-04	1'32"508
13	Timo Glock	Toyota	TF108-01	1'32"528
14	Nelson Piquet	Renault	R28-01	1'32"790
15	Sebastien Bourdais	Toro Rosso	STR02B-03	1'32"915
16	Kazuki Nakajima	Williams	FW30-04	1'32"943
17	David Coulthard	Red Bull	RB4-02	1'33"433
18	Giancarlo Fisichella	Force India	VJM01/05	1'33"501
19	Sebastian Vettel	Toro Rosso	STR02B-04	1'33"562
20	Adrian Sutil	Force India	VJM01/02	1'33"845
21	Anthony Davidson	Super Aguri	SA08-05	1'34"140
22	Takuma Sato	Super Aguri	SA08-06	1'35"725

SAKHIR

Robert Kubica takes a surprise pole position for the first time in his career by making the most of a lighter fuel tank than Massa who had been untouchable up to that point. But the Pole skids too much at the start and Felipe overtakes him straight away. Hamilton gets stuck on the grid and is immediately six places back and then breaks his front wing off Alonso's Renault. It's the start of what turns out to be a hellish race for the Brit. The lead is settled very early on: Räikkönen overtakes Kubica with Heidfeld passing Trulli and then Kovalainen which leaves the two BMWs behind the two Ferraris. They are followed by Heikki, Jarno, Webber and Rosberg, which is how the top eight ends up! Robert is, as planned, the first to pit; Nick is the last but this makes no difference to the overall standings. And the second bout of pit-stops doesn't change anything either. If it's a scrap you're looking for, you have to look further down the field. Between Button and Coulthard, who collide, between Barrichello and Fisichella or between Alonso and Glock. Fernando is unable to get the better of the Toyota and even has to hold off a resurgent Barrichello for a paltry 10th place. And as for Hamilton, rather than tearing back up the field as expected, his race, beset by problems, ends with him finishing way down in 13th, behind the Force India of Fisico who has driven a brilliant race. Lewis loses his lead in the championship to Räikkönen, whilst the consistency of the BMW drivers means the German-Swiss team now leads the constructors' championship.

RESULT

	Driver	Car	Time	Laps	Stops
1	Felipe Massa	Ferrari	1h31'06"970	57	2
2	Kimi Räikkönen	Ferrari	+3"339	57	2
3	Robert Kubica	BMW	+4"998	57	2
4	Nick Heidfeld	BMW	+8"409	57	2
5	Heikki Kovalainen	McLaren	+26"789	57	2
6	Jarno Trulli	Toyota	+41"314	57	2
7	Mark Webber	Red Bull	+45"473	57	2
8	Nico Rosberg	Williams	+55"889	57	2
9	Timo Glock	Toyota	+1'09"500	57	2
10	Fernando Alonso	Renault	+1'17"181	57	2
11	Rubens Barrichello	Honda	+1'17"862	57	2
12	Giancarlo Fisichella	Force India	+1 lap	56	2
13	Lewis Hamilton	McLaren	+1 lap	56	2
14	Kazuki Nakajima	Williams	+1 lap	56	2
15	Sebastien Bourdais	Toro Rosso	+1 lap	56	1
16	Anthony Davidson	Super Aguri	+1 lap	56	2
17	Takuma Sato	Super Aguri	+1 lap	56	2
18	David Coulthard	Red Bull	+1 lap	56	2
19	Adrian Sutil	Force India	+2 laps	55	3

RETIREMENTS

Nelson Piquet	Renault	transmission	40	3
Jenson Button	Honda	collision	19	3
Sebastian Vettel	Toro Rosso	accident	0	0

FASTEST LAP

Heikki Kovalainen	McLaren	1'33"193	49

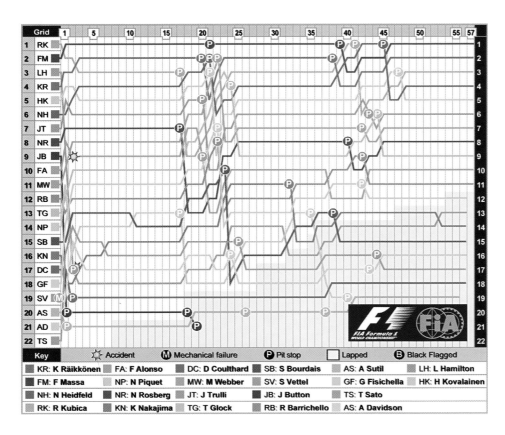

Key ☆ Accident | Ⓜ Mechanical failure | Ⓟ Pit stop | ☐ Lapped | Ⓑ Black Flagged

KR: K Räikkönen	FA: F Alonso	DC: D Coulthard	SB: S Bourdais	AS: A Sutil	LH: L Hamilton
FM: F Massa	NP: N Piquet	MW: M Webber	SV: S Vettel	GF: G Fisichella	HK: H Kovalainen
NH: N Heidfeld	NR: N Rosberg	JT: J Trulli	JB: J Button	TS: T Sato	
RK: R Kubica	KN: K Nakajima	TG: T Glock	RB: R Barrichello	AS: A Davidson	

Spanish Grand Prix

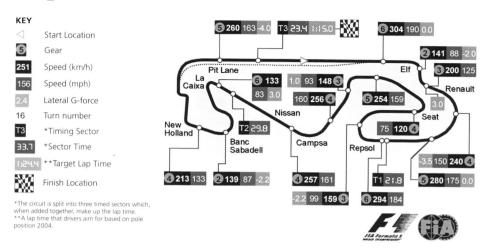

Barcelona, Spain – April 27
Length of the circuit: 4.655 km/2.892 miles
Race: 66 laps
Distance: 307.104 km/190.872 miles
Weather: sunny and dry

QUALIFYING

	Driver	Car	Chassis	Time
1	Kimi Räikkönen	Ferrari	F2008-268	1'21"813
2	Fernando Alonso	Renault	R28-03	1'21"904
3	Felipe Massa	Ferrari	F2008-267	1'22"058
4	Robert Kubica	BMW	F1.08-03	1'22"065
5	Lewis Hamilton	McLaren	MP4-23 04	1'22"096
6	Heikki Kovalainen	McLaren	MP4-23 03	1'22"231
7	Mark Webber	Red Bull	RB4-04	1'22"429
8	Jarno Trulli	Toyota	TF108-02	1'22"529
9	Nick Heidfeld	BMW	F1.08-04	1'22"542
10	Nelson Piquet	Renault	R28-01	1'22"699
11	Rubens Barrichello	Honda	RA108-04	1'21"049
12	Kazuki Nakajima	Williams	FW30-04	1'21"117
13	Jenson Button	Honda	RA108-02	1'21"211
14	Timo Glock	Toyota	TF108-04	1'21"230
15	Nico Rosberg	Williams	FW30-03	1'21"349
16	Sebastien Bourdais	Toro Rosso	STR2B-03	1'21"724
17	David Coulthard	Red Bull	RB4-03	1'21"810
18	Sebastian Vettel	Toro Rosso	STR2B-04	1'22"108
19	Giancarlo Fisichella	Force India	VJM01/05	1'22"516
20	Adrian Sutil	Force India	VJM01/03	1'23"224
21	Anthony Davidson	Super Aguri	SA08-05	1'23"318
22	Takuma Sato	Super Aguri	SA08-06	1'23"496

BARCELONA

Alonso in a reinvigorated Renault (though with how much fuel on board?) surprisingly heads for pole position on his home track until Räikkönen beats him by 91/1000ths of a second in the dying moments. Massa, 3rd on the grid, makes short work of the Spaniard on the first corner with Hamilton stealing 4th place from Kubica. The accident between Sutil and Vettel towards the back brings the safety car out onto the track. With the Ferraris pulling away, Alonso pits early on the 16th lap. The rush of pit-stops propels Kovalainen into the lead on the 22nd lap, precisely the moment his front left tyre chooses to explode as he brakes. The McLaren is stuck under a wall of tyres and there are a few long, anxious minutes before the Finn is pulled free unscathed. The safety car comes back out onto the track. Heidfeld is ordered to stop when practically out of petrol while the pit-lane is still closed. The penalty the German incurs ruins his race. Midway through the race, Alonso, who has climbed back up to 5th, sees his engine explode, as does Rosberg shortly thereafter. Hamilton and Kubica don't let up but are powerless to prevent another Ferrari one-two. The win helps Räikkönen pull away in the championship, which the Scuderia now has a solid lead in. Lewis and Robert salvage something from the wreckage behind the two red cars. A superb 5th place for Webber, ahead of Button, who scored his first points of the season, a lucky Nakajima and Trulli, who deserved better. Heidfeld ends up in 9th place, after a tough battle against… Fisico in his Force India.

RESULT

	Driver	Car	Time	Laps	Stops
1	Kimi Räikkönen	Ferrari	1h38'19"051	66	2
2	Felipe Massa	Ferrari	+3"228	66	2
3	Lewis Hamilton	McLaren	+4"187	66	2
4	Robert Kubica	BMW	5"694	66	2
5	Mark Webber	Red Bull	35"938	66	2
6	Jenson Button	Honda	53"010	66	2
7	Kazuki Nakajima	Williams	58"244	66	2
8	Jarno Trulli	Toyota	59"435	66	3
9	Nick Heidfeld	BMW	63"073	66	3
10	Giancarlo Fisichella	Force India	+1 lap	65	2
11	Timo Glock	Toyota	+1 lap	65	2
12	David Coulthard	Red Bull	+1 lap	65	2
13	Takuma Sato	Super Aguri	+1 lap	65	2

RETIREMENTS

Nico Rosberg	Williams	engine	41	1
Fernando Alonso	Renault	engine	34	1
Rubens Barrichello	Honda	crash	34	2
Heikki Kovalainen	McLaren	accident	21	0
Anthony Davidson	Super Aguri	radiator	8	0
Sebastien Bourdais	Toro Rosso	crash	7	0
Nelson Piquet	Renault	collision	6	0
Adrian Sutil	Force India	collision	0	0
Sebastian Vettel	Toro Rosso	collision	0	0

FASTEST LAP

Kimi Räikkönen	Ferrari	1'21"670	46

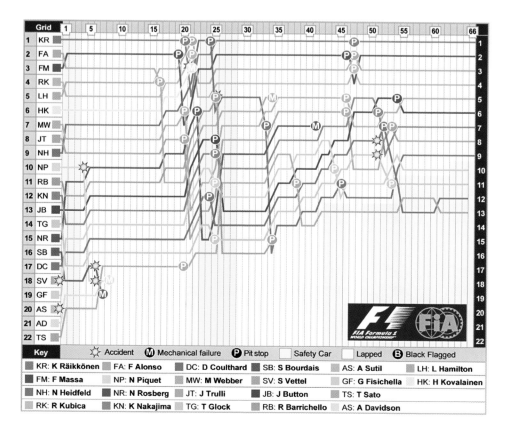

Turkish Grand Prix

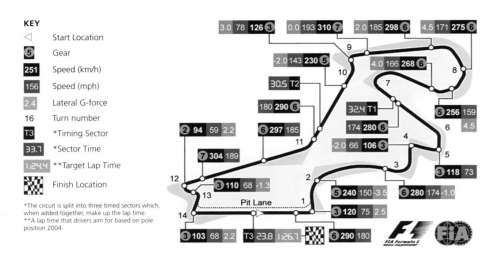

Istanbul, Turkey – May 11
Length of the circuit: 5.338 km/3.317 miles
Race: 58 laps
Distance: 309.356 km/192.258 miles
Weather: sunny and hot

QUALIFYING

	Driver	Car	Chassis	Time
1	Felipe Massa	Ferrari	F2008-267	1'27"617
2	Heikki Kovalainen	McLaren	MP4-23 05	1'27"808
3	Lewis Hamilton	McLaren	MP4-23 04	1'27"923
4	Kimi Räikkönen	Ferrari	F2008-270	1'27"936
5	Robert Kubica	BMW	F1.08-03	1'28"390
6	Mark Webber	Red Bull	RB4-03	1'28"417
7	ernando Alonso	Renault	R28-02	1'28"422
8	Jarno Trulli	Toyota	TF108-05	1'28"836
9	Nick Heidfeld	BMW	F1.08-05	1'28"882
10	David Coulthard	Red Bull	RB4-04	1'29"959
11	Nico Rosberg	Williams	FW30-03	1'26"822
12	Rubens Barrichello	Honda	RA 108-04	1'27"219
13	Jenson Button	Honda	RA 108-02	1'27"298
14	Sebastian Vettel	Toro Rosso	STR2B-04	1'27"412
15	Timo Glock	Toyota	TF108-06	1'27"806
16	Kazuki Nakajima	Williams	FW30-04	1'27"547
17	Nelson Piquet	Renault	R28-01	1'27"568
18	Sebastien Bourdais	Toro Rosso	STR2B-01	1'27"621
19	Giancarlo Fisichella	Force India	VJM01/05	1'27"807
20	Adrian Sutil	Force India	VJM01/02	1'28"625

ISTANBUL

With the best time of the twenty cars (once the Super Aguri had retired), Massa heads Kovalainen, on the front row of the grid for the first time, Hamilton and Räikkönen. The first corner is action-packed: at the rear, Fisico goes flying over Nakajima; at the front, the two Finns collide. Kova has a slow puncture and comes in to change his tyres, which ruins his race. While Felipe can't shake off Lewis, Kimi has to wait for the first pit-stop to get past Kubica, who had passed him at the start. After this round of stops, Hamilton swoops down on Massa. He takes the lead on the 24th lap with a beautiful attacking move and pulls away immediately. But it soon becomes clear that the Englishman is on a three-stop strategy so the Scuderia keeps its head. And indeed the Brazilian retakes the lead and goes on to take his third win running on Turkish soil. Hamilton manages to slip in between the Ferraris. Räikkönen harries him until the end but settles for some good points rather than risking everything. Kubica and Heidfeld's BMWs are not up to battling it out for podium positions this time round and end up 4th and 5th ahead of Alonso, Webber and Rosberg. Regardless of a record number of passes, Kovalainen ends up a pitiful 12th and Barrichello, in his 257th race (thus beating Patrese's record!), has to settle for 14th. With 28 points, Massa is neck and neck with Hamilton and eight points ahead of Kimi.

RESULT

	Driver	Car	Time	Laps	Stops
1	Felipe Massa	Ferrari	1h26'49"451	58	2
2	Lewis Hamilton	McLaren	+3"779	58	3
3	Kimi Räikkönen	Ferrari	+4"271	58	2
4	Robert Kubica	BMW	+21"945	58	2
5	Nick Heidfeld	BMW	+38"741	58	2
6	Fernando Alonso	Renault	+53"724	58	2
7	Mark Webber	Red Bull	+1'04"229	58	2
8	Nico Rosberg	Williams	+1'11"406	58	2
9	David Coulthard	Red Bull	+1'15"270	58	2
10	Jarno Trulli	Toyota	+1'16"344	58	2
11	Jenson Button	Honda	+1 lap	57	1
12	Heikki Kovalainen	McLaren	+1 lap	57	3
13	Timo Glock	Toyota	+1 lap	57	1
14	Rubens Barrichello	Honda	+1 lap	57	1
15	Nelson Piquet	Renault	+1 lap	57	2
16	Adrian Sutil	Force India	+1 lap	57	1
17	Sebastian Vettel	Toro Rosso	+1 lap	57	4

RETIREMENTS

Sebastien Bourdais	Toro Rosso	brakes	25	1
Kazuki Nakajima	Williams	collision	1	1
Giancarlo Fisichella	Force India	spin	0	0

FASTEST LAP

Kimi Räikkönen	Ferrari	1'26"506	20

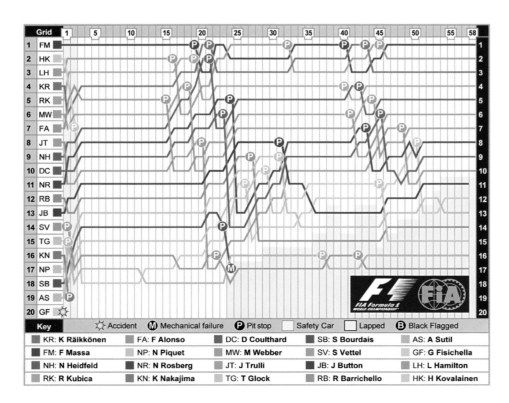

Monaco Grand Prix

KEY

◁ Start Location
5 Gear
251 Speed (km/h)
156 Speed (mph)
2.4 Lateral G-force
16 Turn number
T3 *Timing Sector
33.7 *Sector Time
1:24.4 **Target Lap Time
🏁 Finish Location

*The circuit is split into three timed sectors which, when added together, make up the lap time.
**A lap time that drivers aim for based on pole position 2004.

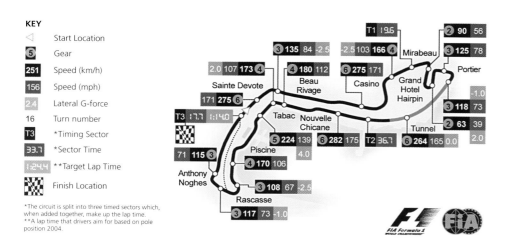

MONACO

Massa, a surprise pole, leads off in the rain ahead of Hamilton, who slips in between the Ferraris. Kovalainen, who'd started in 4th, again has no luck, needing to change his steering wheel. Soon wings fly and shunts increase: Glock, Rosberg, Button, but most dramatically Alonso and Hamilton. Forced to observe a drive-through penalty after a mistake by his mechanics, Räikkönen cedes 2nd to Kubica, which becomes 1st when Massa goes wide at Sainte-Dévote, which Kimi also does. Half way through after the first stops, an unbridled Hamilton is out in front ahead of Massa, Kubica, Webber and an amazing Sutil, who has the fastest lap so far! By lap 50, the track is dry and the drivers change tyres; Kubica gets past Massa. Rosberg spins spectacularly at La Piscine, and the safety car is deployed. As the race restarts, Räikkönen brakes wrong coming out of the tunnel and slams into the unlucky Sutil, who's in 5th and has to retire in tears. Hamilton stays in control and wins majestically from Kubica and Massa. Further back, it's all smiles for Webber, who comes in in 4th, Vettel 5th in the new Toro Rosso, Barrichello in 6th and Nakajima in 7th. Kovalainen manages to salvage one point ahead of a rampant Räikkönen, Alonso, who made too many mistakes, and the languishing Toyotas. Lewis is back on top of the drivers' championship ahead of Kimi, Felipe and Robert. They are only six points apart.

Monte-Carlo, Monaco – May 25
Length of the circuit: 3.340 km/2.075 miles
Race: 78 laps
Distance: 260.520 km/161.887 miles
Weather: overcast and rainy

QUALIFYING

	Driver	Car	Chassis	Time
1	Felipe Massa	Ferrari	F2008-270	1'15"787
2	Kimi Räikkönen	Ferrari	F2008-267	1'15"815
3	Lewis Hamilton	McLaren	MP4-23 04	1'15"839
4	Heikki Kovalainen	McLaren	MP4-23 05	1'16"165
5	Robert Kubica	BMW	F1.08-03	1'16"171
6	Nico Rosberg	Williams	FW30-03	1'16"548
7	Fernando Alonso	Renault	R28-02	1'16"852
8	Jarno Trulli	Toyota	TF108-05	1'17"203
9	Mark Webber	Red Bull	RB4-04	1'17"343
10	David Coulthard	Red Bull	RB4-03	no time
11	Timo Glock	Toyota	TF108-06	1'15"907
12	Jenson Button	Honda	RA108-02	1'16"101
13	Nick Heidfeld	BMW	F1.08-05	1'16"455
14	Kazuki Nakajima	Williams	FW30-04	1'16"479
15	Rubens Barrichello	Honda	RA108-04	1'16"537
16	Sebastien Bourdais	Toro Rosso	STR3-01	1'16"806
17	Nelson Piquet	Renault	R28-02	1'16"933
18	Sebastian Vettel	Toro Rosso	STR3-03	1'16"955
19	Adrian Sutil	Force India	VJM01/02	1'17"225
20	Giancarlo Fisichella	Force India	VJM01/05	1'17"823

RESULT

	Driver	Car	Time	Laps	Stops
1	Lewis Hamilton	McLaren	2h00'42"742	76	2
2	Robert Kubica	BMW	+3"069	76	2
3	Felipe Massa	Ferrari	+4"811	76	2
4	Mark Webber	Red Bull	+19"264	76	1
5	Sebastian Vettel	Toro Rosso	+24"657	76	1
6	Rubens Barrichello	Honda	+28"408	76	1
7	Kazuki Nakajima	Williams	+30"180	76	1
8	Heikki Kovalainen	McLaren	+33"191	76	1
9	Kimi Räikkönen	Ferrari	+33"793	76	4
10	Fernando Alonso	Renault	+1 lap	75	2
11	Jenson Button	Honda	+1 lap	75	3
12	Timo Glock	Toyota	+1 lap	75	3
13	Jarno Trulli	Toyota	+1 lap	75	3
14	Nick Heidfeld	BMW	+4 laps	72	3

RETIREMENTS

Adrian Sutil	Force India	collision	67	1
Nico Rosberg	Williams	spin	59	4
Nelson Piquet	Renault	spin	47	1
Giancarlo Fisichella	Force India	transmission	36	0
David Coulthard	Red Bull	spin	7	0
Sebastien Bourdais	Toro Rosso	spin	7	0

FASTEST LAP

Kimi Räikkönen	Ferrari	1'16"689	74

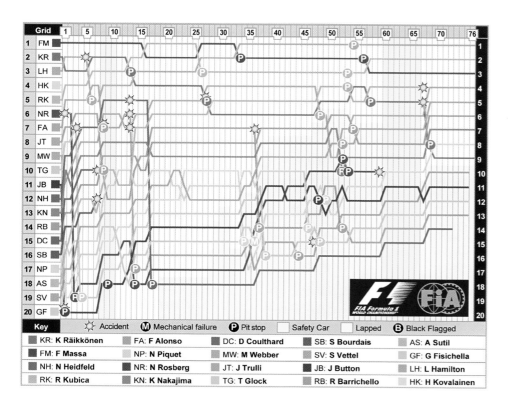

Key
- KR: K Räikkönen
- FM: F Massa
- NH: N Heidfeld
- RK: R Kubica
- FA: F Alonso
- NP: N Piquet
- NR: N Rosberg
- KN: K Nakajima
- DC: D Coulthard
- MW: M Webber
- JT: J Trulli
- TG: T Glock
- SB: S Bourdais
- SV: S Vettel
- JB: J Button
- RB: R Barrichello
- AS: A Sutil
- GF: G Fisichella
- LH: L Hamilton
- HK: H Kovalainen

Key: ☆ Accident · Ⓜ Mechanical failure · Ⓟ Pit stop · □ Safety Car · Lapped · Ⓑ Black Flagged

Canadian Grand Prix

KEY
◁ Start Location
5 Gear
251 Speed (km/h)
156 Speed (mph)
2.4 Lateral G-force
16 Turn number
T3 *Timing Sector
33.7 *Sector Time
1:24.4 **Target Lap Time
🏁 Finish Location

*The circuit is split into three timed sectors which,
when added together, make up the lap time.
**A lap time that drivers aim for based on pole
position 2004

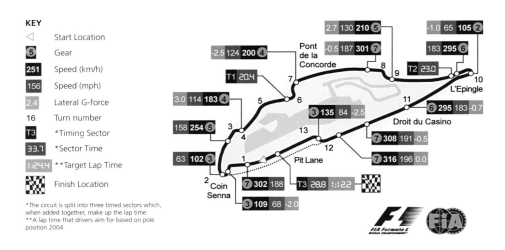

Pont de la Concorde

Droit du Casino

L'Epingle

Coin Senna

Pit Lane

Gilles Villeneuve Circuit, Montreal, Canada – June 8
Length of the circuit: 4.361 km/2.709 miles
Race: 70 laps
Distance: 305.270 km/189.694 miles
Weather: dry and overcast

QUALIFYING

	Driver	Car	Chassis	Time
1	Lewis Hamilton	McLaren	MP4-23 06	1'17"886
2	Robert Kubica	BMW	F1.08-03	1'18"498
3	Kimi Raikkonen	Ferrari	F2008-270	1'18"735
4	Fernando Alonso	Renault	R28-02	1'18"746
5	Nico Rosberg	Williams	FW30-05	1'18"844
6	Felipe Massa	Ferrari	F2008-267	1'19"048
7	Heikki Kovalainen	McLaren	MP4-23 02	1'19"089
8	Nick Heidfeld	BMW	F1.08-07	1'19"633
9	Rubens Barrichello	Honda	RA108-04	1'20"848
10	Mark Webber	Red Bull	RB4-04	no time
11	Timo Glock	Toyota	TF108-06	1'18"031
12	Kazuki Nakajima	Williams	FW30-04	1'18"062
13	David Coulthard	Red Bull	RB4-03	1'18"238
14	Jarno Trulli	Toyota	TF108-05	1'18"327
15	Nelson Piquet	Renault	R28-01	1'18"393
16	Sebastien Bourdais	Toro Rosso	STR3-01	1'18"916
17	Adrian Sutil	Force India	VJM01/02	1'19"108
18	Giancarlo Fisichella	Force India	VJM01/04	1'19"165
19	Jenson Button	Honda	RA108-02	1'23"565
20	Sebastian Vettel	Toro Rosso	STR3-04	no time

MONTREAL

Hamilton takes pole by a mile and opens up a lead from the start. But Sutil's retirement on the 14th lap sees the safety car out on the track. All the leaders dash for the open pit-lane. Kubica and Räikkönen, 2nd and 3rd, refuel quicker than the Brit and are side by side at the end of the pit-lane but come to a stop before the flashing lights. Annoyed at having lost time, Lewis sees the light too late and hits the Ferrari and is himself hit by Rosberg. That's it for the McLaren and the Ferrari! When the race restarts, Heidfeld (who hasn't stopped) is in the lead. The German comes out from his pit-stop half way through the race right under the noses of Kubica and Alonso. They will fight it out for the win. The Pole gets past his team-mate and roars away to such an extent that he even comes back out onto the track in the lead from his second pit-stop. Stuck behind Nick, Alonso ends up losing control of his temper and his car, hitting a wall on the 45th lap. The Spaniard thus clears the way for a spectacular BMW double and Kubica's first win… on the track where he almost lost his life a year earlier. And he leads the championship to boot! Coulthard finally breaks his duck and gets on the podium ahead of the Toyotas of Glock and Trulli on either side of Massa, in 5th, who roars back up through the field after a refuelling problem. Barrichello manages to hold on to two points ahead of Vettel, who was at the back of the grid and gets one after a ding-dong battle with Kovalainen who'd been caught in the traffic.

RESULT

	Driver	Car	Time	Laps	Stops
1	Robert Kubica	BMW	1h36'24"447	70	2
2	Nick Heidfeld	BMW	+16"495	70	1
3	David Coulthard	Red Bull	+23"352	70	1
4	Timo Glock	Toyota	+42"627	70	1
5	Felipe Massa	Ferrari	+43"934	70	3
6	Jarno Trulli	Toyota	+47"775	70	1
7	Rubens Barrichello	Honda	+53"597	70	1
8	Sebastian Vettel	Toro Rosso	+54"120	70	1
9	Heikki Kovalainen	McLaren	+54"433	70	2
10	Nico Rosberg	Williams	+54"749	70	3
11	Jenson Button	Honda	+1'07"540	70	3
12	Mark Webber	Red Bull	+1'11"299	70	2
13	Sebastien Bourdais	Toro Rosso	+1 lap	69	2

RETIREMENTS

Giancarlo Fisichella	Force India	spin	51	2
Kazuki Nakajima	Williams	spin	46	2
Fernando Alonso	Renault	spin	44	1
Nelson Piquet	Renault	brakes	40	2
Kimi Räikkönen	Ferrari	accident	19	1
Lewis Hamilton	McLaren	accident	19	1
Adrian Sutil	Force India	transmission	13	0

FASTEST LAP

Kimi Räikkönnen	Ferrari	1'17"387	14

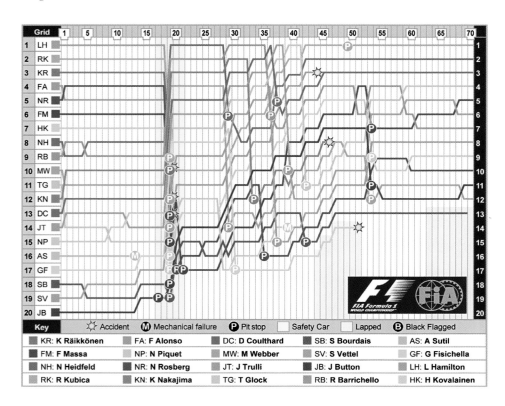

French Grand Prix

KEY

◁ Start Location
5 Gear
251 Speed (km/h)
156 Speed (mph)
2.4 Lateral G-force
16 Turn number
T3 *Timing Sector
33.7 *Sector Time
1:24.4 **Target Lap Time
🏁 Finish Location

*The circuit is split into three timed sectors which, when added together, make up the lap time.
**A lap time that drivers aim for based on pole position 2004.

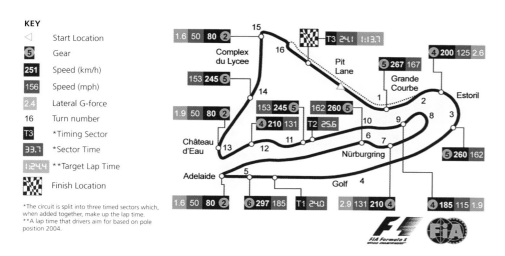

Magny-Cours, France – June 22
Length of the circuit: 4.411 km/2.741 miles
Race: 70 laps
Distance: 308.586 km/191.755 miles
Weather: cloudy

QUALIFYING

	Driver	Car	Chassis	Time
1	Kimi Räikkönen	Ferrari	F2008-270	1'16"449
2	Felipe Massa	Ferrari	F2008-267	1'16"490
3	Lewis Hamilton	McLaren	MP4-23 06	1'16"693
4	Fernando Alonso	Renault	R28-02	1'16"840
5	Jarno Trulli	Toyota	TF108-05	1'16"920
6	Heikki Kovalainen	McLaren	MP4-23 02	1'16"944
7	Robert Kubica	BMW	F1.08-03	1'17"037
8	Mark Webber	Red Bull	RB4-04	1'17"233
9	David Coulthard	Red Bull	RB4-03	1'17"426
10	Timo Glock	Toyota	TF108-06	1'17"596
11	Nelson Piquet	Renault	R28-01	1'15"770
12	Nick Heidfeld	BMW	F1.08-07	1'15"786
13	Sebastian Vettel	Toro Rosso	STR3-03	1'15"816
14	Sebastien Bourdais	Toro Rosso	STR3-01	1'16"045
15	Nico Rosberg	Williams	FW30-05	1'16"235
16	Kazuki Nakajima	Williams	FW30-04	1'16"243
17	Jenson Button	Honda	RA108-02	1'16"306
18	Rubens Barrichello	Honda	RA108-04	1'16"330
19	Giancarlo Fisichella	Force India	VJM01/04	1'16"971
20	Adrian Sutil	Force India	VJM01/02	1'17"053

MAGNY-COURS

The Ferraris, impressive in qualifying, stretch into an immediate lead with Räikkönen, who'd been on pole, ahead of Massa. Alonso, an impressive third on the grid, is passed by Trulli and Kubica at the start but immediately gets back past the BMW. Penalised by ten places on the grid for causing the Montreal crash, Hamilton, 13th, gets a drive-through penalty for a dodgy move on Vettel, which sees him at the very back of the field while team-mate Kovalainen, given a five-place penalty for getting in Webber's way in qualifying, tries in vain to get past Piquet, who shows his potential at last. The pit-stops – Alonso comes in first - let Kubica past the Spaniard and Heikki past Nelsinho, at last. By mid-race, Räikkönen's 4-second lead over Massa is gone. The exhaust breaks on the no. 1 Ferrari and it loses power. Kimi thus makes way for Felipe who heads off to victory and the lead in the championship. As a sign of the Scuderia's total domination, the Finn holds on for second with third going to Trulli (in his first podium finish for two years) who outsprints Kovalainen, who's come back well. Kubica comes in fifth way ahead of the four Renault engines of Webber, Piquet – who scores his first points – Alonso, who kept going backwards, and Coulthard respectively. Button is the only retirement.

RESULT

	Driver	Car	Time	Laps	Stops
1	Felipe Massa	Ferrari	1h31'50"245	70	2
2	Kimi Räikkönen	Ferrari	+17"984	70	2
3	Jarno Trulli	Toyota	+28"250	70	2
4	Heikki Kovalainen	McLaren	+28"929	70	2
5	Robert Kubica	BMW	+30"512	70	2
6	Mark Webber	Red Bull	+40"304	70	2
7	Nelson Piquet	Renault	+41"033	70	2
8	Fernando Alonso	Renault	+43"372	70	2
9	David Coulthard	Red Bull	+51"072	70	2
10	Lewis Hamilton	McLaren	+54"521	70	3
11	Timo Glock	Toyota	+57"738	70	2
12	Sebastian Vettel	Toro Rosso	+58"065	70	2
13	Nick Heidfeld	BMW	+62"079	70	3
14	Rubens Barrichello	Honda	+1 lap	69	2
15	Kazuki Nakajima	Williams	+1 lap	69	2
16	Nico Rosberg	Williams	+1 lap	69	1
17	Sebastien Bourdais	Toro Rosso	+1 lap	69	2
18	Giancarlo Fisichella	Force India	+1 lap	69	2
19	Adrian Sutil	Force India	+1 lap	69	2

RETIREMENT

Jenson Button	Honda	collision	16	1

FASTEST LAP

Kimi Räikkönen	Ferrari	1'16"630	16

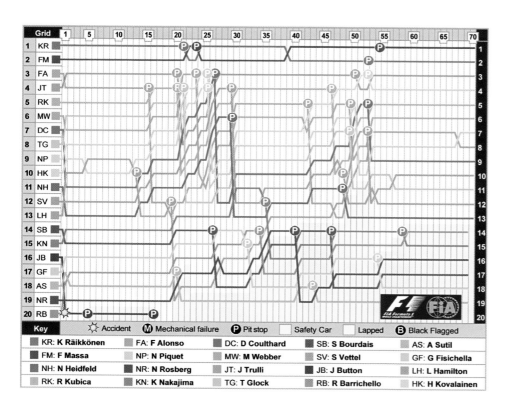

Key				
KR: K Räikkönen	FA: F Alonso	DC: D Coulthard	SB: S Bourdais	AS: A Sutil
FM: F Massa	NP: N Piquet	MW: M Webber	SV: S Vettel	GF: G Fisichella
NH: N Heidfeld	NR: N Rosberg	JT: J Trulli	JB: J Button	LH: L Hamilton
RK: R Kubica	KN: K Nakajima	TG: T Glock	RB: R Barrichello	HK: H Kovalainen

☆ Accident   Ⓜ Mechanical failure   Ⓟ Pit stop   ☐ Safety Car   ☐ Lapped   Ⓑ Black Flagged

British Grand Prix

KEY

◁ Start Location
5 Gear
251 Speed (km/h)
156 Speed (mph)
2.4 Lateral G-force
16 Turn number
T3 *Timing Sector
33.7 *Sector Time
1:24.4 **Target Lap Time
🏁 Finish Location

*The circuit is split into three timed sectors which, when added together, make up the lap time.
**A lap time that drivers aim for based on pole position 2004.

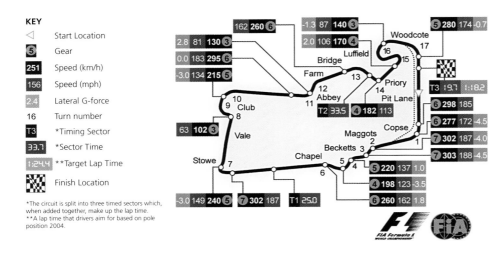

Silverstone, Great Britain – July 6
Length of the circuit: 5.141 km/3.194 miles
Race: 60 laps
Distance: 308.460 km/191.640 miles
Weather: rainy

QUALIFYING

	Driver	Car	Chassis	Time
1	Heikki Kovalainen	McLaren	MP4-23 05	1'21"049
2	Mark Webber	Red Bull	RB4-04	1'21"554
3	Kimi Räikkönen	Ferrari	F2008-270	1'21"706
4	Lewis Hamilton	McLaren	MP4-23 04	1'21"835
5	Nick Heidfeld	BMW	F1.08-07	1'21"873
6	Fernando Alonso	Renault	R28-02	1'22"029
7	Nelson Piquet	Renault	R28-01	1'22"491
8	Sebastian Vettel	Toro Rosso	STR2B-03	1'22"251
9	Felipe Massa	Ferrari	F2008-267	1'19"788
10	Robert Kubica	BMW	F1.08-03	1'23"305
11	David Coulthard	Red Bull	RB4-03	1'20"174
12	Timo Glock	Toyota	TF108-06	1'20"274
13	Sebastien Bourdais	Toro Rosso	STR2B-01	1'20"531
14	Jarno Trulli	Toyota	TF108-05	1'20"601
15	Kazuki Nakajima	Williams	FW30-04	1'21"112
16	Rubens Barrichello	Honda	RA 108-04	1'21"512
17	Jenson Button	Honda	RA 108-02	1'21"631
18	Nico Rosberg	Williams	FW30-05	1'21"668
19	Adrian Sutil	Force India	VJM01/02	1'21"786
20	Giancarlo Fisichella	Force India	VJM01/04	1'21"885

SILVERSTONE

The track is flooded at the start. From 4th on the grid, Hamilton gets straight past Räikkönen and surprise package Webber but Kovalainen, on pole for the first time, holds him off. Not for long; Lewis gets past five laps in and begins an aquatic master class. He leaves his team-mate to battle it out with Kimi and Alonso. Championship leader Felipe Massa, 9th on the grid after a problem in practice, is soon at the back of the field after spinning twice – with more to come! Hamilton changes tyres during his first stop but Räikkönen – who'd been closing on the McLaren – keeps his, convinced that the rain is going to stop. He's wrong. It gets harder! And the Ferrari is soon down in 11th. Nick Heidfeld glides into an excellent 2nd place (and stays there), ahead of Kovalainen, who's struggling, and Kubica, who'd also roared back up the field before making an error. But the best progress is made by Barrichello who'd started the race on his favourite track in 16th. Rubinho goes for 'extreme rain' tyres: a good move which sees him climb to third and score his first podium finish since leaving the Scuderia! Behind the Honda, a battling Räikkönen steals fourth ahead of Kova, a fading Alonso, an ever risk-taking Trulli and Nakajima, who salvages something on a disastrous weekend for Williams. Webber, in trouble from the start, only manages 10th and Massa is a sorry 13th and last, two laps behind Hamilton, triumphant 'at home' and now back ahead of the Ferraris on the leader board.

RESULT

	Driver	Car	Time	Laps	Stops
1	Lewis Hamilton	McLaren	1h39'09"440	60	2
2	Nick Heidfeld	BMW	+1'08"577	60	2
3	Rubens Barrichello	Honda	+1'22"273	60	3
4	Kimi Räikkönen	Ferrari	+1 lap	59	2
5	Heikki Kovalainen	McLaren	+1 lap	59	2
6	Fernando Alonso	Renault	+1 lap	59	2
7	Jarno Trulli	Toyota	+1 lap	59	2
8	Kazuki Nakajima	Williams	+1 lap	59	2
9	Nico Rosberg	Williams	+1 lap	59	3
10	Mark Webber	Red Bull	+1 lap	59	2
11	Sebastien Bourdais	Toro Rosso	+1 lap	59	2
12	Timo Glock	Toyota	+1 lap	59	2
13	Felipe Massa	Ferrari	+2 laps	58	3

RETIREMENTS

Robert Kubica	BMW	spin	39	2
Jenson Button	Honda	spin	38	2
Nelson Piquet	Renault	spin	35	1
Giancarlo Fisichella	Force India	spin	26	0
Adrian Sutil	Force India	spin	10	0
Sebastian Vettel	Toro Rosso	accident	0	0
David Coulthard	Red Bull	accident	0	0

FASTEST LAP

Kimi Räikkönen	Ferrari	1'33"130	18

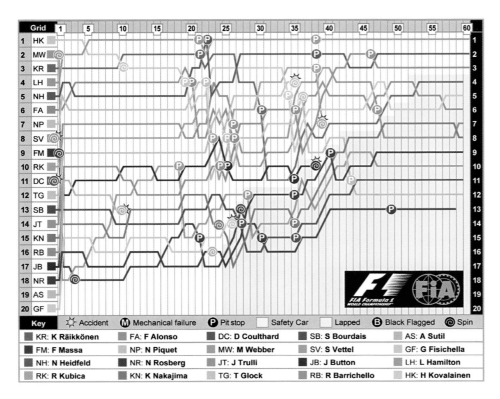

Key	☆ Accident	Ⓜ Mechanical failure	Ⓟ Pit stop	Safety Car	Lapped	Ⓑ Black Flagged	◎ Spin
KR: K Räikkönen	FA: F Alonso	DC: D Coulthard	SB: S Bourdais				AS: A Sutil
FM: F Massa	NP: N Piquet	MW: M Webber	SV: S Vettel				GF: G Fisichella
NH: N Heidfeld	NR: N Rosberg	JT: J Trulli	JB: J Button				LH: L Hamilton
RK: R Kubica	KN: K Nakajima	TG: T Glock	RB: R Barrichello				HK: H Kovalainen

German Grand Prix

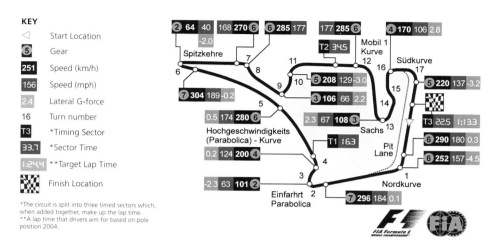

HOCKENHEIM

Hamilton maintains the lead at the start and gradually pulls away. The middle of the race is uneventful – Massa is more than 11 seconds back, Kovalainen 18 – until Glock's rear right-hand suspension gives up the ghost on the last turn. The Toyota smashes into the pit wall backwards. Safety car. Everyone refuels… or rather almost everyone. Incomprehensibly, McLaren leave Hamilton on the track. Naturally, when the race restarts, he's ahead of Piquet and Heidfeld who didn't stop either but the Brazilian (who'd refuelled just before the accident) won't have to stop again and, what with the gap between the drivers gone, he is now favourite! Lewis belts along but comes out from his second pit-stop fifth, behind his team-mate. Hamilton being not one to be contained has swept past Kova and Massa within 17 laps, made the most of Heidfeld's stop and borne down on Piquet, passing him on lap 59. Nelsinho (only 17th in qualifying!) still secures his first podium finish, Renault's first of 2008, with a flattering 2nd place ahead of Massa, who'd had trouble with his brakes. Heidfeld comes home right behind the Ferrari ahead of Kovalainen, who still hasn't had much race luck, a slapdash Räikkönen, a battling Kubica and a decisive Vettel. Lewis savours his victory; he's back in front in the championship.

Hockenheim, Germany – July 20
Length of the circuit: 4.574 km/2.843 miles
Race: 67 laps
Distance: 306.458 km/190.480 miles
Weather: dry and overcast

QUALIFYING

	Driver	Car	Chassis	Time
1	Lewis Hamilton	McLaren	MP4-23 04	1'15"666
2	Felipe Massa	Ferrari	F2008-267	1'15"859
3	Heikki Kovalainen	McLaren	MP4-23 05	1'16"143
4	Jarno Trulli	Toyota	TF108-05	1'16"191
5	Fernando Alonso	Renault	R28-02	1'16"385
6	Kimi Räikkönen	Ferrari	F2008-270	1'16"389
7	Robert Kubica	BMW	F1.08-03	1'16"521
8	Mark Webber	Red Bull	RB4-04	1'17"014
9	Sebastian Vettel	Toro Rosso	STR3-03	1'17"244
10	David Coulthard	Red Bull	RB4-03	1'17"503
11	Timo Glock	Toyota	TF108-02	1'15"508
12	Nick Heidfeld	BMW	F1.08-07	1'15"581
13	Nico Rosberg	Williams	FW30-05	1'15"633
14	Jenson Button	Honda	RA108-02	1'15"701
15	Sebastien Bourdais	Toro Rosso	STR3-01	1'15"858
16	Kazuki Nakajima	Williams	FW30-04	1'16"083
17	Nelson Piquet	Renault	R28-01	1'16"189
18	Rubens Barrichello	Honda	RA108-04	1'16"249
19	Adrian Sutil	Force India	VJM01/02	1'16"657
20	Giancarlo Fisichella	Force India	VJM01/04	1'16"963

RESULT

	Driver	Car	Time	Laps	Stops
1	Lewis Hamilton	McLaren	1h31'20"742	67	2
2	Nelson Piquet	Renault	+5"586	67	1
3	Felipe Massa	Ferrari	+9"339	67	2
4	Nick Heidfeld	BMW	+9"825	67	2
5	Heikki Kovalainen	McLaren	+12"411	67	2
6	Kimi Räikkönen	Ferrari	+14"483	67	2
7	Robert Kubica	BMW	+22"603	67	2
8	Sebastian Vettel	Toro Rosso	+33"282	67	2
9	Jarno Trulli	Toyota	+37"199	67	2
10	Nico Rosberg	Williams	+37"658	67	2
11	Fernando Alonso	Renault	+38"625	67	2
12	Sebastien Bourdais	Toro Rosso	+39"199	67	2
13	David Coulthard	Red Bull	+54"971	67	2
14	Giancarlo Fisichella	Force India	+59"093	67	2
15	Kazuki Nakajima	Williams	+1'00"003	67	2
16	Adrian Sutil	Force India	+1'09"488	67	2
17	Jenson Button	Honda	+1 lap	66	3

RETIREMENTS

Rubens Barrichello	Honda	accident	50	2
Mark Webber	Red Bull	engine	40	2
Timo Glock	Toyota	accident	35	0

FASTEST LAP

Nick Heidfeld	BMW	1'15"987	52

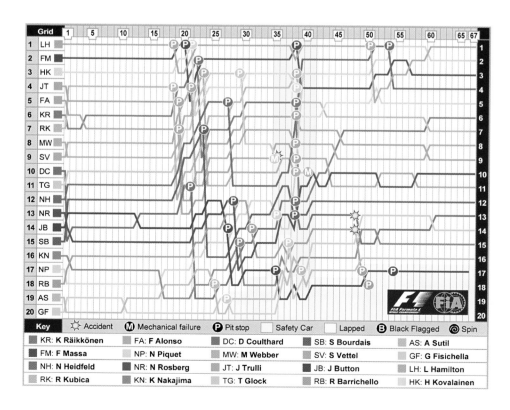

Hungarian Grand Prix

KEY

◁ Start Location

5 Gear

251 Speed (km/h)

156 Speed (mph)

2.4 Lateral G-force

16 Turn number

T3 *Timing Sector

33.7 *Sector Time

1:24.4 **Target Lap Time

🏁 Finish Location

*The circuit is split into three timed sectors which,
when added together, make up the lap time.
**A lap time that drivers aim for based on pole
position 2004.

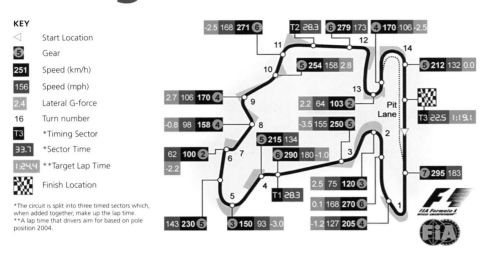

Hungaroring, Budapest, Hungary – August 3
Circuit length: 4.381km /2.722 miles
Race: 70 laps
Distance: 306.663 km/190.560 miles
Weather: sunny

QUALIFYING

	Driver	Car	Chassis	Time
1	Lewis Hamilton	McLaren	MP4-23 07	1'20"899
2	Heikki Kovalainen	McLaren	MP4-23 05	1'21"140
3	Felipe Massa	Ferrari	F2008-269	1'21"191
4	Robert Kubica	BMW	F1.08-05	1'21"281
5	Timo Glock	Toyota	TF108-06	1'21"326
6	Kimi Räikkönen	Ferrari	F2008-270	1'21"516
7	Fernando Alonso	Renault	R28-02	1'21"698
8	Mark Webber	Red Bull	RB4-04	1'21"732
9	Jarno Trulli	Toyota	TF108-05	1'21"767
10	Nelson Piquet	Renault	R28-01	1'22"371
11	Sebastian Vettel	Toro Rosso	STR2B-03	1'20"144
12	Jenson Button	Honda	RA 108-02	1'20"332
13	David Coulthard	Red Bull	RB4-03	1'20"502
14	Sebastien Bourdais	Toro Rosso	STR2B-01	1'20"963
15	Nico Rosberg	Williams	FW30-05	no time
16	Nick Heidfeld	BMW	F1.08-07	1'21"045
17	Kazuki Nakajima	Williams	FW30-04	1'21"085
18	Rubens Barrichello	Honda	RA 108-04	1'21"332
19	Giancarlo Fisichella	Force India	VJM01/05	1'21"670
20	Adrian Sutil	Force India	VJM01/02	1'22"113

HUNGARORING

The McLarens monopolise the front row of the grid; it's thought they'll be untouchable in the race. But as the lights go out, Massa, starting from the clean side of the track, gets past both Kovalainen and Hamilton, going round the latter on the first corner. Further back, Glock (who qualified fifth fastest, his best ever performance) gets past Kubica and Alonso passes Räikkönen. The two men in front quickly pull away. The first run of pit-stops is only cruel to Kubica, who loses three places, whilst several others (Bourdais, Barrichello, Nakajima) play with fire. There are theatrics on lap 40: Hamilton's front left tyre blows and he has to do over half a lap in slow motion. After pitting for the second time, the Briton is now down in sixth, between the two Renaults. Massa seems to have the race won as Räikkönen, who has at last got past Alonso in the pits, bears down on Glock in a stunning third place. Three laps from the finish, the leading Ferrari's V8 emits an enormous puff of smoke. Which means Kova wins the first race of his career ahead of the excellent Glock (first podium finish) and a disappointing Räikkönen who does at least make some headway in the championship, closing the gap on Hamilton, who finishes fifth behind Alonso, by two points. Then come Piquet, Trulli and Kubica, the best-placed driver of a BMW team way off the pace.

RESULT

	Driver	Car	Time	Laps	Stops
1	Heikki Kovalainen	McLaren	1h37'27"067	70	2
2	Timo Glock	Toyota	+11"061	70	2
3	Kimi Räikkönen	Ferrari	+16"856	70	2
4	Fernando Alonso	Renault	+21"614	70	2
5	Lewis Hamilton	McLaren	+23"048	70	2
6	Nelson Piquet	Renault	+32"298	70	2
7	Jarno Trulli	Toyota	+36"449	70	2
8	Robert Kubica	BMW	+48"321	70	2
9	Mark Webber	Red Bull	+58"834	70	2
10	Nick Heidfeld	BMW	+1'07"709	70	2
11	David Coulthard	Red Bull	+1'10"407	70	2
12	Jenson Button	Honda	+1 lap	69	2
13	Kazuki Nakajima	Williams	+1 lap	69	2
14	Nico Rosberg	Williams	+1 lap	69	2
15	Giancarlo Fisichella	Force India	+1 lap	69	2
16	Rubens Barrichello	Honda	+2 laps	68	2
17	Sebastien Bourdais	Toro Rosso	+3 laps	67	3
18	Felipe Massa	Ferrari	+3 laps	67	2

RETIREMENTS

Adrian Sutil	Force India	brakes	62	3
Sebastian Vettel	Toro Rosso	engine	22	1

FASTEST LAP

Kimi Räikkönen	Ferrari	1'21"195	61

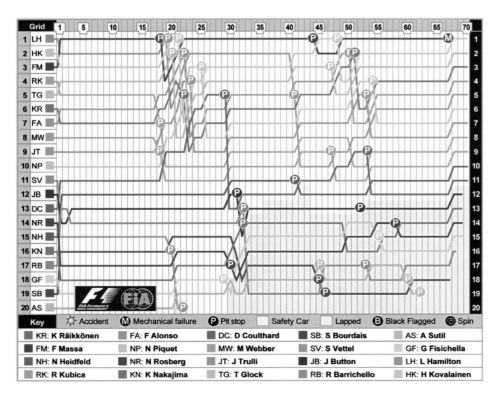

Key	☼ Accident	Ⓜ Mechanical failure	Ⓟ Pit stop	Safety Car	Lapped	Ⓑ Black Flagged	◉ Spin
KR: K Räikkönen		**FA: F Alonso**	**DC: D Coulthard**	**SB: S Bourdais**		**AS: A Sutil**	
FM: F Massa		**NP: N Piquet**	**MW: M Webber**	**SV: S Vettel**		**GF: G Fisichella**	
NH: N Heidfeld		**NR: N Rosberg**	**JT: J Trulli**	**JB: J Button**		**LH: L Hamilton**	
RK: R Kubica		**KN: K Nakajima**	**TG: T Glock**	**RB: R Barrichello**		**HK: H Kovalainen**	

European Grand Prix

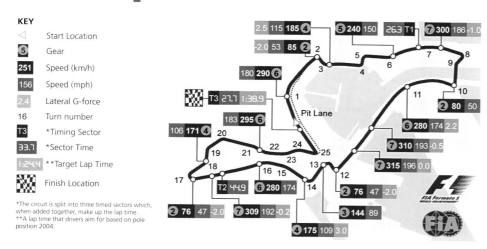

KEY

◁ Start Location
5 Gear
251 Speed (km/h)
156 Speed (mph)
2.4 Lateral G-force
16 Turn number
T3 *Timing Sector
33.7 *Sector Time
1:24.4 **Target Lap Time
🏁 Finish Location

*The circuit is split into three timed sectors which, when added together, make up the lap time.
**A lap time that drivers aim for based on pole position 2004.

Pit Lane

Valencia, Spain – August 24

Circuit length: 5.743 km/3.569 miles
Race: 57 laps
Distance: 327.351 km/203.433 miles
Weather: sunny

QUALIFYING

	Driver	Car	Chassis	Time
1	Felipe Massa	Ferrari	F2008-269	1'38"989
2	Lewis Hamilton	McLaren	MP4-23 07	1'39"199
3	Robert Kubica	BMW	F1.08-05	1'39"392
4	Kimi Räikkönen	Ferrari	F2008-270	1'39"488
5	Heikki Kovalainen	McLaren	MP4-23 05	1'39"937
6	Sebastian Vettel	Toro Rosso	STR3-03	1'40"142
7	Jarno Trulli	Toyota	TF108-05	1'40"309
8	Nick Heidfeld	BMW	F1.08-07	1'40"631
9	Nico Rosberg	Williams	FW30-05	1'40"721
10	Sebastien Bourdais	Toro Rosso	STR3-01	1'40"750
11	Kazuki Nakajima	Williams	FW30-04	1'38"428
12	Fernando Alonso	Renault	R28-02	1'38"435
13	Timo Glock	Toyota	TF108-06	1'38"499
14	Mark Webber	Red Bull	RB4-05	1'38"515
15	Nelson Piquet	Renault	R28-01	1'38"744
16	Jenson Button	Honda	RA108-02	1'38"880
17	David Coulthard	Red Bull	RB4-04	1'39"235
18	Giancarlo Fisichella	Force India	VJM01/05	1'39"268
19	Rubens Barrichello	Honda	RA108-04	1'39"811
20	Adrian Sutil	Force India	VJM01/02	1'39"943

VALENCIA

The new Spanish circuit witnesses total domination by Felipe Massa. Having snatched pole in the very last lap from Hamilton, the Brazilian went on to record his ninth win in Valencia and the race's fastest lap. He holds Lewis and Kubica off brilliantly in the early stages. Räikkönen has already lost a spot to Kovalainen. Local hero Alonso, only 12th on the grid, retires on the very first lap after getting tangled up with Nakajima. The outcome of the race is clear, Massa containing Hamilton, who makes a late first pit-stop, throughout. The only heart-stopping moment for the Brazilian is when he narrowly avoids hitting Sutil in the pits. Lewis secures a valuable 2nd place for the championship (six points ahead of Massa), while Kubica gradually pulls away from his nearest rivals to take 3rd. Räikkönen should have cantered home but the reigning world champion first mows down one of his mechanics and then retires with a broken engine. Good news for Kovalainen who finishes 4th ahead of Trulli, an impressive Vettel (6th in testing; Toro Rosso haven't known the like all season), Glock (who'd cleverly started with a full tank) and Rosberg. Heidfeld, Bourdais and Piquet just miss out on the points.

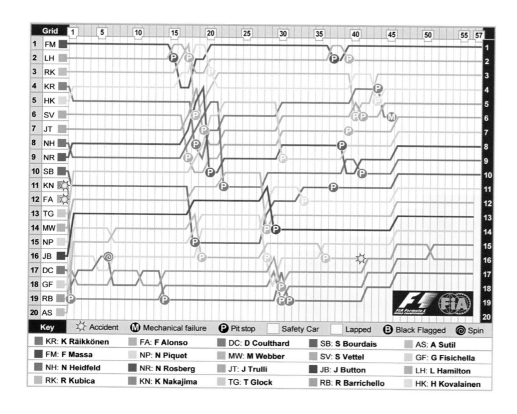

| Grid | | | | | | | | | | | | |

Key

☆ Accident	Ⓜ Mechanical failure	Ⓟ Pit stop	☐ Safety Car	Lapped	Ⓑ Black Flagged	@ Spin

KR: K Räikkönen	FA: F Alonso	DC: D Coulthard	SB: S Bourdais	AS: A Sutil
FM: F Massa	NP: N Piquet	MW: M Webber	SV: S Vettel	GF: G Fisichella
NH: N Heidfeld	NR: N Rosberg	JT: J Trulli	JB: J Button	LH: L Hamilton
RK: R Kubica	KN: K Nakajima	TG: T Glock	RB: R Barrichello	HK: H Kovalainen

RESULT

	Driver	Car	Time	Laps	Stops
1	Felipe Massa	Ferrari	1h35'32"339	57	2
2	Lewis Hamilton	McLaren	+5"611	57	2
3	Robert Kubica	BMW	+37"353	57	2
4	Heikki Kovalainen	McLaren	+39"703	57	2
5	Jarno Trulli	Toyota	+50"684	57	2
6	Sebastian Vettel	Toro Rosso	+52"625	57	2
7	Timo Glock	Toyota	+1'07"990	57	1
8	Nico Rosberg	Williams	+1'11"457	57	2
9	Nick Heidfeld	BMW	+1'22"177	57	2
10	Sebastien Bourdais	Toro Rosso	+1'29"794	57	2
11	Nelson Piquet	Renault	+1'32"717	57	1
12	Mark Webber	Red Bull	+1 lap	56	1
13	Jenson Button	Honda	+1 lap	56	1
14	Giancarlo Fisichella	Force India	+1 lap	56	1
15	Kazuki Nakajima	Williams	+1 lap	56	2
16	Rubens Barrichello	Honda	+1 lap	56	1
17	David Coulthard	Red Bull	+1 lap	56	2

RETIREMENTS

Kimi Räikkönen	Ferrari	engine	45	2
Adrian Sutil	Force India	accident	41	2
Fernando Alonso	Renault	accident	0	0

FASTEST LAP

Felipe Massa	Ferrari	1'38"708	36

Belgian Grand Prix

◁ Start Location

5 Gear

251 Speed (km/h)

156 Speed (mph)

2.4 Lateral G-force

16 Turn number

T3 *Timing Sector

33.7 *Sector Time

1:24.4 **Target Lap Time

🏁 Finish Location

*The circuit is split into three timed sectors which, when added together, make up the lap time.
**A lap time that drivers aim for based on pole position 2004.

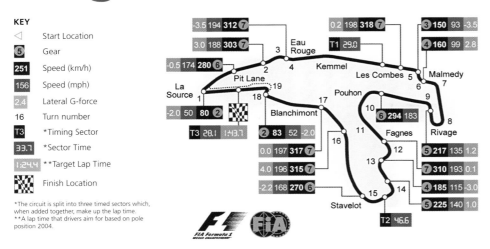

SPA-FRANCORCHAMPS

Hamilton doesn't maintain the advantage of being on pole for long. On just the 2nd lap, he spins at Source and is passed by Räikkönen. The traditional first-corner jostle sees Kovalainen, Heidfeld and Trulli, who'd gone off like a rocket, lose several places. Alonso and Bourdais, by contrast, are 4th and 5th behind Massa. And that's pretty much how things stay till lap 42 of 44, when the rain starts lashing down. Lewis bears down on Räikkönen who must have thought he had the race won. He cuts the final chicane to avoid a crash, lets the Finn back past to avoid, or so he thinks, a penalty and then attacks on the inside at Source. A few hundred metres further and the Englishman is on the grass to avoid Rosberg in a tailspin. Kimi gets back past but then comes off. The Ferrari ends up in the barrier after the heated exchange. Hamilton wins but is relegated to 3rd because of the move at Source. A cautious Massa is given victory and Heidfeld, who dared change to intermediates just two laps from the end, gets past six cars to finish 2nd. A tragic final lap for Bourdais who had been 3rd but is passed by the German, Alonso (4th), Vettel (5th) and Kubica (6th)! The man from Le Mans finishes 7th, ahead of Glock… who loses his point to Webber for having overtaken under the yellow flags. Ouch!

Spa-Francorchamps, Belgium – September 7

Circuit length: 7.004 km/4.352 miles
Race: 44 laps
Distance: 308.176 km/191.500 miles
Weather: overcast and rainy

QUALIFYING

	Driver	Car	Chassis	Time
1	Lewis Hamilton	McLaren	MP4-23 07	1'47"338
2	Felipe Massa	Ferrari	F2008-269	1'47"678
3	Heikki Kovalainen	McLaren	MP4-23 05	1'47"815
4	Kimi Räikkönen	Ferrari	F2008-271	1'47"992
5	Nick Heidfeld	BMW	F1.08-07	1'48"315
6	Fernando Alonso	Renault	R28-02	1'48"504
7	Mark Webber	Red Bull	RB4-05	1'48"736
8	Robert Kubica	BMW	F1.08-05	1'48"763
9	Sebastien Bourdais	Toro Rosso	STR3-04	1'48"951
10	Sebastian Vettel	Toro Rosso	STR3-03	1'50"319
11	Jarno Trulli	Toyota	TF108-05	1'46"949
12	Nelson Piquet	Renault	R28-01	1'46"965
13	Timo Glock	Toyota	TF108-06	1'46"995
14	David Coulthard	Red Bull	RB4-04	1'47"018
15	Nico Rosberg	Williams	FW30-05	1'47"429
16	Rubens Barrichello	Honda	RA108-03	1'48"153
17	Jenson Button	Honda	RA108-05	1'48"211
18	Adrian Sutil	Force India	VJM01/06	1'48"226
19	Kazuki Nakajima	Williams	FW30-04	1'48"268
20	Giancarlo Fisichella	Force India	VJM01/05	1'48"447

RESULT

	Driver	Car	Time	Laps	Stops
1	Felipe Massa	Ferrari	1h22'59"394	44	2
2	Nick Heidfeld	BMW	+9"383	44	3
3	Lewis Hamilton	McLaren	+10"539	44	2
4	Fernando Alonso	Renault	+14"478	44	3
5	Sebastian Vettel	Toro Rosso	+14"576	44	2
6	Robert Kubica	BMW	+15"037	44	2
7	Sebastien Bourdais	Toro Rosso	+16"735	44	2
8	Mark Webber	Red Bull	+42"776	44	2
9	Timo Glock	Toyota	+1'07"045	44	2
10	Heikki Kovalainen	McLaren	+1 lap	43	3
11	David Coulthard	Red Bull	+1 lap	43	2
12	Nico Rosberg	Williams	+1 lap	43	2
13	Adrian Sutil	Force India	+1 lap	43	2
14	Kazuki Nakajima	Williams	+1 lap	43	2
15	Jenson Button	Honda	+1 lap	43	2
16	Jarno Trulli	Toyota	+1 lap	43	2
17	Giancarlo Fisichella	Force India	+1 lap	43	3

RETIREMENTS

Kimi Räikkönen	Ferrari	crash	42	2
Rubens Barrichello	Honda	transmission	19	1
Nelson Piquet	Renault	crash	13	0

FASTEST LAP

Kimi Räikkönen	Ferrari	1'47"930	24

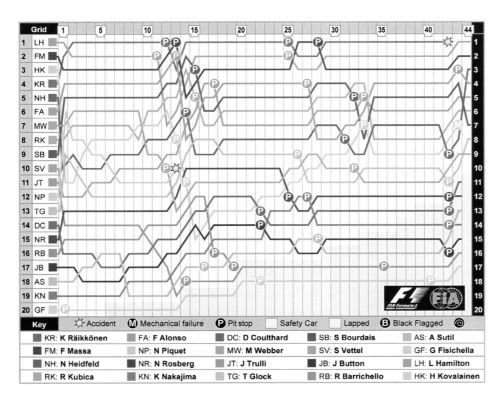

Key	☆ Accident	Ⓜ Mechanical failure	Ⓟ Pit stop	Safety Car	Lapped	Ⓑ Black Flagged	◎
	KR: **K Räikkönen**	FA: **F Alonso**	DC: **D Coulthard**	SB: **S Bourdais**	AS: **A Sutil**		
	FM: **F Massa**	NP: **N Piquet**	MW: **M Webber**	SV: **S Vettel**	GF: **G Fisichella**		
	NH: **N Heidfeld**	NR: **N Rosberg**	JT: **J Trulli**	JB: **J Button**	LH: **L Hamilton**		
	RK: **R Kubica**	KN: **K Nakajima**	TG: **T Glock**	RB: **R Barrichello**	HK: **H Kovalainen**		

Italian Grand Prix

KEY

◁ Start Location
5 Gear
251 Speed (km/h)
156 Speed (mph)
2.4 Lateral G-force
16 Turn number
T3 *Timing Sector
33.7 *Sector Time
1:24.4 **Target Lap Time
▓ Finish Location

*The circuit is split into three timed sectors which, when added together, make up the lap time.
**A lap time that drivers aim for based on pole position 2004.

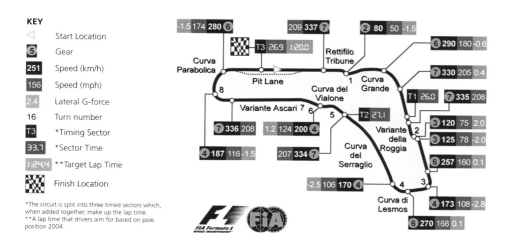

Monza, Italy – September 14
Circuit length: 5.793 km/3.600 miles
Race: 53 laps
Distance: 306.720 km/190.596 miles
Weather: overcast and rainy

QUALIFYING

	Driver	Car	Chassis	Time
1	Sebastian Vettel	Toro Rosso	STR3-03	1'37"555
2	Heikki Kovalainen	McLaren	MP4-23 05	1'37"631
3	Mark Webber	Red Bull	RB4-05	1'38"117
4	Sebastien Bourdais	Toro Rosso	STR3-04	1'38"445
5	Nico Rosberg	Williams	FW30-05	1'38"767
6	Felipe Massa	Ferrari	F2008-269	1'38"894
7	Jarno Trulli	Toyota	TF108-05	1'39"152
8	Fernando Alonso	Renault	R28-02	1'39"751
9	Timo Glock	Toyota	TF108-06	1'39"787
10	Nick Heidfeld	BMW	F1.08-07	1'39"906
11	Robert Kubica	BMW	F1.08-05	1'36"697
12	Giancarlo Fisichella	Force India	VJM01/05	1'36"698
13	David Coulthard	Red Bull	RB4-04	1'37"284
14	Kimi Raikkonen	Ferrari	F2008-271	1'37"522
15	Lewis Hamilton	McLaren	MP4-23 07	1'39"265
16	Rubens Barrichello	Honda	RA108-03	1'36"510
17	Nelson Piquet	Renault	R28-01	1'36"630
18	Kazuki Nakajima	Williams	FW30-04	1'36"653
19	Jenson Button	Honda	RA108-05	1'37"006
20	Adrian Sutil	Force India	VJM01/06	1'37"417

MONZA

An insane weekend! The favourites are routed in a rain-lashed qualifying session – Kubica 11th, Räikkönen 14th, Hamilton 15th – and the red bulls charge with Vettel on pole and Webber and Bourdais on the second row of the grid behind Kovalainen. The two Toro Rosso drivers couldn't have a more different Sunday. A mechanical problem stops Bourdais setting off on the warm-up lap and he starts a lap down from the pits… while his team-mate lords it in the lead, the rain still falling. Even though the track gets drier and drier, the German is never threatened with Kovalainen always well behind. Hamilton livens up the early part of the race by storming up the field to 2nd place before coming in for what he thinks will be his only pit-stop. However, the ever drier track means everyone has to pit to change their 'extreme rain' tyres for intermediates. A stroke of luck for Kubica, Alonso and Heidfeld who also manage to refuel for the only time in the race and see themselves climb to 3rd, 4th and 5th. A catastrophe for Massa, Hamilton, Webber and Räikkönen, who come in behind them in that order, and worse still for Rosberg and the Toyotas languishing further back. Meanwhile a 21-year-old becomes the youngest race-winner in history and gives Toro Rosso a moment of unprecedented glory. Who could have predicted that?

RESULT

	Driver	Car	Time	Laps	Stops
1	Sebastian Vettel	Toro Rosso	1h26'47"494	53	2
2	Heikki Kovalainen	McLaren	+12"512	53	2
3	Robert Kubica	BMW	+20"471	53	1
4	Fernando Alonso	Renault	+23"903	53	2
5	Nick Heidfeld	BMW	+27"748	53	2
6	Felipe Massa	Ferrari	+28"816	53	2
7	Lewis Hamilton	McLaren	+29"912	53	2
8	Mark Webber	Red Bull	+32"048	53	2
9	Kimi Räikkönen	Ferrari	+39"468	53	2
10	Nelson Piquet	Renault	+54"445	53	2
11	Timo Glock	Toyota	+58"888	53	2
12	Kazuki Nakajima	Williams	+1'02"015	53	2
13	Jarno Trulli	Toyota	+1'05"954	53	2
14	Nico Rosberg	Williams	+1'08"635	53	2
15	Jenson Button	Honda	+1'13"370	53	2
16	David Coulthard	Red Bull	+1 lap	52	2
17	Rubens Barrichello	Honda	+1 lap	52	2
18	Sebastien Bourdais	Toro Rosso	+1 lap	52	2
19	Adrian Sutil	Force India	+2 laps	51	3

RETIREMENT

Giancarlo Fisichella	Force India	accident	11	0

FASTEST LAP

Kimi Räikkönen	Ferrari	1'28"047	53

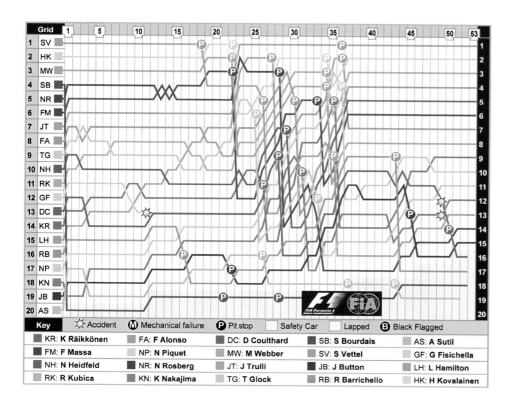

Key ☆ Accident Ⓜ Mechanical failure Ⓟ Pit stop ☐ Safety Car ☐ Lapped Ⓑ Black Flagged

KR: K Räikkönen	FA: F Alonso	DC: D Coulthard	SB: S Bourdais	AS: A Sutil
FM: F Massa	NP: N Piquet	MW: M Webber	SV: S Vettel	GF: G Fisichella
NH: N Heidfeld	NR: N Rosberg	JT: J Trulli	JB: J Button	LH: L Hamilton
RK: R Kubica	KN: K Nakajima	TG: T Glock	RB: R Barrichello	HK: H Kovalainen

Singapore Grand Prix

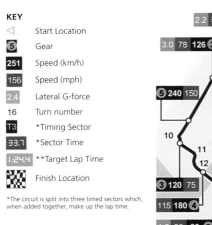
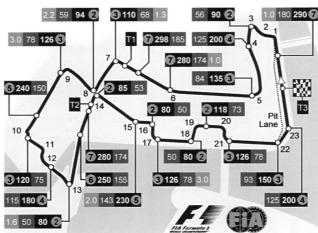

SINGAPORE

The 800th Grand Prix, and the first to be raced at night. Having secured pole in authoritative fashion, Massa gets away ahead of Hamilton, who is gradually reeled in by Räikkönen. 13th lap: Piquet hits the wall. Safety car. Disastrous pit-stop for Massa, who pulls the fuel hose away with him. It takes Ferrari ages to remove it and the Brazilian rejoins the field in last place. When the race restarts, Rosberg is in the lead ahead of Trulli and Fisichella (neither Italian having yet pitted) but, like Kubica, the German has a drive-through penalty for pitting with an almost empty tank when the pit-lane was still closed. Nico makes the most of a clear track to belt along and comes back out in 3rd whilst Robert loses everything. And who inherits the lead? Alonso, 15th on the grid after problems in qualifying, but having had the good fortune to stop before his team-mate's crash. The Spaniard is never under threat and gives Renault its first win in two years. A superb race for Rosberg in 2nd who holds Hamilton off to the end to get the best result of his career. Räikkönen tries to steal 4th place from Glock after the safety car comes out again following an accident involving Sutil and... hits the wall, rounding off the Scuderia's misery with Massa finishing 13th and now seven points adrift of Lewis. Vettel, Heidfeld, Coulthard and Nakajima wrap up the remaining points.

Marina Bay, Singapore – September 28
Circuit length: 5.067 km/3.149 miles
Race: 61 laps
Distance: 309.087 km/192.089 miles
Weather: hot and humid

QUALIFYING

	Driver	Car	Chassis	Time
1	Felipe Massa	Ferrari	F2008-269	1'44"801
2	Lewis Hamilton	McLaren	MP4-23 07	1'45"465
3	Kimi Räikkönen	Ferrari	F2008-270	1'45"617
4	Robert Kubica	BMW	F1.08-05	1'45"779
5	Heikki Kovalainen	McLaren	MP4-23 05	1'45"873
6	Nick Heidfeld	BMW	F1.08-07	1'45"964
7	Sebastian Vettel	Toro Rosso	STR2B-03	1'46"244
8	Timo Glock	Toyota	TF108-06	1'46"328
9	Nico Rosberg	Williams	FW30-05	1'46"611
10	Kazuki Nakajima	Williams	FW30-04	1'47"547
11	Jarno Trulli	Toyota	TF108-05	1'45"038
12	Jenson Button	Honda	RA 108-02	1'45"133
13	Mark Webber	Red Bull	RB4-04	1'45"212
14	David Coulthard	Red Bull	RB4-03	1'45"298
15	Fernando Alonso	Renault	R28-02	no time
16	Nelson Piquet	Renault	R28-01	1'46"037
17	Sebastien Bourdais	Toro Rosso	STR2B-01	1'46"389
18	Rubens Barrichello	Honda	RA 108-04	1'46"583
19	Adrian Sutil	Force India	VJM01/02	1'47"940
20	Giancarlo Fisichella	Force India	VJM01/05	no time

RESULT

	Driver	Car	Time	Laps	Stops
1	Fernando Alonso	Renault	1h57'16"304	61	2
2	Nico Rosberg	Williams	+2"957	61	3
3	Lewis Hamilton	McLaren	+5"917	61	2
4	Timo Glock	Toyota	+8"155	61	2
5	Sebastian Vettel	Toro Rosso	+10"268	61	2
6	Nick Heidfeld	BMW	+11"101	61	2
7	David Coulthard	Red Bull	+16"387	61	2
8	Kazuki Nakajima	Williams	+18"489	61	2
9	Jenson Button	Honda	+19"885	61	2
10	Heikki Kovalainen	McLaren	+26"902	61	2
11	Robert Kubica	BMW	+27"975	61	3
12	Sebastien Bourdais	Toro Rosso	+29"432	61	3
13	Felipe Massa	Ferrari	+35"170	61	3
14	Giancarlo Fisichella	Force India	+43"571	61	1
15	Kimi Räikkönen	Ferrari	+4 laps	57	1

RETIREMENTS

Jarno Trulli	Toyota	hydraulics	50	1
Adrian Sutil	Force India	accident	49	2
Mark Webber	Red Bull	transmission	29	1
Rubens Barrichello	Honda	electronics	14	1
Nelson Piquet	Renault	accident	13	0

FASTEST LAP

Kimi Räikkönen	Ferrari	1'45"599		14

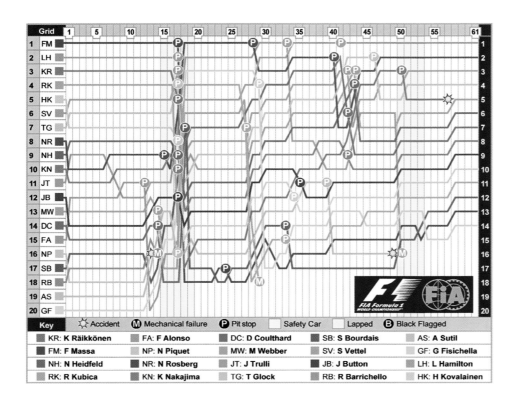

Japanese Grand Prix

KEY

◁ Start Location

5 Gear

251 Speed (km/h)

156 Speed (mph)

2.4 Lateral G-force

16 Turn number

T3 *Timing Sector

33.7 *Sector Time

1:24.4 **Target Lap Time

▓ Finish Location

*The circuit is split into three timed sectors which, when added together, make up the lap time.
**A lap time that drivers aim for based on pole position 2004

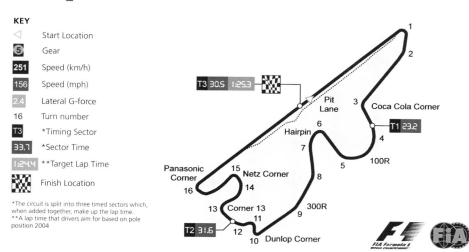

T3 30.5 1:25.3

Pit Lane
3 Coca Cola Corner
T1 23.2
6
Hairpin
7
4
100R
5
Panasonic Corner
15 Netz Corner
8
16
14
13 Corner 13
300R
11
T2 31.6 12
9
10 Dunlop Corner

FUJI

Hamilton loses the 1st place he had earned in qualifying right at the start. But in trying to get back past Räikkönen at any cost on the first corner, the Briton jams his wheels and front brakes, veers right and forces the Ferrari to go wide too without actually touching it. Towards the back of the field, a broken suspension sees Coulthard crash. Lewis gets past Massa on the 2nd lap but the Brazilian collides with him. Both men are given a drive-through penalty for the contentious moves. Kubica and Alonso make the most of the confusion to open up a lead in front. The Spaniard uses the first round of pit-stops to get ahead of the Pole. Fernando is untroubled for the rest of the race and notches up his second successive win. Robert has to contend with a resurgent Räikkönen. The two men very nearly touch but the BMW Sauber stays ahead. A good race from Piquet who finishes 4th ahead of Trulli. Bourdais comes in an excellent 6th… and immediately has the result taken away from him, the stewards giving him a 25-second penalty for obstructing Massa when it was the Ferrari which flung itself at the Toro Rosso! A shameful punishment which gives three points to Vettel but, more importantly, two to Massa, who had muscled his way past Webber. Felipe is now just five points behind Hamilton, who finished 12th. Bad day for McLaren as Kovalainen, a potential race-winner, saw his engine fail on lap 16.

Fuji, Japan – October 12

Circuit length: 4.563 km/2.835 miles
Race: 67 laps
Distance: 305.721 km/189.975 miles
Weather: cool and overcast

QUALIFYING

	Driver	Car	Chassis	Time
1	Lewis Hamilton	McLaren	MP4-23 06	1'18"404
2	Kimi Räikkönen	Ferrari	F2008-270	1'18"644
3	Heikki Kovalainen	McLaren	MP4-23 04	1'18"821
4	Fernando Alonso	Renault	R28-02	1'18"852
5	Felipe Massa	Ferrari	F2008-269	1'18"874
6	Robert Kubica	BMW	F1.08-05	1'18"979
7	Jarno Trulli	Toyota	TF108-05	1'19"026
8	Timo Glock	Toyota	TF108-07	1'19"118
9	Sebastian Vettel	Toro Rosso	STR3-03	1'19"638
10	Sebastien Bourdais	Toro Rosso	STR3-04	1'20"167
11	David Coulthard	Red Bull	RB4-03	1'18"187
12	Nelson Piquet	Renault	R28-01	1'18"274
13	Mark Webber	Red Bull	RB4-04	1'18"314
14	Kazuki Nakajima	Williams	FW30-04	1'18"594
15	Nico Rosberg	Williams	FW30-05	1'18"672
16	Nick Heidfeld	BMW	F1.08-07	1'18"835
17	Rubens Barrichello	Honda	RA108-03	1'18"882
18	Jenson Button	Honda	RA108-05	1'19"100
19	Adrian Sutil	Force India	VJM01/06	1'19"163
20	Giancarlo Fisichella	Force India	VJM01/05	1'19"910

RESULT

	Driver	Car	Time	Laps	Stops
1	Fernando Alonso	Renault	1h30'21"892	67	2
2	Robert Kubica	BMW	+5"283	67	2
3	Kimi Räikkönen	Ferrari	+6"400	67	2
4	Nelson Piquet	Renault	+20"570	67	1
5	Jarno Trulli	Toyota	+23"767	67	2
6	Sebastian Vettel	Toro Rosso	+39"207	67	2
7	Felipe Massa	Ferrari	+46"158	67	3
8	Mark Webber	Red Bull	+50"811	67	1
9	Nick Heidfeld	BMW	+54"120	67	1
10	Sebastien Bourdais	Toro Rosso	+59"085	67	2
11	Nico Rosberg	Williams	+1'02"096	67	1
12	Lewis Hamilton	McLaren	+1'18"900	67	3
13	Rubens Barrichello	Honda	+1 lap	66	1
14	Jenson Button	Honda	+1 lap	66	1
15	Kazuki Nakajima	Williams	+1 lap	66	2

RETIREMENTS

Giancarlo Fisichella	Force India	gearbox	21	1
Heikki Kovalainen	McLaren	engine	16	2
Adrian Sutil	Force India	tyres	8	0
Timo Glock	Toyota	hydraulics	6	0
David Coulthard	Red Bull	accident	1	0

FASTEST LAP

Felipe Massa	Ferrari	1'18"426	55

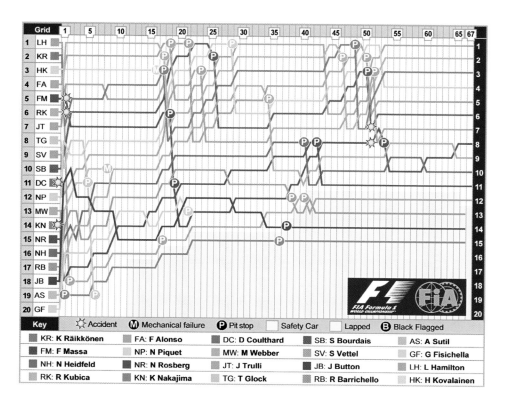

Grid	1	5	10	15	20	25	30	35	40	45	50	55	60	65	67
1 LH															
2 KR															
3 HK															
4 FA															
5 FM															
6 RK															
7 JT															
8 TG															
9 SV															
10 SB															
11 DC															
12 NP															
13 MW															
14 KN															
15 NR															
16 NH															
17 RB															
18 JB															
19 AS															
20 GF															

Key ☆ Accident Ⓜ Mechanical failure Ⓟ Pit stop Safety Car Lapped Ⓑ Black Flagged

KR: K Räikkönen	FA: F Alonso	DC: D Coulthard	SB: S Bourdais	AS: A Sutil
FM: F Massa	NP: N Piquet	MW: M Webber	SV: S Vettel	GF: G Fisichella
NH: N Heidfeld	NR: N Rosberg	JT: J Trulli	JB: J Button	LH: L Hamilton
RK: R Kubica	KN: K Nakajima	TG: T Glock	RB: R Barrichello	HK: H Kovalainen

Chinese Grand Prix

KEY

◁ Start Location
5 Gear
251 Speed (km/h)
156 Speed (mph)
2.4 Lateral G-force
16 Turn number
T3 *Timing Sector
33.7 *Sector Time
1:24.4 **Target Lap Time
🏁 Finish Location

*The circuit is split into three timed sectors which,
when added together, make up the lap time.
**A lap time that drivers aim for based on pole
position 2004.

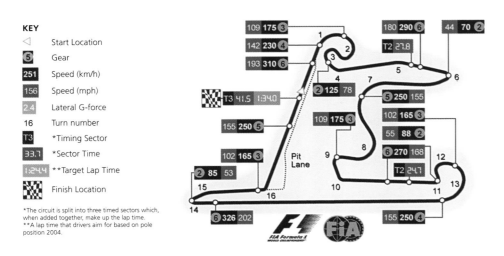

Shanghai, Zhuhai, China – October 19
Circuit length: 5.451 km/3.387 miles
Race: 56 laps
Distance: 305.066 km/189.568 miles
Weather: overcast

SHANGHAI

A clear run for Lewis Hamilton who was already imperious in testing. The Englishman keeps the Ferraris of Räikkönen and Massa behind him at the start where Trulli and Bourdais collide in the middle of the pack. There's a nice battle for 4th place between Alonso and Kovalainen which the Spaniard wins. Kubica, poor in qualifying (11th), starts with a very heavy fuel load and gets no higher than 3rd – during the first round of pit-stops – at any point in the race. Kova gets a puncture on lap 34, falls down the pecking order and ends up retiring. The second wave of pit-stops causes as little change in positions as the first. Nothing will stop Hamilton sailing to the ninth win of his career (and a hat-trick of bests as he also records the fastest lap). In the last few laps, Ferrari ask Kimi, not surprisingly, to let Felipe past. Finishing 2nd, the Brazilian is now seven points behind Lewis in the championship which will be settled in Brazil. By notching up 14 points, the Scuderia has almost secured the constructors' championship. With Alonso 4th and Piquet 8th, Renault guarantees itself 4th place in the constructors championship behind BMW Sauber with Heidfeld in 5th and Kubica 6th, the Pole well off the pace. The two points for 7th go to Glock thanks to a one-stop strategy.

QUALIFYING

	Driver	Car	Chassis	Time
1	Lewis Hamilton	McLaren	MP4-23 06	1'36"303
2	Kimi Räikkönen	Ferrari	F2008-270	1'36"645
3	Felipe Massa	Ferrari	F2008-269	1'36"889
4	Fernando Alonso	Renault	R28-02	1'36"927
5	Heikki Kovalainen	McLaren	MP4-23 04	1'36"930
6	Mark Webber	Red Bull	RB4-05	1'37"083
7	Nick Heidfeld	BMW	F1.08-07	1'37"201
8	Sebastian Vettel	Toro Rosso	STR3-03	1'37"685
9	Jarno Trulli	Toyota	TF108-05	1'37"934
10	Sebastien Bourdais	Toro Rosso	STR3-04	1'38"885
11	Nelson Piquet	Renault	R28-01	1'35"722
12	Robert Kubica	BMW	F1.08-05	1'35"814
13	Timo Glock	Toyota	TF108-07	1'35"937
14	Rubens Barrichello	Honda	RA108-03	1'36"079
15	Nico Rosberg	Williams	FW30-05	1'36"210
16	David Coulthard	Red Bull	RB4-03	1'36"731
17	Kazuki Nakajima	Williams	FW30-04	1'36"863
18	Jenson Button	Honda	RA108-05	1'37"053
19	Adrian Sutil	Force India	VJM01/06	1'37"730
20	Giancarlo Fisichella	Force India	VJM01/05	1'37"739

RESULT

	Driver	Car	Time	Laps	Stops
1	Lewis Hamilton	McLaren	1h31'57"403	56	2
2	Felipe Massa	Ferrari	+14"925	56	2
3	Kimi Räikkönen	Ferrari	+16"455	56	2
4	Fernando Alonso	Renault	+18"370	56	2
5	Nick Heidfeld	BMW	+28"923	56	2
6	Robert Kubica	BMW	+33"219	56	2
7	Timo Glock	Toyota	+41"722	56	1
8	Nelson Piquet	Renault	+56"645	56	2
9	Sebastian Vettel	Toro Rosso	+1'04"339	56	2
10	David Coulthard	Red Bull	+1'14"842	56	1
11	Rubens Barrichello	Honda	+1'25"061	56	2
12	Kazuki Nakajima	Williams	+1'30"847	56	1
13	Sebastien Bourdais	Toro Rosso	+1'31"457	56	2
14	Mark Webber	Red Bull	+1'32"422	56	2
15	Nico Rosberg	Williams	+1 lap	55	2
16	Jenson Button	Honda	+1 lap	55	2
17	Giancarlo Fisichella	Force India	+1 lap	55	1

RETIREMENTS

10	Heikki Kovalainen	McLaren	tyres	49	2
13	Adrian Sutil	Force India	gearbox	13	0
16	Jarno Trulli	Toyota	collision	2	0

FASTEST LAP

Lewis Hamilton	McLaren	1'36"325	13

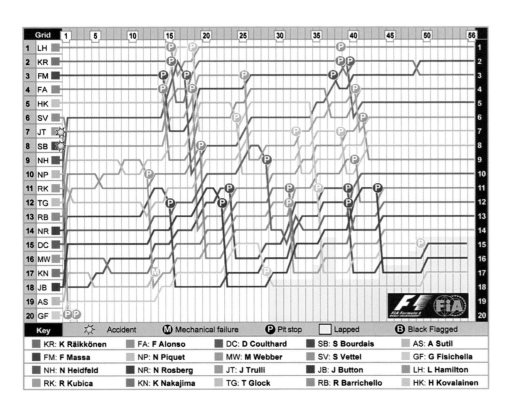

Brazilian Grand Prix

KEY

◁ Start Location
5 Gear
251 Speed (km/h)
156 Speed (mph)
2.4 Lateral G-force
16 Turn number
T3 *Timing Sector
33.7 *Sector Time
1:24.4 **Target Lap Time
🏁 Finish Location

*The circuit is split into three timed sectors which, when added together, make up the lap time.
**A lap time that drivers aim for based on pole position 2004

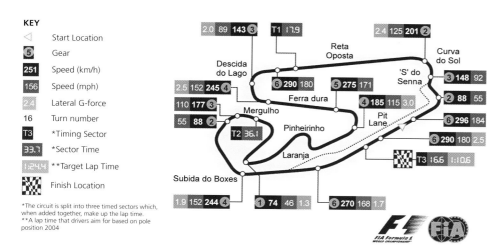

Interlagos Circuit, Sao Paulo, Brazil – November 2
Circuit length: 4.309 km/2.677 miles
Race: 71 laps
Distance: 305.909 km/190.067 miles
Weather: overcast and rainy

QUALIFYING

	Driver	Car	Chassis	Time
1	Felipe Massa	Ferrari	F2008-269	1'12"368
2	Jarno Trulli	Toyota	TF108-05	1'12"737
3	Kimi Räikkönen	Ferrari	F2008-271	1'12"828
4	Lewis Hamilton	McLaren	MP-23 07	1'12"830
5	Heikki Kovalainen	McLaren	MP-23 05	1'12"917
6	Fernando Alonso	Renault	R28-02	1'12"967
7	Sebastian Vettel	Toro Rosso	STR2B-03	1'13"082
8	Nick Heidfeld	BMW	F1.08-07	1'13"297
9	Sebastien Bourdais	Toro Rosso	STR2B-04	1'14"105
10	Timo Glock	Toyota	TF108-07	1'14"230
11	Nelson Piquet	Renault	R28-01	1'12"137
12	Mark Webber	Red Bull	RB4-05	1'12"289
13	Robert Kubica	BMW	F1.08-05	1'12"300
14	David Coulthard	Red Bull	RB4-03	1'12"717
15	Rubens Barrichello	Honda	RA 108-03	1'13"139
16	Kazuki Nakajima	Williams	FW30-04	1'12"800
17	Jenson Button	Honda	RA 108-05	1'12"810
18	Nico Rosberg	Williams	FW30-05	1'13"002
19	Giancarlo Fisichella	Force India	VJM01/05	1'13"426
20	Adrian Sutil	Force India	VJM01/06	1'13"508

INTERLAGOS

Pure madness! Massa, who must finish in the top two to win the championship, secures pole ahead of Trulli, Räikkönen and Hamilton down in 4th. Just a few minutes before the race is due to begin, the heavens open. All the drivers set off in wets. Coulthard ends his last Grand Prix in the rails at the start. Safety car. When the race gets going again, there are no changes in the leading positions. After the first round of pit-stops, Vettel, who had pitted early, is breathing down Massa's neck! Hamilton, who needs to finish in the top five, is currently 6th behind the amazing Fisichella and it takes him half a dozen laps to get past him. After Vettel's second stop – he is on a three-stop strategy – Lewis gets up to 4th with Glock hot on his tails. Up ahead, Räikkönen is reeling Alonso in and Massa is cruising. But with seven laps to go the rain starts again. Some come into the pits, some don't, and Hamilton, who does, is now 5th behind Glock, who doesn't. But Vettel passes him on the penultimate lap! Last lap: Massa crosses the line first ahead of Alonso and Räikkönen. Jubilation in the Ferrari camp... until they see that, in the dying moments, Glock has been passed on the last corner by Vettel and, more importantly, by Hamilton, who finishes 5th, thereby winning the championship by a single point. Heart-stopping stuff!

RESULT

	Driver	Car	Time	Laps	Stops
1	Felipe Massa	Ferrari	1h34'11"435	71	3
2	Fernando Alonso	Renault	+13"298	71	3
3	Kimi Räikkönen	Ferrari	+16"235	71	3
4	Sebastian Vettel	Toro Rosso	+38"011	71	4
5	Lewis Hamilton	McLaren	+38"907	71	3
6	Timo Glock	Toyota	+44"368	71	2
7	Heikki Kovalainen	McLaren	+55"074	71	3
8	Jarno Trulli	Toyota	+1'08"433	71	2
9	Mark Webber	Red Bull	+1'19"666	71	3
10	Nick Heidfeld	BMW	+1 lap	70	3
11	Robert Kubica	BMW	+1 lap	70	3
12	Nico Rosberg	Williams	+1 lap	70	3
13	Jenson Button	Honda	+1 lap	70	4
14	Sebastien Bourdais	Toro Rosso	+1 lap	70	3
15	Rubens Barrichello	Honda	+1 lap	70	4
16	Adrian Sutil	Force India	+2 laps	69	3
17	Kazuki Nakajima	Williams	+2 laps	69	3
18	Giancarlo Fisichella	Force India	+2 laps	69	3

RETIREMENTS

Nelson Piquet	Renault	accident	0	0
David Coulthard	Red Bull	accident	0	0

FASTEST LAP

Felipe Massa	Ferrari	1'13"736	36

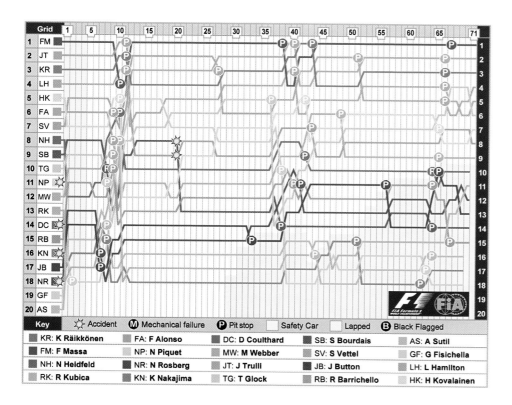

Grid																	

1	FM
2	JT
3	KR
4	LH
5	HK
6	FA
7	SV
8	NH
9	SB
10	TG
11	NP
12	MW
13	RK
14	DC
15	RB
16	KN
17	JB
18	NR
19	GF
20	AS

Key: ☆ Accident Ⓜ Mechanical failure ℗ Pit stop Safety Car Lapped Ⓑ Black Flagged

KR: K Räikkönen	FA: F Alonso	DC: D Coulthard	SB: S Bourdais	AS: A Sutil
FM: F Massa	NP: N Piquet	MW: M Webber	SV: S Vettel	GF: G Fisichella
NH: N Heidfeld	NR: N Rosberg	JT: J Trulli	JB: J Button	LH: L Hamilton
RK: R Kubica	KN: K Nakajima	TG: T Glock	RB: R Barrichello	HK: H Kovalainen

Championships

F1 DRIVERS

#	Driver	Cars	Australia	Malaysia	Bahrein	Spain	Turkey	Monaco	Canada	France	Great Britain	Germany	Hungary	Europe	Belgium	Italy	Singapore	Japan	China	Brazil	Points
1	Lewis Hamilton (GB)	McLaren-Mercedes	10	4	0	6	8	10	R	0	10	10	4	8	6	2	6	0	10	4	98
2	Felipe Massa (BR)	Ferrari	R	R	10	8	10	6	4	10	0	6	0	10	10	3	0	2	8	10	97
3	Kimi Räikkönen (SF)	Ferrari	1	10	8	10	6	0	R	8	5	3	6	R	R	0	0	6	6	6	75
4	Robert Kubica (PL)	BMW-Sauber	R	8	6	5	5	8	10	4	R	2	1	6	3	6	0	8	3	0	75
5	Fernando Alonso (E)	Renault	5	1	0	R	3	0	R	1	3	0	5	R	5	5	10	10	5	8	61
6	Nick Heidfeld (D)	BMW-Sauber	8	3	5	0	4	0	8	0	8	5	0	0	8	4	3	0	4	0	60
7	Heikki Kovalainen (SF)	McLaren-Mercedes	4	6	4	R	0	1	0	5	4	4	10	5	0	8	0	R	R	2	53
8	Sebastian Vettel (D)	Toro Rosso-Ferrari	R	R	R	R	0	4	1	0	R	1	R	3	4	10	4	3	0	5	35
9	Jarno Trulli (I)	Toyota	R	5	3	1	0	0	3	6	2	0	2	4	0	0	R	4	R	1	31
10	Timo Glock (D)	Toyota	R	R	0	0	0	0	5	0	0	R	8	2	0	0	5	R	2	3	25
11	Mark Webber (AUS)	Red Bull-Renault	R	2	2	4	2	5	0	3	0	R	0	0	1	1	R	1	0	0	21
12	Nelson Piquet jr (BR)	Renault	R	0	R	R	0	R	R	2	R	8	3	0	R	0	R	5	1	R	19
13	Nico Rosberg (D)	Williams-Toyota	6	0	1	R	1	R	0	0	0	0	0	1	0	0	8	0	0	0	17
14	Rubens Barrichello (BR)	Honda	R	0	0	R	0	3	2	0	6	R	0	0	R	0	R	0	0	0	11
15	Kazuki Nakajima (J)	Williams-Toyota	3	0	0	2	R	2	R	0	1	0	0	0	0	0	1	0	0	0	9
16	David Coulthard (GB)	Red Bull-Renault	R	0	0	0	0	R	6	0	R	0	0	0	0	0	2	R	0	R	8
17	Sebastien Bourdais (F)	Toro Rosso-Ferrari	2	R	0	R	R	R	0	0	0	0	0	0	2	0	0	0	0	0	4
18	Jenson Button (GB)	Honda	R	0	R	3	0	0	0	R	R	0	0	0	0	0	0	0	0	0	3
19	Giancarlo Fisichella (I)	Force India-Ferrari	R	0	0	0	R	R	R	0	R	0	0	0	0	R	0	R	0	0	0
20	Adrian Sutil (D)	Force India-Ferrari	R	R	0	R	0	R	R	0	R	0	R	R	0	0	R	R	R	0	0
21	Takuma Sato (J)	Super Aguri-Honda	R	0	0	0	–	–	–	–	–	–	–	–	–	–	–	–	–	–	0
22	Anthony Davidson (GB)	Super Aguri-Honda	R	0	0	R	–	–	–	–	–	–	–	–	–	–	–	–	–	–	0

F1 CONSTRUCTORS

#	Team	Australia	Malaysia	Bahrein	Spain	Turkey	Monaco	Canada	France	Great Britain	Germany	Hungary	Europe	Belgium	Italy	Singapore	Japan	China	Brazil	Points
1	Scuderia Ferrari Marlboro	1	10	18	18	16	6	4	18	5	9	6	10	10	3	0	8	14	16	172
2	Vodafone McLaren Mercedes	14	10	4	6	8	11	0	5	14	14	14	13	6	10	6	0	10	6	151
3	BMW Sauber F1 Team	8	11	11	5	9	8	18	4	8	7	1	6	11	10	3	8	7	0	135
4	ING Renault F1 Team	5	1	0	0	3	0	0	3	3	8	8	0	5	5	10	15	6	8	80
5	Panasonic Toyota Racing	0	5	3	1	0	0	8	6	2	0	10	6	0	0	5	4	2	4	56
6	Scuderia Toro Rosso	2	0	0	0	0	4	1	0	0	1	0	3	10	10	4	3	0	5	39
7	Red Bull Racing	0	2	2	4	2	5	6	3	0	0	0	0	1	1	2	1	0	0	29
8	AT&T Williams	9	0	1	2	1	2	0	0	1	0	0	1	0	0	9	0	0	0	26
9	Honda Racing F1 Team	0	0	0	3	0	3	2	0	6	0	0	0	0	0	0	0	0	0	14
10	Force India F1 Team	0	0	0	0	0	0	0	0	0	0	0	0	0	0	0	0	0	0	0
11	Super Aguri F1 Team	0	0	0	0	–	–	–	–	–	–	–	–	–	–	–	–	–	–	0

GP2 SERIES
Champion

Giorgio Pantano (I)   Racing Engineering   Dallara-Renault   76 points

A1 GP
Champion 2007/2008

Team Switzerland   168 points

INDYCAR SERIES
After a secession of twelve years, Champ Car and Indy Racing League merged and became the IndyCar Series.

Champion
Scott Dixon (NZ)   Target Chip Ganassi Racing   Dallara-Honda   646 points

Scott Dixon also won the Indianapolis 500 Race. For the first time, a woman won a championship race (Danica Patrick at Motegi, Japan).

FORMULA NIPPON
Champion

Tsugio Matsuda (J)   Lawson Team Impul   Lola-Toyota   93,5 points

A new era

After three seasons of winter competition so as not to clash with the F1 calendar, the A1GP World Cup of Motorsport series started season four. As **Pierre van Vliet** explains, the championship has met with limited success in Europe, with the notable exception of the races held at Zandvoort and Brands Hatch, whereas in more distant lands, such as South Africa, India and Australia, it's been enthusiastically greeted by the crowds. What is new is a partnership with Ferrari no less!
The series' undisputable operational success, with 25 cars of surprising design (based on the old F3000 Lolas and all powered by the same Zytek V8 engine) from as many countries, still left the observers as sceptical as its economic chances seemed unlikely. With investment of nigh on $300 million, balancing the books seemed a long way off. None of which has prevented the series' Chairman Tony Teixeira from turning to Ferrari to provide engines for the next six seasons of A1GP. Much to the surprise of the cynics, the Ferrari era World Cup got under way at the start of October in Zandvoort, the opening round originally scheduled for Mugello in September having been cancelled. The car that looks like the Ferrari F2004 has had a true baptism of fire. Only 17 cars were ready which meant that such high-profile teams as Germany, the UK, India and Mexico were left on the sidelines but the staying power and sheer will of those taking part still commanded respect. And a clever decision to deduct the points from a single race in the championship standings meant that the collateral damage for those who missed the first outing due to a lack of time or parts to assemble all the cars would be minimised.

In spite of the inclement weather, the public turned out in force in Zandvoort to attend the first meeting of the 2008/2009 season and to discover the A1GP 'powered by Ferrari'.

So a new era has begun and the quality of the material on offer in the shape of this good-looking car combined with the undeniable talents of the series' very successful marketing heralds a bright future. The system of franchises per country, which are mostly held by rich motor-racing enthusiasts who have decided to marry their image to that of their country, provides a solid foundation upon which to develop the only single-seater racing world championship which sets itself apart from the sacrosanct Formula 1. We shall follow A1GP's development with interest in the months and years to come and wish good speed to those brave enough to take part in a trail-blazing discipline. The partnership with Ferrari, while no doubt expensive, is a real chance for the series' image, its sporting legitimacy and technical credibility. Thus, the first leg at Zandvoort under heavy rain saw 17 cars on the track and only seven cross the finishing line at the end of the second race. After Malaysia had come home ahead of New Zealand and France in the initial battle, it

was the experienced Loïc Duval who won the second round from young Kiwi Earl Bamber and Malaysia's excellent gentleman driver Fairuz Fauzy. Three countries might well have monopolised the season's first podium but other countries, such as Korea and Monaco, both new in this motor sport World Cup, scored their first points. The competition's favourites are still to be found on the list of previous winners, i.e. France, Switzerland (with their 2007-2008 champion Neel Jani) and Germany (Christian Vietoris having replaced Nico Hülkenberg). Oddly, for a number of drivers whose careers have come to a standstill, A1GP can almost become an end in itself: Loïc Duval, exiled in Japan in Formula Nippon, has long given up dreaming of Formula 1, as has Neel Jani (a former Red Bull F1 test driver) after a fairly failed attempt at Champ Car in the US. But others see the series as a springboard to the summer programmes in Europe or the States: promising Mexican teenager Esteban Gutierrez (crowned European Formula BMW champion aged 17) and New Zealand hopeful

Revealed in Zandvoort, the young Earl Bamber seems promised to a bright future.

The podium in Zandvoort, from left to right: Fauzy (Malaysia), Duval (France) and Bamber (New Zealand).

Earl Bamber, a revelation at Zandvoort, fit into this category. Former F1 drivers' involvement with some of the franchises, whether as advisers or national team managers, is important in bringing A1GP publicity. After Emerson Fittipaldi, Alan Jones, Jan Lammers, Alex Yoong and even Alain Prost and Olivier Panis, the 2008-2009 season's new boy comes from the US, their team having been entrusted to Michael Andretti, the man in charge of the powerful AGR (Andretti Green Racing) Indy Car outfit. While the American car may have been driven by the youngster Charlie Kimball in Zandvoort, it has been established that Marco Andretti (son of Michael and grandson of Mario) and Danica Patrick (the first female winner in Indy Car) will also defend the honour of the star-spangled banner. Champions of this calibre, who are real stars in the USA, aim to make the most of the winter series to hone their training on road or city circuits in time for the American Indy Car season. This bridge between the US and the rest of the world, absent from F1, could be exploited by A1GP to establish a reputation in areas of the world where currently little is known about it. And the fact that this is motor-racing in the form of national teams in emerging markets which have had little to do with the sport till now, such as India, Pakistan, Lebanon, China and now Korea, is no small string to the bow of a series whose potential is still far from being fully exploited. In these times of economic stagnation, A1GP's experience will perhaps one day be its best asset.

A1GP POWERED BY FERRARI

The new A1GP series car, powered by Ferrari, is comparable – in looks, at least – to an F1 from four or five years ago. Its shape is reminiscent of the F2004 which saw Michael Schumacher to his seventh world championship. Maranello's South African engineer Rory Byrne, acted as a consultant on the design of the A1GP project working with the A1GP design team lead by Technical Director John Travis. The

Pete da Silva, Rory Byrne

Emerson Fittipaldi   Alan Jones   Alain Prost, Nicolas Prost   Michael Andretti

result is fantastic: a car with a distinct shape bearing a family resemblance to its glorious older sibling. A more modern design with better aerodynamics and the use of Michelin tyres have reduced lap time by about 4 seconds in equal conditions compared to the Lolas. The chassis is powered by a series engine (the GT2 version of the 430 Modena 4.5l V8 developed by Michelotto under the guidance of Jean-Jacques His) generating 600 hp, with a Ferrari transmission (made by engineer Anton Stipinovich) and the latest electronics by Magnetti Marelli, long-time partners of the Scuderia. Operation on the ground remains the realm of the A1GP team, led by John Wickham, with each participating team only allowed to carry out maintenance on the tracks to avoid parallel development and the accompanying spiralling costs.

It is interesting to note that the sport's promoters are reflecting about an A2GP category with less sophisticated and less powerful cars, still in conjunction with Ferrari, to meet the demand of a growing number of countries who would like to participate in a series that would cost less and be open to less experienced drivers.

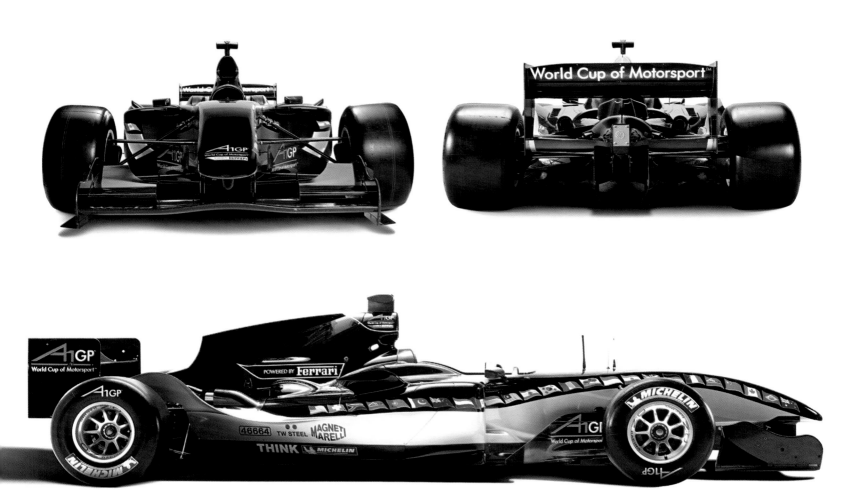

The A1GP has adopted the shark-fin engine cover, all the rage in F1. The Ferrari V8 engine, descended from the 430 GT, generates 600 hp.

Audi's eighth

Historians will have to delve deep into the history books to establish the last time the winners in all four categories at Le Mans had a completely reliable race, but in 2008 Audi, Porsche, Aston Martin and Ferrari achieved just that in their respective classes.
Audi had a strategically superb race to take its eighth win at Le Mans, its third since it introduced the diesel-powered R10 TDI in 2006, ahead of the superior Peugeot 908. The two manufacturers, each fielding 5.5-litre V12 diesel-powered sport prototypes, left the gasoline cars far behind as their competition escalated over the first six months of the 2008 season. In qualifying, two of the three Peugeots were more than five seconds clear of Audi's best, and nearly eight seconds faster than in 2007. Stephane Sarrazin set a pole position lap of 3'18"513, 247.16 km/h (153.57 mph).
Having established the Le Mans regulations to provide a test bed for new technology, all cars, including the diesels, ran with high performance biofuel incorporated into the Shell-supplied fuel. Tank sizes were reduced by 10% for the diesel LMP1 cars, from 90 litres to 81, and the air restrictor sizes for gasoline powered cars were increased by 3%. Homologated engines were also permitted in LMP1, including Aston Martin's 6-litre V12 taken from the DBR9, which was mated to a Lola chassis. Air restrictor breaks were awarded for road-car based engines, and for air conditioning systems in the closed cars.
The ACO confirmed its commitment to increasing lap times for the LMP1 cars to 3'30" in race conditions to avoid having to make major changes to the 13.629 km circuit, and to do so would reduce the turbo boost pressure of the diesels, along with the air restrictor sizes of the gasoline powered cars.
During the Le Mans week, Hideki Noda and Mike Newton were victims of a phenomenon new to sports car racing in 2008 when their Lolas slid sideways, and took flight. No fewer than five such accidents happened prior to the race, prompting the ACO to promise an urgent review of its aerodynamic rules and consider rushing through new rules, reducing downforce and increasing drag.
Andrew Cotton reviews the race and the winning teams.

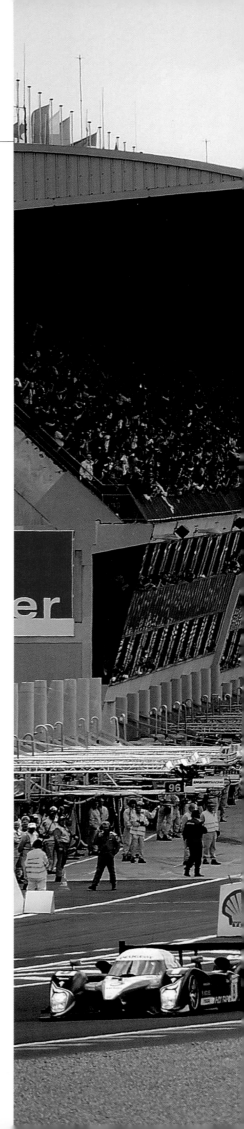

3'18"513 against 3'23"847: over five seconds separated the fastest Peugeot from the fastest Audi, underlining the superiority of the French cars in qualifying.

The Kristensen/Capello/McNish Audi No.2 was driven
harder and faster than the two sister cars from the start,
and the drivers were ruthless in traffic as they clung to the
tail of the Peugeots before the rain set in. The three drove
quadruple stints throughout, averaging lap times within
seconds of each other. The No.1 and No.3 Audis soon
settled into a supporting role to deliver Audi its eighth win.

Porsche's RS Spyder faced increased competition in the American Le Mans Series from a revised Acura LMP2 chassis, but in Europe the Porsche set new standards for the class. Le Mans was their first race of longer than 12 hours, and the van Merksteijn car won the LMP2 class.

Peugeot mechanics were stretched to their limit prior to the race after Alexander Wurz crashed one 908 HDI FAP in the LMS race at Spa, Marc Gene destroyed another chassis at the test day, and Ricardo Zonta crashed the No.9 car in second qualifying on Thursday. During the race, each of the Peugeots overheated and stopped to have their radiators cleaned. Whether the rain, which arrived during the night, helped Peugeot due to being less demanding on the engines, or hindered them due to set-up, will long be debated.

Ferrari and Porsche both invested heavily in their 2008 GT2 contenders, Porsche with a four-litre engine and Ferrari with aerodynamic, engine and exhaust updates which improved power delivery. The Risi Competizione 430 GT was followed by two other Ferraris in the class, the fastest Porsche finishing 4th. The class will form the base for the new GT1 regulations in 2010, satisfying the needs of Ferrari, Porsche, Aston Martin and General Motors.

The GT1 winning Aston Martin DBR9 carried only minor updates since last year, while the improved fuel economy of arch rival Corvette was negated by the weather and the safety car. After 24 hours, the Aston Martin crossed the line just over one minute ahead of the Corvette.

As the party gets into full swing after dusk for many of the spectators, night time sees a lot of action for the teams. The cool air means that the cars can run faster and run softer tyres for longer. They run different colour headlights for each class to help those in slower cars work out closing speeds and reduce the risk of accidents. Still, in the dark it is easy to make a mistake, like here the Courage No.5, right in front of the pits…

Maserati's third

The FIA GT 2008 season continued with the television-friendly two-hour race format. The Spa 24 hours was the only longer variant – and in Bucharest, the championship also experimented with two one-hour races. The cars were unchanged from 2007 as teams prepare for an all-new GT formula which will begin the integration process in 2009, and will be compulsory in both the FIA GT Championship and the Le Mans-sanctioned races in 2010. Series promoter Stephane Ratel was instrumental in bringing together the warring factions of the Automobile Club de l'Ouest and the Fédération Internationale de l'Automobile to harmonise the rules.

Andrew Cotton was in Spa for the 24 Hours. There were just 11 GT1 cars entered, as teams anticipate the new formula to render the existing machinery obsolete. They included Aston Martin DBR9s, Corvette C6.Rs and Maserati MC12s. The GT2 class was again well subscribed with Ferrari 430s and Porsche 997s, whilst the field was completed with G2 and G3 classes for cars that, for various reasons, do not compete in the championship. Maserati dominated the final two-thirds of the race, the fifth in the Championship, after its principal rivals were either involved in accidents or delayed before the event was seven hours old. Swiss driver Steve Zacchia crashed the pole-sitting Saleen S7R on the final lap of the warm-up and the car could not take its place at the head of the grid. Christophe Bouchut seriously damaged the Selleslagh Racing Team Corvette C6.R on Thursday, which put the Frenchman in hospital. The car was repaired for the race but, after an early lead, retired with brake problems. With two of the fastest cars out so early, the Maseratis were challenged by the JetAlliance Aston Martin DBR9 and the Phoenix Carsport Racing Corvette C6.R. Intelligent pit work saw the Maseratis lead at six hours. During the seventh hour, Karl Wendlinger lost control of his Aston Martin and crashed, hitting Mike Hezemans' Corvette while the two cars ran fourth and fifth overall. The Aston Martin retired, the Corvette had a long stop to repair the front suspension and returned to the competition only to have a fuel leak cause a fire on Sunday morning. The second Phoenix Corvette caught fire, the PekaRacing Saleen was damaged, the IPB Spartak Racing Lamborghini had a gearbox failure and the Gigawave Motorsport Aston Martin DBR9 team admitted that it did not have the outright speed to challenge the Maseratis. The Vitaphone Racing team ran in first and second places for the remainder of the race. Peugeot driver Stephane Sarrazin, making a guest appearance in the Maserati, followed his Le Mans 24 hours drive with another quite brilliant night stint to assure his car of victory, Belgian co-driver Eric van de Poele's historic fifth win at the event, and Maserati's third in four years.

Belgian Eric van de Poele won his record fifth Spa
24 hours and Michael Bartels, with co-driver Andrea
Bertolini, took a big step towards their second drivers'
title. It was the team's first win of the year and their
third podium. Leading at the six and 12-hour marks as
well as winning overall gave them a maximum score and
put them 13 points clear of their team-mates Miguel
Ramos and Alexandre Negrao. The Vitaphone Maserati
team led from the sixth hour, but the advantage of the
No.1 MC12 was sealed after another exceptional drive
during the night by Frenchman Stephane Sarrazin.

Marcel Fässler started the 60th edition of the Spa 24 hours from the head of the field in his 7-litre, V8-powered Phoenix Racing Corvette C6.R. The Swiss driver had been beaten to pole position by Pedro Lamy in the Larbre Competition Saleen S7R, but the Portuguese watched as his co-driver Steve Zacchia crashed at the Raidillon during Saturday's warm up.

For the first time in its history, the race started from the Formula One grid, positioned before La Source. Dutch Xavier Maassen in the Selleslagh Corvette made the most of the heavy braking zone into the hairpin to move into the lead while behind, the chaos caused by using this inappropriate grid sent cars in all directions. Maassen led for two laps before he suffered brake problems and retired.

The Gigawave team was new to the FIA GT Championship with its Aston Martin DBR9, but regular drivers Allan Simonsen and Philipp Peter scored podium positions in the first two races. The team withdrew from Oschersleben due to a technical fault, but bounced back at Spa, its debut in a 24-hour race. Together with double Le Mans winner Darren Turner, Simonsen and Peter claimed another podium. Their Aston Martin never had the pace to challenge the Maseratis, but moved into 3rd place in the sixth hour and stayed there to the end of the race.

The BMS Scuderia Italia team unexpectedly switched from Porsche to Ferrari this season. BMS successfully defended its Spa 24 hours GT2 title with the new, Pirelli-shod Ferrari 430 GT. Paolo Ruberti, Matteo Malucelli, Joel Camathias and Davide Rigon resisted strong pressure to win the GT2 class from the Prospeed Porsche and the championship-leading AF Corse Ferrari, penalised by long stops to repair air jacks.

The Mühlner Motorsport Porsche 997 GT3 Cup S of Heinz-Josef Barnes, Mark Thomas, Marc Basseng and Jean-Francois Hemroulle started from the G3 pole position, and finished 13th overall, winning the class for Cup-specification cars. For the team, based in the village of Francorchamps, it was its third 1-2 finish at the Spa 24 hours, and its seventh class win at the race. Basseng and Hemroulle completed almost 17 of the 24 hours between them at electrifying pace, finishing five laps clear of the sister car. The G3 class featured a diverse set of manufacturers including Porsche, Ferrari, Lamborghini, Dodge and Ascari.

Audi R10 TDI

LMP1

Audi did not have a magic formula that would dramatically increase performance against Peugeot in the Le Mans Series. Over the short 1000 km distances, and on twisty circuits, the R10 TDI conceded three wins to Peugeot in three races prior to Le Mans. At Barcelona in April, the problem that had overheated the Audi front brake discs at Sebring was cured, but despite official power figures of more than 650 hp and 1100 Nm of torque, unchanged since the car's launch in December 2005, performance was still lacking. At Le Mans, Audi needed to rely on its strategic brilliance to worry its French rivals into making a mistake over the long distance. Audi had devised a plan that concentrated on efficiency in both the pits and the car. The team changed tyres and drivers fewer times. From the start, Audi quadruple stinted its drivers which gave consistency, particularly when the weather changed on from dry to wet shortly before dawn, and when conditions were difficult on Sunday morning. Audi was able to complete 12 laps on a tank of fuel compared with Peugeot's 11. Both cars ran 81-litre

fuel tanks defined by the regulations but were lighter than in 2007 with minimum weight of 900 kg. In the ALMS, the Audi continued to run at 925 kg. At Le Mans, Tom Kristensen was outstanding during the night, getting the Audi into the lead in the pit stops, and the R10 TDIs were able to double and triple stint their wet weather tyres while Peugeot could not. Audi had also made the right call on wet weather tyres the moment the rain fell, giving Kristensen, Allan McNish and Rinaldo Capello enough of an advantage to convince Peugeot that it could not catch up without a strategic gamble. McNish was given the option of taking the chequered flag but his response was "whatever is best strategically for the team." That meant that, for only the second time in his eight wins at Le Mans, Kristensen took the chequered flag following a scheduled quadruple stint. While the winning R10 TDI ran flawlessly, the two remaining Audis, driven by Marco Werner, Frank Biela and Emanuele Pirro in the No.1 car, the No.3 by Alexandre Premat, Mike Rockenfeller and Lucas Luhr, did not.

Neither had the pace on track to win, and both had mechanical problems: No.1 had a clutch failure on Sunday, and No.3 a filter problem which cost them a place on the Le Mans podium.

Peugeot 908 HDi FAP

LMP1

The year of development was visible in the 2008 version of the 908 HDI FAP. The cars still passed the record 258,000-strong crowd at barely a whisper, revving to 5500 rpm, but were faster, stronger, more reliable than their debut in 2007, and a third car was entered at Le Mans giving more tactical options. This was a race that Peugeot expected to win having been dominant in the Le Mans Series, at the test day and in qualifying, but the race was lost to Audi with slow pit stops and through driver error.

The cars ran new bodywork worth up to a second per lap at Le Mans, but lost time on Saturday night with dirty windscreens and all three cars lost further time having their radiators cleaned during the night. Other problems, particularly bodywork change, were costly. The most reliable car was driven by Nicolas Minassian, Marc Gene and Jacques Villeneuve, but the former Formula One World Champion was not fast, and the Spaniard was recovering from a crash at the test day which wrote off one of the team's race chassis.

Despite setting up the car to understeer, they had the speed to win by two clear laps and eventually finished second. Two of the three Peugeots had breathtaking pace. Franck Montagny on Saturday night hauled his car into the lead with a series of blistering laps before Christian Klien spun into the gravel. The third car, driven by pole-winner Stephane Sarrazin, Pedro Lamy and Alexander Wurz, led the first two hours before suffering a piston failure in the gear selection process.

Porsche RS

LMP2

Porsche's RS Spyder had never contested a race of more than 12 hours, but the German manufacturer was confident that its engines and gearboxes would last at Le Mans; in the American Le Mans Series the 3.4-litre V8 engines, revving to 10,600 rpm and producing 478 hp and 370 Nm of torque, are returned to the factory for a re-build after 30 hours of running. The weight of the cars was increased to 800 kg for Le Mans (from 775) and the fuel tank reduced to 80 litres (from 90). The winning team at Le Mans was managed by Frans Verschuur, a former driver who made a business running Renault Méganes and Clios in the Dutch championship. Endurance racing is not new to the team having run in the Dubai 24 hours. Though the RS Spyder is an altogether different league the team, with drivers Peter van Merksteijn and Jos Verstappen, won two of the opening three Le Mans Series races. Jeroen Bleekemolen joined the duo at Le Mans. The team runs as van Merksteijn Motorsport, after the steel magnate who finances the operation and performs

well as a driver, too. The purple and white Porsche ran almost completely without fault, delayed during the night only by a slight front-end vibration. They had time to fix the fault as the Team Essex Porsche, which led into the night, had an engine problem which reduced power until the team changed the electrics and the injectors.

Aston Martin DBR9

GT1

The factory Aston Martin DBR9s and the Corvette C6.Rs
faced each other in the GT1 class at Le Mans on four occasions,
winning two each.

The Aston Martin Racing team had not competed with the
DBR9s since Le Mans 2007, but it had not been inactive, joining
Charouz Racing Systems to run the Lola Coupé in the LMP1
class, which features a 6-litre V12 engine taken from the DBR9.
The factory DBR9s, running in the colours of Gulf oil, were
essentially the same as in 2007 and maximum power quoted
remained at 575 hp, and torque at 700 Nm at 5250 rpm. General
Motors had worked on fuel efficiency from its 7-litre V8 engine,
which should have been an advantage, but that was negated by
a safety car period on Saturday night and by the rain on Sunday.
The two Corvettes each lost time, one with an alternator
failure, another having the brake pads and discs changed, and
the second Aston Martin also had an alternator failure.
In 2008, if the race was not perfect, it could not be won,
and David Brabham, Antonio Garcia and Darren Turner
just had the perfect race.

Ferrari 430 GT

GT2

Ferrari has held the upper hand over Porsche for 18 months ahead of Le Mans 2008, winning the 2007 FIA GT Championship and the American Le Mans Series. In the Sarthe, the Texas based Risi Competizione team added a Le Mans victory to the score.

Ferrari produced a new aerodynamic package and updates to its 4-litre V8 engine, producing more than 400 hp at 6800 rpm and more than 400 Nm of torque delivered through the Ferrari 6-speed gearbox. The marque benefited from a numerical superiority over Porsche which was represented by just three cars. The Risi Competizione team had a dismal start to its defence of the ALMS title, with just three points from four races, and an accident at Salt Lake City left the team with repair work before transporting the cars to Le Mans. Despite the difficult conditions in 2008, Jaime Melo, with Mika Salo and Gianmaria Bruni, drove a faultless race to take a comfortable victory. Salo had one unscheduled pit stop when he flat spotted a tyre, but the car was otherwise perfect, surrendering pole position to the Porsches but

running stronger and more reliably in the race.

Ferrari filled the podium, with BMS Scuderia Italia and Farnbacher Racing taking 2rd and 3rd places after the Virgo Motorsport team retired with engine failure.

Maserati MC12

GT1

Since its debut in the FIA GT Championship at Imola in 2004, the Maserati MC12 has been one of the most controversial GT cars ever produced. Based on its Fiat stablemate, the Ferrari Enzo, the MC12 uses the same floorplan and mid-mounted 6-litre V12 engine. The race version was initially built to regulations which were subsequently replaced. It was therefore not eligible for racing without extensive modifications, which included reducing the rear overhang and rear wing, and concessions from governing bodies. The car, engineered by Giorgio Ascanelli who is now at Toro Rosso, was expensive at one million euros in 2005, lifting the bar further than the Prodrive-supplied 550 Maranello, though stable championship regulations ensured longevity for both models. Rival teams racing feared the potential of the Italian super car, and so a performance balancing structure was introduced. The FIA was given the power to reduce the size of the rear wing, the minimum weight of the car, and even reduce the capacity of the fuel tank when the races

were still three hours in duration and fuel economy mattered. The MC12 was accepted into the FIA GT Championship, and by IMSA in the US in 2005, though the ACO refused to acknowledge it and it was not eligible to score points towards the GT1 title in the American Le Mans Series. The car was extremely popular with the crowds in the US, running in Maserati blue with the famous trident on its roof, but only

contested one season before it was garaged. In Europe the car was not dominant, but was successful from the outset, winning in its debut season at Oschersleben in 2004, the second of its two races before it was fully accepted to score points. German driver Michael Bartels, who won the Imola race that year ahead of the two debutant MC12s, convinced his sponsor, telemedicine service company Vitaphone, to switch from their unreliable Saleen S7R and buy two MC12s for the 2005 season. Since then, Vitaphone Racing has won the teams' title every year and in 2006 Bartels was the champion driver with Andrea Bertolini, while Thomas Biagi won the title with the team in 2007. Vitaphone Racing's performance at the Spa 24 hours, a race which carries double points for the championship, has been particularly impressive. It won in 2005, the first time that the MC12 contested a 24-hour race, and repeated the feat in 2006. In 2007, it was in contention for the win when

Belgian Eric van de Poele spun into the gravel on Sunday afternoon, but in 2008 there were no such problems. With the main rivals dropping out of the race before midnight, the two Maseratis cruised to a comfortable 1-2 and extended their lead at the head of the teams' title, claiming the maximum of 36 points, and putting Bartels and Bertolini in a strong position to win the drivers' title for a second time together.

ENDURANCE :: LE MANS 24 HOURS RESULTS

Circuit des 24 Heures, Le Mans, France – June 14-15
Circuit length: 13.629 km
Distance covered by the winning team: 5192 km
Weather conditions: partly sunny with some showers

LMP1
LMP2
GT1
GT2

No. MAKE AND TYPE   HOURLY POSITIONS

No.	MAKE AND TYPE	1	2	3	4	5	6	7	8	9	10	11	12	13	14	15	16	17	18	19	20	21	22	23	24
2	Audi R10 TDI	4	2	1	1	2	3	3	2	2	2	2	2	1	2	1	1	1	1	1	1	1	1	1	1
7	Peugeot 908 Hdi-FAP	3	4	3	2	1	2	2	1	1	1	1	1	2	1	2	2	2	2	2	2	2	2	2	2
9	Peugeot 908 Hdi-FAP	2	3	2	3	3	1	1	3	3	3	3	3	4	4	3	3	3	3	3	3	3	3	3	3
3	Audi R10 TDI	6	5	4	4	4	4	4	4	5	4	4	4	3	3	4	4	4	4	4	4	4	4	4	4
8	Peugeot 908 Hdi-FAP	1	1	27	16	13	10	7	6	6	6	9	7	7	6	6	6	6	6	6	5	6	5	5	5
1	Audi R10 TDI	5	6	5	5	5	5	5	5	4	5	5	5	5	5	5	5	5	5	5	6	5	6	6	6
17	Pescarolo Judd	12	11	9	7	8	7	9	10	8	7	6	6	6	7	7	7	7	7	7	7	7	7	7	7
5	Courage-Oreca Judd	10	8	7	6	6	6	6	7	7	8	7	8	9	9	9	9	8	8	8	8	8	8	8	8
10	Lola Aston Martin	9	32	47	43	31	28	25	20	16	14	15	13	13	12	12	11	11	11	11	11	11	10	10	9
34	Porsche RS Spyder	15	14	11	11	14	12	12	12	11	10	10	10	10	10	11	8	9	9	9	9	9	9	9	10
18	Pescarolo Judd	13	13	13	12	12	14	13	14	12	12	12	12	11	10	10	10	10	10	10	10	10	11	11	11
31	Porsche RS Spyder	16	12	12	10	11	12	14	13	13	11	11	11	11	13	13	15	15	15	13	13	12	12	12	12
9	Aston Martin DBR9	29	26	22	20	21	21	22	19	19	16	16	15	17	15	15	12	12	12	12	12	13	13	13	13
63	Corvette C6.R	26	25	23	23	20	19	19	21	20	17	17	16	16	17	16	14	14	14	14	14	14	14	14	14
64	Corvette C6.R	28	27	24	21	22	26	26	24	23	20	20	19	19	18	17	16	16	16	16	16	16	15	15	15
7	Aston Martin DBR9	30	28	25	24	23	23	23	22	21	18	18	18	18	19	20	18	17	17	17	17	17	16	16	16
72	Corvette C6.R	33	29	28	29	27	27	28	26	25	24	22	20	21	20	19	17	18	18	18	18	18	17	17	17
35	Pescarolo Judd	24	23	19	18	18	17	18	18	18	15	14	14	14	14	14	13	13	13	15	15	15	18	18	18
82	Ferrari 430 GT	41	38	34	33	29	30	30	28	28	28	25	26	24	22	22	21	21	20	19	19	19	19	19	19
40	Lola AER	23	21	20	25	19	25	24	23	22	19	19	17	15	16	18	19	19	19	22	22	21	21	20	20
73	Corvette C6.R	34	37	35	35	33	31	32	30	29	27	24	25	23	21	21	20	20	22	21	21	22	20	21	21
97	Ferrari 430 GT	45	41	38	37	37	35	35	32	31	30	28	28	28	26	25	23	23	23	23	23	23	22	22	22
90	Ferrari 430 GT	47	40	41	39	38	36	36	33	32	31	29	30	29	29	27	25	25	26	26	25	24	23	23	23
14	Creation AIM	17	15	31	26	43	45	41	39	37	35	33	34	32	31	29	27	24	24	24	24	26	24	24	24
99	Ferrari 430 GT	50	47	46	42	39	37	37	34	33	32	30	29	30	30	28	26	26	25	30	29	27	26	25	25
4	Pescarolo Judd	27	24	21	22	24	20	21	25	24	22	21	22	25	24	24	24	28	28	27	28	25	25	26	26
77	Porsche 997 GT3 RSR	43	39	37	34	30	32	31	29	38	40	38	37	36	34	35	33	32	31	31	30	29	27	27	27
50	Saleen S7R	31	31	43	48	47	43	42	40	40	38	36	35	33	32	31	30	29	29	29	31	30	29	28	28
32	Zytek 07S	22	17	18	28	26	22	27	37	35	34	32	32	37	35	34	32	30	30	28	27	28	28	29	29
59	Aston Martin DBR9	36	33	30	32	28	29	29	27	26	25	23	23	22	23	22	35	34	34	33	31	33	30	30	30
26	Radical AER	32	36	32	40	36	42	39	38	36	36	35	33	34	33	33	31	31	32	32	33	32	31	31	31
80	Porsche 997 GT3 RSR	40	50	51	50	48	43	43	47	46	44	42	42	40	40	37	37	36	35	35	34	34	33	32	32
11	Dome Judd S102	8	9	6	8	7	8	8	8	14	26	26	24	27	28	30	28	27	27	25	26	31	32	33	33
55	Lamborghini Murcielago	54	54	54	52	49	46	45	45	45	43	43	43	43	38	38	37	36	36	36	35	35	34	34	34
24	Courage Mugen	18	22	49	51	51	51	50	48	47	47	45	44	44	42	40	39	38	39	39	37	36	35	35	35(NC)

RETIREMENTS

No.	MAKE AND TYPE	1	2	3	4	5	6	7	8	9	10	11	12	13	14	15	16	17	18	19	20	21	22	23	24
96	Ferrari 430 GT	48	42	40	38	35	34	33	31	30	29	27	27	26	25	23	22	22	21	20	20	20		engine	
16	Pescarolo Judd	7	7	8	13	10	11	11	11	10	9	8	9	8	8	8		engine							
23	Creation Judd	38	48	45	41	41	38	40	42	41	41	39	38	35	36	36	34	33	33	34	35		accident		
45	Zytek WF01	19	18	17	17	17	18	17	36	34	33	31	31	31	27	26	29		accident						
33	Lola Judd	20	20	15	15	16	16	16	16	15	13	13	21	20		engine									
20	Epsilon Euskadi Judd	14	16	16	14	15	15	15	15	27	37	40	40	42	43	42	40	39	38	37	38	gearbox			
22	Courage-Oreca YGK	53	53	50	47	46	44	45	44	42	42	41	42	41	41	39	38	37	37	38	gearbox				
21	Epsilon Euskadi Judd	21	19	14	19	45	47	48	49	48	48	46	46	45	44	43	41	40	40	4	38		gearbox		
6	Courage-Oreca Judd	11	10	10	9	9	9	9	10	9		accident													
44	Lola Mazda	39	34	29	30	32	41	43	41	39	39	37	39		gearbox										
12	Lola Judd	25	44	36	27	25	24	20	17	17	12		engine												
78	Ferrari 430 GT	44	43	39	36	34	33	34	35					driveshaft											
25	Lola MG	55	52	48	46	42	39	38	43	43	44	44	45		accident										
19	Lola AER	37	30	26	44	48	50	49	47	46	46		engine												
53	Aston Martin DBR9	35	35	33	31	40	40		engine																
94	Spyker C8	49	46	44	45	44	48		engine																
85	Spyker C8	46	45	42	49		engine																		
76	Porsche GT3 RSR	42	49		accident																				
41	Zytek 07S	51	51		accident																				
83	Ferrari 430 GT	52		accident																					

FINAL STANDINGS

	Grid	No.	Class	Car	Team	Drivers	Laps	Km/h	Best lap
1	4	2	LMP1	Audi R10 TDI	Audi Sport North America	Capello R./Kristensen T./McNish A.	381	216.300	3'24"152
2	3	7	LMP1	Peugeot 908 Hdi-FAP	Team Peugeot Total	Gene M./Minassian N/Villeneuve J.	381	215.624	3'21"438
3	2	9	LMP1	Peugeot 908 Hdi-FAP	Peugeot Sport Total	Montagny F./Klien C./Zonta R.	379	215.009	3'20"600
4	5	3	LMP1	Audi R10 TDI	Audi Sport Team Joest	Luhr L./Premat A./Rockenfeller M.	374	212.273	3'23"939
5	1	8	LMP1	Peugeot 908 Hdi-FAP	Team Peugeot Total	Lamy P./Sarrazin S./Wurz A.	368	208.567	3'19"394
6	7	1	LMP1	Audi R10 TDI	Audi Sport North America	Biela F./Pirro E./Werner M.	367	208.103	3'25"166
7	11	17	LMP1	Pescarolo Judd	Pescarolo Sport	Primat H./Tinseau C./Treluyer B.	362	205.457	3'30"610
8	10	5	LMP1	Courage-Oreca Judd	Team Oreca Matmut	Ayari S./Duval L./Groppi L.	357	202.577	3'30"543
9	6	10	LMP1	Lola Aston Martin	Charouz Racing System	Mucke S./Enge T./Charouz J.	354	200.685	3'28"131
10	14	34	LMP2	Porsche RS Spyder	Van Merksteijn Motorsport	Van Merksteijn P./Verstappen J./Bleekemolen J.	354	200.346	3'34"188
11	18	18	LMP1	Pescarolo Judd	Rollcentre Racing	Barbosa J./Ickx V./Gregoire S.	352	199.537	3'35"601
12	16	31	LMP2	Porsche RS Spyder	Team Essex	Elgaard C./Nielsen J./Maassen S.	347	196.271	3'36"562
13	36	009	LMGT1	Aston Martin DBR9	Aston Martin Racing	Brabham D./Garcia A./Turner D.	344	195.159	3'49"387
14	31	63	LMGT1	Corvette C6.R	Corvette Racing	Fellows R./O'Connell J./Magnussen J.	344	194.565	3'50"650
15	35	64	LMGT1	Corvette C6.R	Corvette Racing	Gavin O./Beretta O./Papis M.	341	193.477	3'49"707
16	37	007	LMGT1	Aston Martin DBR9	Aston Martin Racing	Frentzen H-H./Piccini A./Wendlinger K.	339	191.927	3'49"820
17	39	72	LMGT1	Corvette C6.R	Luc Alphand Aventures	Alphand L./Moreau G./Policand J.	335	189.954	3'54"006
18	28	35	LMP2	Pescarolo Judd	Saulnier Racing	Ragues P./Lahaye M./Cheng Cong F.	333	189.026	3'44"293
19	48	82	LMGT2	Ferrari F430 GT	Risi Competizione	Melo J./Salo M./Bruni G.	326	184.620	4'02"086
20	26	40	LMP2	Lola AER	Quifel ASM Team	Amaral M./ Pla O./Smith G.	325	183.999	3'41"064
21	42	73	LMGT1	Corvette C6.R	Luc Alphand Aventures	Blanchemain J.L./Goueslard P./Pasquali L.	325	183.823	3'57"217
22	49	97	LMGT2	Ferrari F430 GT	BMS Scuderia Italia	Malucelli M./Ruberti P./Babini F.	318	180.452	4'02"776
23	47	90	LMGT2	Ferrari F430 GT	Farnbacher Racing	Ehret P./Kaffer P./Nielsen L-E.	317	179.965	4'03"381
24	21	14	LMP1	Creation Aim	Creation AIM	Hall S./Mowlem J./Goossens M.	316	178.962	3'39"052
25	50	99	LMGT2	Ferrari F430 GT	JMB Racing	Aucott B./Ferte A./Daoudi S.	312	176.993	4'04"738
26	27	4	LMP1	Pescarolo Judd	Saulnier Racing	Nicolet J./Faggionato M./Hein R.	311	176.082	3'44"289
27	44	77	LMGT2	Porsche 997 GT3 RSR	Team Felbermayr-Proton	Davison A./Henzler W./Felbermayr H. Sen	309	174.873	4'00"709
28	33	50	LMGT1	Saleen S7R	Larbre Competition	Bouchut Ch./Bornhauser P./Smet D.	306	173.021	3'51"727
29	19	32	LMP2	Zytek 07S	Barazi Epsilon	Barazi J./Vergers M./Moseley S.	304	172.546	3'39"082
30	40	59	LMGT1	Aston Martin DBR9	Team Modena	Fittipaldi C./Borcheller T./Menten J.	302	171.202	3'53"086
31	30	26	LMP2	Radical AER	Bruichladdich Radical	Rostan M./Devlin B./Jeannette G.	297	168.612	3'46"031
32	46	80	LMGT2	Porsche 997 GT3 RSR	Flying Lizard Motorsports	Neiman S./Bergmeister J./Van Overbeek J.	289	164.008	3'59"887
33	8	11	LMP1	Dome Judd S102	Dome Racing Team	Ito D./Tachikawa T./Kataoka T.	272	153.834	3'29"504
34	38	55	LMGT1	Lamborghini Murcielago	IPB Spartak Racing	Rusinov R./Kox P./Hezemans M.	266	150.981	3'55"713
35	22	24	LMP1	Courage Mugen	Terramos	Terada Y./Takahashi K./Katoh H.	224	126.966	3'41"589

RETIREMENTS

45	96	LMGT2	Ferrari F430 GT	Virgo Motorsport	Bell R./Mullen T./Sugden T.	289	184.166	4'01"559
9	16	LMP1	Pescarolo Judd	Pescarolo Sport	Collard E./Boullion J.C./Dumas R.	238	211.375	3'31"114
32	23	LMP1	Creation Judd	Autocon	Lewis M./Willman B./McMurry C.	224	166.744	3'43"217
24	45	LMP2	Zytek WF01	Embassy Racing	Hughes W./Kane J./Foster J.	213	183.153	3'42"676
20	33	LMP2	Lola Judd	Speedy Racing Team Sebah	Bellicchi A./Pompidou X./Zacchia S.	194	195.870	3'37"472
17	20	LMP1	Epsilon Euskadi Judd	Epsilon Euskadi	Burgueno A./De Castro M.A./Valles A.	189	138.367	3'35"401
55	22	LMP1	Courage-Oreca YGK	Tokai University YGK	Suzuki T./Kageyama M./Kurosawa H.	185	142.754	3'52"274
15	21	LMP1	Epsilon Euskadi Judd	Epsilon Euskadi	Gounon JM./Johansson S./Nakano S.	158	118.657	3'37"638
13	6	LMP1	Courage-Oreca Judd	Team Oreca Matmut	Panis O./Fassler M./Pagenaud S.	147	220.320	3'30"147
34	44	LMP2	Lola Mazda	Kruse Schiller Motorsport	de Pourtales J./Noda H./Simonsen A.	147	174.588	3'46"061
12	12	LMP1	Lola Judd	Charouz Racing System	Pickett G./Graf K./ Lammers J.	146	202.842	3'35"596
52	78	LMGT2	Ferrari F430 GT	AF Corse SRL	Vilander T./Biagi T./Montanari C.	111	194.067	4'04"091
25	25	LMP2	Lola MG	RML	Erdos T./Newton M./Wallace A.	100	125.741	3'43"082
23	19	LMP1	Lola AER	Chamberlain Synergy	Evans G./Berridge B./Streton A.	87	133.338	3'41"859
41	53	LMGT1	Aston Martin DBR9	Vitaphone Racing Team	Hardman P./Leventis N./Negrao A.	82	180.360	3'55"102
54	94	LMGT2	Spyker C8 Laviolette	Speedy Racing Team	Chiesa A./Leuenberger B./Alexander-David I.	72	174.905	4'07"980
51	85	LMGT2	Spyker C8 Laviolette	Snoras Spyker Squadron	Dumbreck P./Kellleners R./Vasiliev A.	43	192.381	4'07"225
43	76	LMGT2	Porsche 997 GT3 RSR	Imsa Performance Matmut	Narac R./Lietz R./Long P.	26	197.333	4'02"717
29	41	LMP2	Zytek 07S	Trading Performance	Ojjeh K./Gosselin C.Y./Sharpe A.	22	185.055	3'52"339
53	83	LMGT2	Ferrari F430 GT	Risi Competizione	Krohn T./Jonsson N./Van De Poele E.	12	195.896	4'06"199

AMERICAN LE MANS SERIES
Champions

LMP1 Drivers

Lucas Luhr (D)	Audi Sport North America	Audi R10 TDI	219 points
Marco Werner (D)	Audi Sport North America	Audi R10 TDI	219 points
LMP1 Teams	Audi Sport North America		230 points

LMP2 Drivers

Romain Dumas (F)	Penske Racing	Porsche RS Spyder	203 points
Timo Bernhard (D)	Penske Racing	Porsche RS Spyder	203 points
LMP2 Teams	Penske Racing		210 points

GT1 Drivers

Jan Magnussen (DK)	Corvette Racing	Corvette C6.R	238 points
Johnny O'Connell (USA)	Corvette Racing	Corvette C6.R	238 points
GT1 Teams	Corvette Racing		250 points

GT2 Drivers

Jörg Bergmeister (D)	Flying Lizard Motorsports	Porsche 911 GT3 RSR	188 points
Wolf Henzler (D)	Flying Lizard Motorsports	Porsche 911 GT3 RSR	188 points
GT2 Teams	Flying Lizard Motorsports		213 points

LE MANS SERIES
Champions

LMP1 Drivers

Alexandre Premat (F)	Audi Sport Team Jöst	Audi R10 TDI	32 points
Mike Rockenfeller DF)	Audi Sport Team Jöst	Audi R10 TDI	32 points
LMP1 Manufacturers	Audi		62 points
LMP1 Teams	Audi Sport Team Jöst		35 points

LMP2 Drivers

Jos Verstappen (NL)	Van Merksteijn Motorsport	Porsche RS Spyder	48 points
LMP2 Manufacturers	Porsche		86 points
LMP2 Teams	Van Merksteijn Motorsport		48 points

GT1 Drivers

Patrice Goueslard (F)	Luc Alphand Aventures	Corvette C6.R	42 points
Guillaume Moreau (F)	Luc Alphand Aventures	Corvette C6.R	42 points
GT1 Manufacturers	Corvette		48 points
GT1 Teams	Luc Alphand Aventures		42 points

GT2 Drivers

Robert Bell (GB)	Virgo Motorpsort	Ferrari 430 GT	40 points
GT2 Manufacturers	Ferrari		74 points
GT2 Teams	Virgo Motorpsort		40 points

Circuit Spa-Francorchamps, Belgium – August 2-3
Circuit length: 7.004 km
Distance covered by the winning team: 4041 km
Weather conditions: cloudy, some showers

GT1
GT2
G3
G2

No. MAKE AND TYPE   HOURLY POSITIONS

No.	Make and Type	1	2	3	4	5	6	7	8	9	10	11	12	13	14	15	16	17	18	19	20	21	22	23	24
1	Maserati MC12	3	5	6	3	5	1	1	1	1	1	1	1	1	2	2	1	1	1	1	1	1	1	1	1
2	Maserati MC12	4	3	5	2	3	2	2	2	2	2	2	2	2	1	1	2	2	2	2	2	2	2	2	2
10	Aston Martin DBR9	5	6	3	5	4	3	3	3	3	3	3	3	3	3	3	3	3	3	3	3	3	3	3	3
15	Maserati MC12	19	17	13	8	8	7	5	7	6	7	7	6	6	5	5	5	5	5	5	4	4	4	4	4
77	Ferrari F430 GT	10	12	11	9	10	9	10	9	8	8	8	7	7	6	6	6	6	6	6	5	5	5	5	5
61	Porsche 997 RSR	11	10	9	10	11	12	8	8	9	9	9	8	8	7	7	7	7	7	7	6	6	6	6	6
50	Ferrari F430 GT	13	14	10	11	12	10	9	10	10	10	10	9	9	8	8	8	8	8	8	7	7	7	7	7
8	Lamborghini Murcielago	7	8	7	7	7	6	4	4	4	4	4	4	4	10	14	13	11	11	11	11	10	10	9	8
55	Ferrari F430 GT	18	20	20	20	18	18	16	16	13	12	11	10	10	9	9	9	9	9	9	8	8	8	8	9
57	Ferrari F430 GT	25	19	19	18	20	20	17	17	15	13	12	11	11	11	10	10	10	10	10	10	9	9	10	10
56	Ferrari F430 GT	14	13	14	13	13	14	13	12	12	20	22	19	17	17	15	14	13	12	12	12	11	11	11	11
76	Porsche 997 RSR	9	9	8	12	15	13	25	30	30	28	28	25	24	22	22	22	19	17	16	15	13	13	12	12
123	Porsche 911 GT3 Cup S	31	24	24	23	21	22	19	19	16	14	13	14	14	15	13	15	15	13	13	13	12	12	13	13
124	Porsche 911 GT3 Cup S	22	31	31	31	30	27	29	26	25	25	23	22	19	18	17	17	14	14	14	14	14	14	14	14
112	Ferrari 430 GT3	32	29	22	21	22	21	18	20	20	17	15	13	16	16	21	20	17	16	15	15	15	15	15	15
160	Porsche 911 GT3 Cup S	17	25	25	28	23	23	21	22	17	18	15	13	14	16	16	16	18	18	18	18	16	16	16	16
62	Ferrari F430 GT	16	16	16	16	16	17	14	13	14	19	17	12	12	12	11	11	18	19	17	17	18	18	17	17
145	Porsche 911 GT3 Cup S	33	26	28	27	28	28	24	23	21	22	21	21	18	19	20	21	20	20	19	19	19	19	18	18
75	Porsche 997 RSR	27	21	21	24	26	26	22	21	18	15	14	17	21	20	19	19	22	24	23	20	20	20	20	19
141	Porsche 911 GT3 Cup S	37	36	33	35	32	34	34	32	31	30	29	29	26	25	25	24	24	23	22	21	21	21	21	20
6	Corvette C6.R	1	2	1	1	2	4	7	5	5	5	5	5	5	4	4	4	4	4	4	9	17	17	19	21
106	Ferrari 430 GT3	29	28	29	29	27	30	31	29	28	27	26	24	23	23	23	23	22	21	23	22	22	22	22	22
174	Ferrari 430 GT3	28	38	38	39	39	39	39	38	36	33	33	31	30	29	28	26	26	26	25	24	23	23	23	23

RETIREMENTS

No.	Make and Type	1	2	3	4	5	6	7	8	9	10	11	12	13	14	15	16		
59	Porsche 997 RSR	20	18	17	19	19	19	15	14	23	21	19	16	15	13	12	12	drivetrain	
70	Ferrari F430 GT	24	23	26	30	24	24	20	18	19	16	16	23	20	21	18	18	21	accident
122	Ascari KZ1R	23	22	23	25	29	29	26	25	24	23	27	27	27	26	24	25	25	head gasket
108	Porsche 911 GT3 Cup S	26	30	30	26	25	25	23	24	22	24	20	20	22	gearbox				
4	Saleen S7R	8	7	18	14	9	8	6	6	7	6	6	body damage						
116	Dodge Viper CC	35	35	36	32	31	31	28	27	26	26	24	engine						
102	Porsche 996 Bi-Turbo	36	32	34	37	36	36	35	36	37	37	36	34	34	31	31	fire		
51	Ferrari F430 GT	15	15	15	15	14	16	12	11	11	11	accident							
115	Lamborghini Gallardo	30	39	39	38	38	37	37	34	32	32	32	30	electricity					
60	Porsche 997 RSR	12	11	12	17	17	15	11	15	driveshaft									
33	Aston Martin DBR9	2	1	2	6	6	5	accident											
101	Gillet Vertigo	34	27	27	22	35	35	33	33	driveshaft									
5	Corvette C6.R	6	4	4	4	1	11	accident/fire											
175	Ferrari 430 GT3	38	37	35	34	33	33	accident											
140	Porsche 911 GT3 Cup S	39	33	32	33	37	drivetrain												
121	Ferrari 430 GT3	41	40	accident															
3	Corvette C6.R	40	41	accident															
7	Saleen S7R	DNS/accident during warm up																	

FINAL STANDINGS

	Grid	No.	Class	Car	Team	Drivers	Laps	Km/h	Best lap
1	6	1	GT1	Maserati MC 12	Vitaphone Racing Team	Bertolini A./Bartels M./Sarrazin S./Van De Poele E.	577	168.07	2'17"109
2	4	2	GT1	Maserati MC 12	Vitaphone Racing Team	Negrao A./Ramos M./Lemeret S./Pier Guidi A.	575	167.48	2'16"997
3	8	10	GT1	Aston Martin DBR9	Gigawave Motorsport	Turner D./Simonsen A./Peter P/Thompson A.	570	165.93	2'17"176
4	9	15	GT1	Maserati MC 12	JMB Racing	Ferte A./Aucott B./Daoudi S.	561	163.31	2'18"537
5	12	77	GT2	Ferrari F430 GT	BMS Scuderia Italia	Malucelli M./Ruberti P./Camathias J./Rigon D.	555	161.42	2'23"186
6	16	61	GT2	Porsche 997 RSR	Prospeed Competition	Collard E./Westbrook R./Lieb M.	552	160.77	2'23"076
7	41	50	GT2	Ferrari F430 GT	AF Corse	Bruni G./Vilander T./Melo J./Salo M.	550	160.18	2'22"776
8	7	8	GT1	Lamborghini Murcielago	IPB Spartak Racing	Kox P./Rusinov R./Lammers J./Enge T.	544	158.22	2'16"916
9	18	55	GT2	Ferrari F430 GT	CR Scuderia	Mullen T./Niarchos C./Piccini A./Shedden G.	543	158.15	2'24"195
10	33	57	GT2	Ferrari F430 GT	Kessel Racing	Moser H./Del Monte F./Vannelet G./Palma A.	541	157.53	2'23"741
11	14	56	GT2	Ferrari F430 GT	CR Scuderia	Kirkaldy A./Bell R./Müller D./Sutton J.	536	156.11	2'23"566
12	13	76	GT2	Porsche 997 RSR	IMSA Performance Matmut	Lietz R./Narac R./Long P.	520	151.23	2'22"596
13	23	123	G3	Porsche 911 GT3 Cup S	Mühlner Motorsport	Thomas M./Bermes H.J./Basseng M./Hemroulle J.F.	518	150.88	2'28"265
14	26	124	G3	Porsche 911 GT3 Cup S	Mühlner Motorsport	Huisman D./Khan I./Voerman R./Van Splunteren P.	513	149.37	2'29"165
15	29	112	G3	Ferrari 430 GT3	Francois Jakubowski (AS Events)	Campbell C./Jakubowski F./Barde A./Zangarelli M.	506	147.38	2'28"950
16	27	160	G3	Porsche 911 GT3 Cup S	Prospeed Competition	Heylen J./Dermont D./Lamot F./Loix D.	505	147.05	2'27"964
17	17	62	GT2	Ferrari F430 GT	Scuderia Ecosse	Davis J./Babini F./Monfardini F.	503	146.22	2'24"151
18	31	145	G3	Porsche 911 GT3 Cup S	Christian Kelders (First Motorsport)	Kelders C./Duval F./Greisch P./Kerkhove C.	501	145.80	2'29"204
19	20	75	GT2	Porsche 997 RSR	Juniper Racing	Baird C./Twigg M./Juniper S./Forbes R.	472	137.43	2'25"540
20	39	141	G3	Porsche 911 GT3 Cup S	Olivier Baron (Emeraude Racing)	Noziere P./Brouard R./Stepec T./Samon T.	468	136.26	2'34"506
21	1	6	GT1	Corvette C6.R	Phoenix Carsport Racing	Fässler M./Hezemans M./Deletraz J.D./Gollin F.	460	158.74	2'16"518
22	35	106	G3	Ferrari 430 GT3	Delahaye Racing	Coens D./Fumal A./Schroyen J./Faggionato M.	459	133.69	2'30"755
23	37	174	G3	Ferrari 430 GT3	Gael Lesoudier (Sport Garage)	Brandela R./Lesoudier G./Peyroles A./Lester H.	402	124.94	2'30"152

RETIREMENTS

	Grid	No.	Class	Car	Team	Drivers	Laps	Km/h	Best lap
	19	59	GT2	Porsche 997 RSR	Trackspeed Racing	Pompidou X./Williams R./Sugden T./Ashburn D.	382	154.47	2'24"424
	30	70	GT2	Ferrari F430 GT	Easy Race SRL	Baguette B./Basso M./Tenchini G./Plati R.	350	142.26	2'27"080
	24	122	G3	Ascari KZ1R	David Jones (Team Eurotech)	Jones D./Jones G./Jordan M.	323	127.94	2'28"638
	25	108	G3	Porsche 911 GT3 Cup S	Ice Pole Racing Team	Duez M./Sougnez L./Wautoers K./Muytjens O.	267	148.58	2'29"844
	10	4	GT1	Saleen S7R	PekaRacing	Longin A./Kumpen A./Mollekens K./Bouvy F.	255	157.15	2'18"591
	36	116	G3	Dodge Viper CC	Patrick Chaillet (Signa Motorsport)	Geofroy C./Chaillet P./Galand B./Roscoux P.Y.	229	144.88	2'32"088
	21	102	G2	Porsche 996 Bi-Turbo	McDonalds Racing	Kaufmann W./Talkanitsa A./Ullmann P./Heyer K.	229	104.42	2'26"703
	11	51	GT2	Ferrari F430 GT	AF Corse	Biagi T./Montanari C./Farnbacher S./Russo A.	225	159.21	2'23"517
	32	115	G3	Lamborghini Gallardo	S-Berg Racing	Rich M./Knauss H./Kraihamer D./Kuzminykh V.	196	114.51	2'30"550
	15	60	GT2	Porsche 997 RSR	Prospeed Competition	Henzler W./Palttala M./Forsten M./Horion G.	183	162.51	2'23"682
	2	33	GT1	Aston Martin DBR9	Jetalliance Racing	Wendlinger K./Sharp R./Müller A./Litchner-Hoyer L.	151	169.08	2'16"453
	34	101	G2	Gillet Vertigo	Belgian Racing	Leinders B./Kuppens R./Martin M.	145	138.93	2'28"839
	5	5	GT1	Corvette C6.R	Phoenix Carsport Racing	Menten J./Margaritis A./Schlünssen R./Alzen U.	140	175.42	2'16"506
	38	175	G3	Ferrari 430 GT3	Eddy Renard (Sport Garage)	Renard E./Hissom R./Lacroix Wasover S./Thirion P.	122	146.85	2'32"098
	40	140	G3	Porsche 911 GT3 Cup S	Olivier Baron (Emeraude Racing)	Fournet P./Baron O./Corbel A.A./Ferreira M.	92	151.41	2'34"870
	28	121	G3	Ferrari 430 GT3	Exagon Engineering	Helary E./Desbrueres D./Desbrueres C./Radermecker V.	31	92.28	2'28"861
	3	3	GT1	Corvette C6.R	Selleslagh Racing Team	Maassen X./Soulet M./Pillon C./Bouchut C.	12	90.59	2'18"149
	DNS (1) 7		GT1	Saleen S7R	Larbre Competition	Vosse V./Franchi G./Lamy P./Zacchia S.	0	n.a.	n.a.

COUPE DU ROI

A race within the race, the Coupe du Roi (King's Cup) is a relay affair involving teams of three G3 cars. At Spa, JMB Racing was the only contender, running Ferraris 430 GT3s No.180, 181 and 182 for drivers Scheier J.B./Ballay P., Kuteman P./Carbagnati A. and Comar N./Rambeaud P.; thus they won, even though two (No.180 and 181) of their three cars crashed during their stint.

FIA GT CHAMPIONSHIP
Leaders (after 9 of 10 rounds)

GT1 Drivers

Andrea Bertolini (I)	Vitaphone Racing Team	Maserati MC 12	66 points
Michael Bartels (D)	Vitaphone Racing Team	Maserati MC 12	66 points
GT1 Teams	Vitaphone Racing Team		118.5 points

GT2 Drivers

Toni Vilander (SF)	AF Corse	Ferrari F430	85 points
Gianmaria Bruni (I)	AF Corse	Ferrari F430	85 points
GT2 Teams	AF Corse		124 points

JAPANESE SUPER GT SERIES
Leaders (after 8 of 9 rounds)

Drivers

Satoshi Motoyama (J)	Nismo	Nissan GT-R	74 points
Benoit Treluyer (F)	Nismo	Nissan GT-R	74 points
Teams	Petronas Toyota Team Tom's		87 points

The Seat Leon was the class of the field

The regulations for the World Touring Car Championship came under more scrutiny than ever in 2008, writes **Charles Bradley**, as the job of balancing front- and rear-wheel drive, as well as petrol- and turbodiesel-powered 2-litre engines threatened to overshadow the whole business of racing on the track. Seat and BMW locked horns both on and off the track, while Chevrolet and Honda played somewhat of a supporting role.

Over the winter, under the auspices of Seat Sport chief Jaime Puig, Seat ironed out the technical issues that blighted the 2007 end-of-season races. Seat retained its A-list drivers, led by former British Touring Car champions Yvan Muller and Gabriele Tarquini, (still a winner in his mid-40s) and added comeback kid Rickard Rydell to its six-car line-up.

The FIA Bureau reserved the right to monitor the turbo pressure of the 2-litre motor, as well as the injection settings, and make changes as it saw fit. It also gave them an extra five-kg weight penalty from the start of the season, making the Seat 25 kg heavier than its rivals. Straight from the opening round in Brazil, the whistling Leons were like silent assassins to the BMWs and Chevrolets in a straight line, using all their torque to ease away. Double victory there led to the first of many arguments over equality from its rivals, and they repeated the feat next time out in Mexico – this time filling the top six places in race two and once again leaving the rest trailing in their wake.

A rev limit was imposed by the FIA Bureau on the yellow machines for round three at Valencia – Seat's home turf, of course – and it had the desired effect of letting someone else (in this case, Chevrolet) win for a change. Then, before the next round of the streets of Pau, BMW was given its 15-kg weight break, which relegated Seat from the winners' circle – but it was still racking up consistent podium finishes to keep ahead. To highlight its ability to carry the success ballast, Tarquini scored an astonishing win at Brno in the Czech Republic, despite carrying an extra 55 kg. Another clear sign that the Leon was the class of the '08 field.

After its run of success with Andy Priaulx and the Racing Bart Mampaey squad, the BMW looked a bit long in the tooth this season. A diesel power-plant was evaluated and rejected over the winter, so tweaks were restricted to engine (now boasting 280 hp), gearbox and aerodynamics. After taking the fight to Seat in the opening round, the BMWs struggled mightily in Mexico for round two and even had to play second fiddle to the Chevrolets in Valencia. Finally, its time came at Pau, where – after the marque received a 15-kg weight break – Farfus scored victory by an outrageous margin of almost 18 seconds. A typically canny drive by Priaulx earned him the win in race two around the French street track. BMW stuck to its petrol guns in the face of the diesel Seat onslaught, but may have to revisit that experimental oil-burning engine for next year's campaign.

In the Chevrolet camp, coming off the back of seven wins last year, the RML-run trio of works Lacettis were expected to be a major force in 2008. With no budget available to explore the diesel route, it also lost a couple of its engine dispensations, but was compensated by a 20-kg weight break instead. In its fourth season of competition, the Lacetti was the first to break the Seat stranglehold with a double success at Valencia for Huff and Menu. While the massed Seat and BMW ranks waged their war for title honours, Chevrolet did a good job of poaching around the fringes, accruing some decent results when the circumstances suited its package. The same could be said for Honda, eventually booking a first victory in the second heat at Imola.

Yvan Muller led the World Touring Car Championship
for much of the season in his Seat Leon, the 39-year
old Frenchman aiming to go one place better than his
runner-up spot in 2007. His strongest competition came
from within the Spanish squad, as fellow ex-BTCC
champion Gabriele Tarquini, in his third year with
the Seat outfit, pushed him hard for title honours.

Yvan Muller heads the charge along with Rickard
Rydell off the startline for the opening round in
Curitiba. Right from the beginning, it was clear that
the torque of the turbodiesel Seats was going to be
a huge advantage as they were able to outdrag the
BMWs and Chevrolets, which were faster in the
corners and enjoyed better tyre consistency, on the
straights. It would set the trend for much of the
season.

TOURING CARS :: **RESULTS**

BMW's Andy Priaulx is mired in the midfield here at Pau, but he judged this race to perfection to finish 8th and ensure himself of pole position the following day to dominate in a soaking-wet weather conditions. He kept himself in the title hunt by stealthy performances like this, and Pau was one of the few tracks where the BMW boasted a healthy performance advantage over Seat.

A tale of two Mullers: Yvan might be leading here in his Seat, but it is his namesake Jorg who is going to win this race at Brands Hatch for BMW. It was Jorg's first win of the season, and he would back that up with a fourth place in race two making it his most successful weekend of the season. Chevrolet would also win at Brands, thanks to its former BTCC champion Alain Menu.

WTCC – WORLD TOURING CAR CHAMPIONSHIP STANDINGS
(after 10 races out of 12)

	Drivers	Car	March 2 Curitiba		April 6 Puebla		May 18 Valencia		June 1 Pau		June 15 Brno		July 13 Estoril		July 27 B.Hatch		August 31 Osch.		September 21 Imola		October 5 Monza		October 26 Okayama		November 16 Macau		Points
1	Y. Muller (F)	Seat	10	4	3	5	5	1	8	2	1	4	6	8	8	0	0	1	10	4	10	5					95
2	G. Tarquini (I)	Seat	4	10	4	6	8	4	4	5	3	10	0	0	2	4	0	0	4	0	8	10					86
3	R. Huff (GB)	Chevrolet	0	0	0	0	10	8	5	4	0	0	5	4	0	0	8	6	5	6	3	0					64
4	R. Rydell (S)	Seat	8	2	8	8	0	2	3	6	0	0	10	1	0	0	3	0	8	3	0	0					62
5	A. Priaulx (GB)	BMW	5	8	0	1	2	6	1	10	0	1	3	6	6	0	0	4	0	2	6	0					61
6	J. Gene (E)	Seat	0	1	10	4	6	3	6	0	0	0	4	0	0	0	4	5	0	0	2	8					53
7	J. Müller (D)	BMW	6	5	0	0	4	5	0	0	4	2	0	2	10	5	0	0	1	8	0	0					52
8	F. Porteiro (E)	BMW	3	6	0	0	0	0	0	0	8	5	1	5	3	8	1	10	0	0	0	0					50
9	N. Larini (I)	Chevrolet	0	0	6	0	3	0	2	8	0	0	8	3	0	0	0	0	3	5	4	6					48
10	A. Farfus (BR)	BMW	0	3	0	0	0	0	10	3	5	6	0	0	0	3	10	3	2	1	0	1					47

	Manufacturers																									Points
1	Seat		18	15	18	18	14	7	14	11	8	15	16	18	13	9	9	13	18	7	18	18					277
2	BMW		11	14	7	8	8	11	13	13	18	14	7	11	16	14	13	14	5	10	9	7					223
3	Chevrolet		0	7	11	10	14	18	9	12	8	6	13	7	6	13	14	9	9	11	9	11					197
4	Honda		-	-	-	-	3	3	2	2	5	4	0	0	3	2	2	0	6	10	2	2					46

DTM – DEUTSCHE TOURENWAGEN MASTERS (GERMANY)
Champion

Drivers
Timo Scheider (D)   Audi Sport Team Abt   Audi A4 DTM   75 points
Teams   Mercedes-Benz Bank AMG Mercedes   109 points

BTCC – BRITISH TOURING CAR CHAMPIONSHIP
Champion

Drivers
Fabrizio Giovanardi (I)   VX Racing   Vauxhall Vectra   262 points
Manufacturers   Vauxhall   697 points
Teams   VX Racing   537 points

AUSTRALIAN V8 SUPERCARS
Leaders (after 11 of 14 rounds)

Drivers
Jamie Whincup (AUS)   Team Vodafone   Ford Falcon BF   2616 points
Teams   Team Vodafone   4383 points

NASCAR SPRINT CUP (USA)
Leaders (after 33 of 36 rounds)

Drivers
Jimmie Johnson (USA)   Hendrick Motorsports   Chevrolet Impala SS   6248 points
Manufacturers   Chevrolet   198 points

A battle between Citroën and Ford

Despite starting the 2008 season with four consecutive World Rally Championships under his belt, Sebastien Loeb was in no mood to relinquish his crown, reports **Keith Oswin**. As the season unfolded it quickly emerged that, team-mate Dani Sordo aside, only Ford's Mikko Hirvonen and newcomer Jari-Matti Latvala were capable of taking the fight to the Frenchman. While the Citroën lead driver and the car were familiar, for 2008 the team had a fresh face at the helm. New man in charge Olivier Quesnel took up the reins following the retirement of Citroën's legendary leader Guy Fréquelin. Like Fréquelin, Quesnel has also played an important role in the motorsport industry. After having managed Patrick Tambay's career, he started in racing in 1978 in the competition department of the Simca Racing Team, and then took part in the creation of Peugeot Sport, directed by Jean Todt. For Loeb the highlight of the season undoubtedly came with his first place in Finland, making him only the fourth non-Scandinavian to win the most technical event of the year. Loeb also avenged his 2007 New Zealand defeat with an equally dramatic victory on the event furthest from home as the Ford challenge collapsed on the final stage. Team tactics came to the fore in 2008 after new rules ended the days of reverse seeding. The drivers started in their championship order on the opening day and in their position order for the subsequent two days. It was a rule that forced teams to play tactical games to get favourable start positions on events where loose surfaces meant that running first wasn't always the best place to be. New also for 2008 was the switch to Pirelli as the tyre supplier. With only one compound available no one could be sure that they had an advantage. Add in the rule that denied teams the opportunity to cut the tread pattern on all but asphalt rallies and the ban on anti-deflation 'mousse' inserts, and you had a recipe for clever thinking among the drivers and some nervous moments for team managers hoping that a rogue puncture wouldn't blow their drivers' chances – literally. While Citroën and Ford fought tooth and nail for the title, Subaru continued to struggle until the arrival of the new hatchback version of the Impreza. Chris Atkinson matured into a genuine contender for victory while Petter Solberg fell into the shadow of the Australian on too many occasions and his position in the team looked tenuous for a while. The 2008 season will be remembered for another tight battle between Citroën and Ford, the emergence of Subaru from the shadows of recent years and the arrival of Suzuki in the premier league. What the future holds remains to be seen as the technical specification of the next generation of cars was the subject of great debate and little resolution during 2008. Whether it will bring in new teams or cause the current batch to pull out will be talked about until it all starts again in Ireland on February 1 next year, with the new rotation system decreeing that the traditional opener in Monte-Carlo is dropped from the series…

The calm before the storm. The World Rally Championship contenders line up in the parc fermé on the famous harbour front in Monaco. It was not here, in this little corner of paradise, where the first battle of the season would take place, but high in the mountains behind the Principality.

Dani Sordo may have won the opening stage of the season but from then on it was Sebastien Loeb all the way to a record fifth win on the Monte-Carlo Rally to get his 2008 challenge under way. The Frenchman was in dominant form with the Citroën C4 to take victory by almost three minutes over Ford's new team leader Mikko Hirvonen. It meant that everyone was following form and playing catch-up from then on.

Swedish Rally. Jari-Matti Latvala may have been the new kid on Ford's block but he claimed his maiden WRC win on only the second event of the year. Sweden was more like a gravel rally at times because of reduced snow cover, but the Finn was undaunted by the challenge.

The Middle East had never been represented in the WRC until this season but the arrival of Jordan in the 2008 calendar changed all that. After a slow start to the season Mikko Hirvonen got his title bid on track with victory amid the smooth roads and rocky landscape of this ancient land. Set on some of the lowest stages on earth the event proved to be a huge hit although filming from military helicopters reminded visitors that this was a region recently blighted by recent conflict. With Sebastien Loeb struggling home in 10th place, Citroën's number two Dani Sordo (following page) claimed a vital second place.

219

After a couple of dismal seasons with the previously successful saloon Impreza, Subaru launched its new hatchback version in Greece. It was a bold move but was rewarded with 2nd place for a rejuvenated Petter Solberg whose position in the team was coming under fire.

Sebastien Loeb racked up his fourth win of the season in Sardinia to add to his successes in Monte-Carlo, Mexico and Argentina. He would take a further victory in Greece before the mid-season break although non-finishes in Sweden and Jordan dented his title challenge.

The flamboyant Italian Gigi Galli was drafted into one of two satellite teams run by Ford. On his home event in Sardinia he flew spectacularly high en route to 4th place but later in the season a major shunt in Germany saw him suffer a broken leg. The Italian was sidelined for the remainder of the season and was left to consider whether he wanted to continue in the sport after his recovery.

Sebastien Loeb kicks up two wheels in his chase of the Ford pair in Turkey. Tactics came into play for the first time in 2008 with Ford pulling its drivers back at the end of each leg to force Loeb to lead into the next day's stages. Citroën team manager Olivier Quesnel was furious but Loeb was philosophical and just got on with the task of beating Ford over the long haul of the season.

Mikko Hirvonen gets all crossed up in the air on his
home event in Finland. Finns are used to winning
on home soil but this time the locals had to watch
helpless as Frenchman Sebastien Loeb stole their crown
from under their noses. Hirvonen could only manage
2nd behind Loeb and ahead of Chris Atkinson as
the established order was turned upside down on the
most technical of all rallies in the championship.

No room for error here as Jari-Matti Latvala's Ford takes off on the narrow mountain roads of Turkey. Ford's 1-2 on the final event of the first half of the season brought an historic 100th consecutive points finish for the Blue Oval team, the first time that this has ever been achieved in the WRC.

Ever the bridesmaid in 2008, Dani Sordo flips his Citroën in the German scenery on his way to another 2nd place. There was no surprise as team leader Sebastien Loeb claimed his seventh successive victory on this event – the only driver to have won the rally since its arrival in the championship in 2002. Sordo's event started badly but once he got the car's set-up sorted out he was a solid back-up to his team mate.

Dani Sordo went into the final day of New Zealand lying 3rd but expecting to have to sacrifice the position to help his team leader in his quest for a fifth consecutive title. By the end of the event he didn't need to panic as Ford's dramas handed Citroën a surprise 1-2, the Spaniard tracking Loeb over the finish line to extend the French team's advantage in the Manufacturers' Championship.

The arrival of the new hatchback Subaru Impreza brought the Japanese manufacturer back into the frame for podium finishes in 2008 but it was still not enough to bring a third team into contention for outright victory. Petter Solberg (seen here in New Zealand) was openly critical of progress and, for a while, it seemed that he was no longer in favour with the team, especially as team-mate Chris Atkinson was outrunning him on overall results.

Clever tactics put Ford into a solid position going into the Whaanga Coast stage of the New Zealand rally. However, a brush with a rock ended Jari-Matti Latvala's challenge while Mikko Hirvonen (pictured) lost victory after a puncture dropped him to 3rd behind the two Citroëns and seriously damaged his and Ford's title hopes in one of the most dramatic finishes of the season. If anyone thought that the 2007 event couldn't be bettered they were wrong…

The rear view of Sebastien Loeb's Citroën C4 was
all anyone saw of the World Champion who took
back-to-back victories on the two final asphalt events of
2008; Spain (here) and Corsica. Loeb continued to be
simply unbeatable on asphalt and while Ford may have
got closer than before the Frenchman always had the
advantage – a fair assessment of his season as a whole.

WRC – WORLD RALLY CHAMPIONSHIP

STANDINGS
(AFTER 14 ROUNDS OUT OF 15)

	Drivers	Car	January 24-27 Monte-Carlo	February 8-10 Sweden	February 29-March 3 Mexico	March 28-30 Argentina	April 24-27 Jordan	May 16-18 Sardinia	May 29-June 1 Acropolis	June 13-15 Turkey	July 31-August 3 Finland	August 15-17 Germany	August 28-31 New Zealand	October 2-5 Spain	October 10-12 France	October 21-November 2 Japan	November 5-7 Great Britain	Points
1	Sebastien Loeb (F)	Citroën	10	R	10	10	0	10	10	6	10	10	10	10	10	6		112
2	Mikko Hirvonen (SF)	Ford	8	8	5	4	10	8	6	10	8	5	6	6	8	10		102
3	Dani Sordo (E)	Citroën	0	3	0	6	8	4	4	5	5	8	8	8	R	R		59
4	Chris Atkinson (AUS)	Subaru	6	0	8	8	6	3	R	0	6	3	R	2	3	5		50
5	Jari-Matti Latvala (SF)	Ford	0	10	6	0	2	6	2	8	0	0	R	3	5	8		50
6	Petter Solberg (N)	Subaru	4	5	0	R	R	0	8	3	3	4	5	4	4	1		41
7	Francois Duval (B)	Ford	5	-	-	-	-	-	-	-	-	6	R	5	6	R		32
8	Henning Solberg (N)	Ford	0	0	4	R	5	2	1	4	4	2	0	0	0	R		22
9	Gigi Galli (I)	Ford	3	6	R	2	1	5	R	R	R	R	-	-	-	-		17
10	Matthew Wilson (GB)	Ford	0	R	3	R	4	0	3	2	0	0	0	0	1	2		15
11	Urmo Aava (EE)	Citroën	-	0	-	-	R	1	5	R	0	1	4	0	2	-		13
12	Federico Villagra (RA)	Ford	-	-	2	3	3	0	0	0	R	-	1	0	-	0		9
13	Toni Gardemeister (SF)	Suzuki	R	2	R	R	R	R	0	R	1	0	2	0	0	3		8
14	Andreas Mikkelsen (N)	Ford	-	4	-	-	-	-	-	0	0	0	-	1	0	-		8
15	Conrad Rautenbach (ZW)	Citroën	-	-	-	5	0	0	0	1	0	0	R	-	-	R		6
16	Per-Gunnar Andersson (S)	Suzuki	1	-	-	0	R	0	0	R	R	0	3	0	0	4		4
17	Jean-Marie Cuoq (F)	Peugeot	2	-	-	-	-	-	-	-	-	-	-	-	-	-		2
18	Matti Rantanen (SF)	Ford	-	-	-	-	-	-	-	-	2	-	-	-	-	-		2
19	Andreas Aigner (A)	Mitsubishi	-	-	-	1	-	-	0	0	R	-	R	-	-	-		1
20	Sebastien Ogier (F)	Citroën	-	1	-	0	0	-	-	0	0	-	R	0	-			1
21	Juho Hanninen (SF)	Mitsubishi	-	1	-	-	-	-	0	-	0	-	0	0	0	0		1

	Manufacturers																	Points
1	Citroën Total WRT		11	4	10	16	9	14	15	11	15	18	18	18	10	6		175
2	BP Ford Abu Dhabi WRT		8	18	11	7	13	14	10	18	9	7	6	11	14	18		164
3	Subaru WRT		10	6	9	8	6	3	8	3	9	7	5	6	7	6		93
4	Stobart VK M-Sport Ford WRT		8	8	3	3	7	5	3	4	4	6	0	4	6	2		64
5	Suzuki WRT		2	3	0	1	0	1	3	0	2	1	7	0	1	7		28
6	Munchi's Ford WRT		-	-	6	4	4	2	0	3	0	-	3	0	0	-		22

Junior WRC

Champion

Sebastien Ogier (F)	Citroën	46 points

Production WRC

Champion

Andreas Aigner (A)	Mitsubishi	36 points

Culture

HERITAGE

COLLECTION

LOOKING BACK

An architectural milestone

With BMW World and its new museum, BMW is now in possession of an excellent ensemble of fine architecture. **Jürgen Lewandowski** reports.

Since 1973, the BMW 4-cylinder and its associated museum, designed by Viennese architect Karl Schwanzer, with its unmistakable bowl, have been modern architectural icons – but the high-rise building needed to be brought up to date 35 years on, which couldn't have come at a better time as BMW had long been dreaming of creating a unique distribution centre. BMW World has been built in the last few years on one side of the Petuelring whilst on the other side, the 4-cylinder has been refurbished and a dramatic extension including redesign of the BMW Museum has begun. The spectacular BMW World architecture was conceived by Vienna architects Coop Himmelb(l)au, who created a double cone with a 16,500 m² roof which is held up by just eleven supports – behind it is a structural masterpiece which has never been built to the same design. A number of restaurants, shops and exhibition spaces come together under the floating roof; BMW World's

main function is to provide buyers who want to pick their new BMW up right there at the delivery centre with a special experience. Here they are presented with their new car in a unique environment – and then drive out from BMW World onto the street and home. Before that point, it is recommended they enter the 4-cylinder via a narrow, elegant bridge where the completely refurbished museum, spread out over 5000 m², recounts the history of the building not purely chronologically but according to developments. The museum also sees itself as something of an urban transport building made up of components of habitat influenced by mobility: streets, squares, bridges and houses. The system of ramps connects 25 exhibition areas comprising seven comprehensive themes with 125 exhibits. 'History, continuity and the future,' is the slogan of this extraordinary museum which, with the BMW World and the 4-cylinder high-rise, combines amazing architecture with exciting displays.

From the air, the round logo on the museum roof makes perfectly clear who the owner of the impressive facility is. On the left, across the street, is the huge BMW World with its solar-panel-covered roof whilst on the right is the so-called 4-cylinder building, BMW's administrative centre and the heart of the worldwide company. Beyond are the Milbertshofen factory buildings.

The bowl of the museum is one of the most important BMW symbols – the building is listed and remains unchanged from the outside, but inside the museum everything has been completely rearranged. In the background is the 291 m tall television tower, built in 1968.

The visitors first enter a reception area. From there, a
sloping paved multi-storey ramp leads them through
the museum which has a multitude of themed stands
and spaces that recount the company's history.

Art Cars. Kunst in Bewegung.
Art Cars. Art in motion.

Art Car Collection gilt als außergewöhnliche Kunstsammlung „rollender Kunstwerke".
haben international bekannte Künstler BMW Automobile gestaltet. Kunst und Technik
r eine gemeinsame Plattform. Die primär farblich und grafisch neu gestalteten Renn-
enfahrzeuge reflektieren in ihrer Gesamtheit die Entwicklung von Kunst, Design und Tech-
Als angesehene und gefragte Kunstobjekte kommen sie weltweit in Museen zum Einsatz.
volle Kollektion umfasst in chronologischer Reihenfolge die Werke folgender Künstler:
r Calder, Frank Stella, Roy Lichtenstein, Andy Warhol, Ernst Fuchs, Robert Rauschenberg,
Jagamara Nelson, Ken Done, Matazo Kayama, Cesar Manrique, A. R. Penck, Esther
u, Sandro Chia, David Hockney, Jenny Holzer, Olafur Eliasson.

The winner. In the very first year that BMW entered Formula 1 with its 1.5-litre turbocharged, 4-cylinder engine, Brazilian driver Nelson Piquet won the 1982 Canadian Grand Prix with the 1400 hp at his disposal. And one year later, Piquet was crowned World champion in the Brabham-BMW – no manufacturer has managed to win the title so quickly ever since. There's now a new Formula 1 car up on the wall; in autumn 2005, the Bavarians took over Peter Sauber's Swiss racing team and on June 8, 2008 won the Canadian Grand Prix.

The Art Car. The history is well-known; the French auctioneer Hervé Poulain, who also loved to race, wanted BMW to ready him a car that would be competitive at the Le Mans 24 hours – in exchange he offered the labours of an artist friend. So Alexander Calder transformed a 3.0 CSL Coupé into a 'mobile' which, in his view, "floated above everything, aloof from the hectic events of the race".

The prototype. Way ahead of its time, the BMW Turbo was, in 1972, not just to impress the public with its avant-garde shape but also ushered in new technological advances – for example, it sported the first malleable front and rear bumpers to be used in Europe. The Turbo – of which only two models were made – was designed by the then French chief designer Paul Bracq and was equipped with a 2-litre turbocharged 280 hp 4-cylinder engine. It weighed a mere 1272 kg and could reach speeds of 250 km/h.

241

How fast will it go?

The Bonneville (Utah, USA) Speed Week should rank right up there with the 24 Hours of Le Mans, the Monaco Grand Prix and the Indy 500. **'LandSpeed' Louise Ann Noeth**, a speed freak all her life and a salt flats specialist, introduces us to the fastest place on earth.

Popularity has its drawbacks. With 468 cars, trucks and motorcycles heading to the Bonneville Salt Flats for the 60th annual Speedweek time trials in August 2008, officials were determined to ease the agony of four-hour wait times in staging lane lines experienced by racers the previous year.

They needed, and got, great salt, hard salt, white salt that stayed tough the entire week to support three separate race courses for speed record hopefuls. With two short, and one long course, 2488 timed runs were made resulting in 172 certified event records: 63 bikes and 109 cars.

Land speed racing (LSR) asks and answers the eternal speed question: how fast will it go? With every vehicle that leaves the starting line goes a hope that an idea, rather a combination of ideas will bear fast fruit.

Unlike many other forms of motorsports where regulations and restrictions abound, LSR is rooted in freedom of mechanical expression. Safety rules are strictly enforced, most written with the blood and bad luck of another, but if you can dream it up, build and make it safe, you earn the right to take a trip down the great white dyno.

The sport is comprised of many classes divided by body style, engine type and size. Divisions also take into account vehicles running on pump gas and those that opt for exotic

fuel mixtures as well as supercharged and naturally aspirated induction. Electrics, turbines, diesels round things out and on the horizon are classes for hydrogen, E85 and other emerging fuels and propulsion methods.

To set a record, entrants must qualify by making a pass that exceeds the current record, and then make another record run. The two speeds are averaged and compared down to the third decimal place. Before a new record is declared, the vehicle must submit to a technical inspection to ensure it is running with class rules. This year, the fastest record set was 360 mph by 'Fast Freddie' Dannenfelzer in his lakester.

Spectators are welcome on the starting line, in the pits and along the edge of the race course to watch the action, but must bring their own shade, water and chairs, there are no grandstands, no air-conditioned suites, no infield. Bonneville, for all its beauty, is still as treacherous and forbidding as it was in pioneer days, yet remains one of the best natural raceways on earth.

With drivers and riders suited up in protective gear, the race vehicle is rolled to the starting line. The SCTA/BNI official, in contact with the timing tower three miles down course, waits for the "course all-clear" message before releasing the next vehicle on its speed quest journey. Due to the need for very tall gearing, most vehicles are pushed off the line engaging first gear after attaining approximately 50 mph.

Patriarch John Vesco debuted the 444 car in 1957 and attracted national attention due to its slim, low profile. Although seriously re-worked by sons Rick and Don through the years, the car is a testament to how long a racing heritage can endure in the sport. The late Don Vesco drove the Team Vesco Turbinator, another family streamliner, to the World Wheel-Driven record in 2001 averaging 458 mph. Today, Rick's children are poised to drive the family hot rod.

Car co-owner Ron Main along with co-owner and driver George Poteet, are determined to squeeze 400 mph out of their 4-cylinder Chrysler engine with their new Speed Demon streamliner. The inaugural debut at Speedweek set a new class record of 343.494 mph, so they are well on their way to big speed. Note the tight cockpit with double fire suppression bottles aimed at the driver. A parachute slows the car down after its run.

Hipster Bobby Green yearned for years to go land speed racing, but when he did it had to be with a belly tank lakester, what he considered the heart and soul of land speed racing. The belly tank body style was the brain child of racer Bill Burke who realized during his stint in the service all the abandoned fuel tanks from military planes could be easily adapted to become streamlined bodies for land speed cars without too much metal shaping work. The Old Crow set two land speed records at 104 and 135 mph during the 2008 Speedweek.

Speedweek at the Bonneville Salt Flats is racer heaven. Seven full and hopefully velocity-laden days of answering the nagging question: how fast will it go? The Burke Family's 881 modified sports car carried grandson Joshua Burke into the record books with a 206 mph average.

Streamliners, like the 1212 car, are the slipperiest and usually the fastest. These machines enclose the driver, engine and wheels with as aerodynamic a body shape as possible for a futuristic appearance that looks fast sitting still. Oft times the cars' front wheels are staggered in a configuration to retain a diminutive frontal area while the motorcycle versions use retractable outrigger skids to stay upright while stopped.

Ray Scherr owns
the 'Best of the Best'

Ray Scherr, a relatively newcomer to the collector car scene, was officially presented with the Louis Vuitton Classic Concours Award for the 1938 Alfa Romeo 8C 2900 with which he won Best of Show at the 2007 Meadow Brook Concours d'Elegance (see AY55). The contenders were the six Best of Show winners of the major concours d'elegance in the world, making his 8C the "Best of the Best". The ceremony took place at the North American International Auto Show in Detroit in January 2008, in the presence of Yves Carcelle, Chairman of Louis Vuitton. Ray is American, was born in 1948, and lives with his wife Janet and two children in Westlake Village, California. **Christian Philippsen**, who chaired the judges' panel, submitted him to the Automobile Year questionnaire.

RAY SCHERR, YVES CARCELLE, CHRISTIAN PHILIPPSEN

AUTOMOBILE YEAR: You won the Louis Vuitton Classic Concours Award, what does it represent for you?
RAY SCHERR: Receiving the Louis Vuitton award was a wonderful surprise considering how the award is chosen and the other eligible cars. The Louis Vuitton company represents style, sophistication, beauty and quality workmanship which the Alfa 2.9 represents as well.

AY: How did your passion for cars start?
RS: As a young boy I would ride in the family car and look at all the shiny cars and hope that someday I would be driving one as well.

AY: What is it in cars that you like?
RS: So many different senses like beauty, design, looks, colour, power, sound, smell …

AY: Which is the favourite car from your collection and why?
RS: I like so many cars in my collection that it's very difficult to single out one. But if I had to choose one it would be my 300 SL Roadster.

AY: Is there a car you'd love to own but don't yet?
RS: A blower Bentley.

AY: Is there a car, recent or older, you don't understand?
RS: The interior controls of the newer cars, i.e. Bentley, Mercedes, etc. are very difficult to operate.

AY: Which cars are in your garage?
RS: I have an eclectic collection of about 50 cars including both American and European pre- and post-war cars. All my cars are driven regularly. My favourites include my 1911 Simplex, 1913 Mercer, 1930 734 Packard Speedster, 1933 Stutz Super Bearcat, 1932 Marmon V16 Convertible Coupe, 1958 Ferrari Tour de France, 1937 Bugatti 57 SC Atalante and, of course, my 1938 Alfa Romeo 8 C 2900.

AY: What are you driving daily?
RS: 1971 Mercedes-Benz 3.5 convertible.

AY: Which are your favourite car events?
RS: Pebble Beach, Meadow Brook, Amelia Island.

AY: How do you see the collector's cars scene evolve in the next 10 to 20 years?
RS: Less cars, more buyers.

AY: What are your personal car-related goals in the next 10 years?
RS: To get my collection down to 20-25 cars that I drive.

AY: If you could change something in the world of cars, what would it be?
RS: Make the new cars more user-friendly.

AY: Apart from cars, do you have other interests in life?
RS: Yes, I have a passion for jazz guitars, music, food and family.

AY: How do you relax?
RS: I drive.

AY: Which is your favourite place in the world?
RS: New York.

AY: Which is your favourite hotel/resort?
RS: The Regency in New York.

AY: Which is your favourite restaurant?
RS: Josie Restaurant in Santa Monica, California.

AY: Which is your favourite music?
RS: Jazz: Johnny Smith, Hank Garland, Martin Taylor and Herbie Hancock.

AY: Which is your favourite movie?
RS: The Godfather.

AY: Which is your favourite book?
RS: The Charm School by Nelson DeMille.

AY: What are you particularly proud of?
RS: My family and kids.

AY: Do you have a hero?
RS: Roy Rogers, Paul Newman and Ray Kroc, to name a few, the fictitious character Sherlock Holmes also.

AY: Any advice to youngsters?
RS: Patience, use your un-commonsense, loyalty, honesty and hard work will eventually prevail.

AY: Thank you.

Beauty Queens

Keith Bluemel, **Johann Lemercier**, **Christian Philippsen** and **Jonathan Stein** once more attended the most select concours d'elegance in the world, the ones whose winners are nominated for the Louis Vuitton Classic Concours Award.

CAVALLINO CLASSIC
Palm Beach, Florida, January 26

The 16th annual Cavallino Classic gathering opened the season attracting a spectacular selection of Ferraris to the sunshine state. The event encompasses track activity, a touring rally, together with social functions and dinners, but the highlight is undoubtedly the prestigious concours on the croquet lawn and adjacent golf links at the splendid ocean-side Breakers Hotel.

Although there had been many successful open Ferraris by the late fifties, cabriolets featuring proper folding soft tops had only been produced in relatively small numbers. The first series of Pinin Farina cabriolets was built during 1957 and 1958. Peter Kalikow, the current owner of this lovely example, has had the car for over twenty years. It won the Best of Show, Road Car trophy. The Pinin Farina design is very elegant and beautifully balanced, featuring covered headlights in the wing extremities, with vertical rubber faced bumperettes below them, flanking the wide and low shallow oval egg crate grille.

This Ferrari 166 MM berlinetta with bodywork by Carrozzeria Touring was bought new by Giannino Marzotto, and finished in blue due to his father, Count Gaetano Marzotto, telling his son to "stop racing those red cars"! Ten days after his 22nd birthday he entered the 1950 Mille Miglia co-driven by his friend Marco Crosara, and led virtually the full distance, to become the youngest driver ever to win the epic road race. Its current owner, Jack Croul, has had it magnificently restored to its original colour scheme, wowing the judges to take the Best of Show, Competition Car award.

AMELIA ISLAND CONCOURS D'ELEGANCE
Amelia Island, Florida, March 9

For 2008, founder Bill Warner celebrated the Amelia Island
Concours d'Elegance 13th year. As one of the world's top
concours, it's no wonder that the fairways of The Golf
Club at Amelia Island were jammed with spectators. The
crowd was attracted by the approximately 300 fabulous
cars on display. Entries included a vast variety of cars,
including Model T Fords, European and American Classics,
coachbuilt American sports cars, exclusive European Grand
Touring cars and racers of many varieties.

At the Amelia Island Concours d'Elegance, there are two Best of Show awards: Sam and Emily Mann's ex-Clark Gable 1935 Duesenberg J topped the Concours d'Elegance while the 1957 Ferrari 335 Sport entered by Peter Sachs of Scuderia N.E. bested all other sports and racing cars in the Concours de Sport. Founder Bill Warner is holding the microphone, whilst Parnelli Jones is standing in front of the Ferrari with its trophy.

Thomas Flyer was the 2008 featured marque and there were 14 entered. No class of Thomas automobiles would be complete without the very car that won the 1908 New York to Paris race, presented by the National Automobile Museum in Reno, Nevada.

For many, the highlight of the Amelia Island Concours weekend wasn't the car display, but the Saturday morning Legends of Trans Am presentation replete with driving heroes from the series' heyday. Panelists included Tony Adamovicz, George Follmer, Dan Gurney, Sam Posey, and other top drivers who played a critical role in the series' success, surrounding honoree Parnelli Jones.

To support the Legends of Trans-Am programme, a stellar selection of the cars that ran in the original Trans-Am series was assembled. Entries included one of Mark Donohue's Penske Camaros, as well as one of his AMC Javelins, an ex-Parnelli Jones Mustang, a Dodge Challenger driven by Sam Posey and an ex-Dan Gurney Mercury Cougar.

CONCORSO D'ELEGANZA VILLA D'ESTE
Cernobbio, Italy, April 26-27

The grounds of Villa d'Este are, without doubt, one of the most majestic settings of the major international concours d'elegance. The restricted space afforded by the lake-side location makes for a small but eclectic field, with just 55 cars or so competing in eight classes, but what the concours may lose in quantity is more than made up for in terms of quality. The select group of cars admitted is complemented by a special display devoted to concept cars and prototypes, conferring a welcome contemporary touch to this most classic of events.

The esplanade around the 500-year old plane tree overlooking lake Como is traditionally dedicated to the cream of 1920s and 1930s automobile production. In the foreground, a Mercedes-Benz 680 S sporting Erdmann & Rossi coachwork and a Castagna-bodied Isotta Fraschini 8A can be seen between two Bentleys. Access to the Villa d'Este is strictly upon invitation and highly exclusive, but the second part of the event taking place at the nearby Villa Erba is open to the public and attracts more collectors and enthusiasts every year, proof of the growing success of the Concorso.

Ferraris have often been on the Roll of Honour at Villa d'Este in recent years, and this latest edition was no exception as the jury awarded Best of Show (BMW Group Trophy) to Jack Croul's 166 MM berlinetta by Touring, which had already won the Cavallino Classic Best of Show, Competition Car award. The sheer beauty and race-oriented simplicity of its lines is matched by an illustrious pedigree, for this very car won the Mille Miglia in 1950 with Count Giannino Marzotto at the wheel, and took part in the 24 Hours of Le Mans that same year driven by Raymond Sommer and Dorino Serafini.

Well-known Mexican collector Arturo Keller took home the coveted Coppa d'Oro award, attributed by the vote of Villa d'Este's discerning public, a deserved recognition for his magnificent Mercedes-Benz 540 K Autobahnkurier. The side profile highlights the ideal proportions of the coupé coachwork, with the swooping roofline echoing the curve of the front wings. Only two 540 Ks were originally built to this design.

Owned by Antonius Meijer, this Bugatti Type 57 SC from 1937 took home the Girard-Perregaux, Trophy (Special Prize by the jury). The beautiful lines of the Atalante coupé – originally penned by Jean Bugatti – were here further enhanced by Alsatian coachbuilder Gangloff: long sweeping tail, faired-in headlights, steeply inclined windscreen and front wings rising above the radiator all contribute to its supreme elegance.

A triumphant icon of French styling from the streamlined era, the Delahaye 135 M Figoni & Falaschi roadster is always a winner at concours d'elegance on both sides of the Atlantic. Designed by Geo Ham for the Parisian coachbuilder Figoni & Falaschi, this rare example owned by Peter Mullin was exhibited at the Paris Salon in 1937. It took home the BMW Group Italia trophy awarded by public vote at Villa Erba, on the second day of the concours.

Futuristic visions from three great Turin design houses, the 1967 Dino 206 S Competizione Pininfarina owned by Jim Glickenhaus, Ron Spindler's 1968 Bizzarrini Manta Italdesign and Chris Hrabalek's 1971 Lancia Stratos HF Prototipo Bertone (seen from left to right) were brought together for the first time – their vivid colours and adventurous shapes contrasting with the classicism of the Villa d'Este. The Stratos won the class, and was even considered for Best of Show.

MEADOW BROOK CONCOURS D'ELEGANCE
Rochester, Michigan, August 3

The Meadow Brook Concours d'Elegance celebrated 100 years of the Ford Model T, 100 years of General Motors and the magnificent 8-litre Bentley. The weather was glorious and the attendance was up substantially, which surely warmed the heart of second year chairman Larry Smith and a team that included GM Vice Chairman Bob Lutz as chief judge and a good selection of auto industry luminaries.

The Meadow Brook Concours d'Elegance celebrates a record three Best of Show awards every year. The motorcycle award was given to Berland Sullivan's 1940 four-cylinder Indian. After having won the Concours d'Elegance at Amelia Island, Sam and Emily Mann's ex-Clark Gable Duesenberg Model J scored another first with Best of Show, American Cars, while its European counterpart was bestowed upon Judge Joseph Cassini's 1927 Isotta Fraschini Tipo 8A roadster which Rudolph Valentino had commissioned from Fleetwood Metal Body.

Elegance is not taken lightly at Meadow Brook. Paul Emple's 1930 Minerva AL three-position drophead coupé by VandenPlas – recipient of the Most Elegant Car award – shares modeling duties in the fashion show that is part of the concours each year.

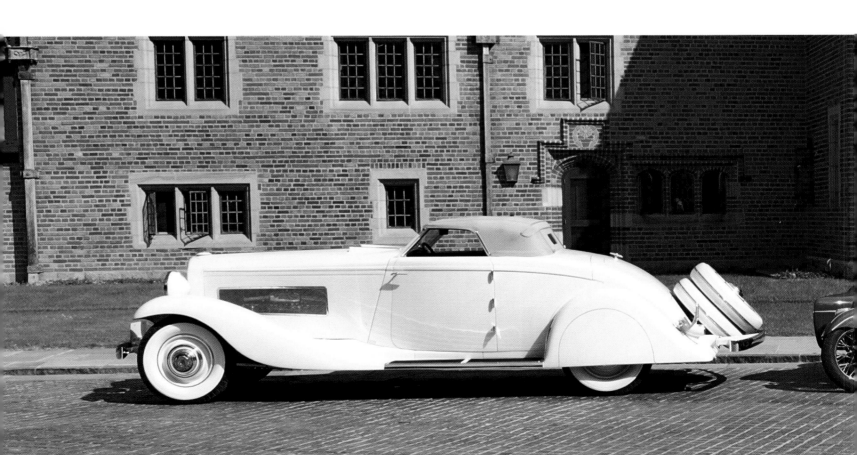

To celebrate 100 years of General Motors, the organisers
worked closely with the auto giant to mount a special
display of Bill Mitchell era concept cars, including the 1959
Sting Ray racer which Mitchell campaigned in SCCA
competition. Other cars in the display included the Mako
Shark, Manta Ray, Monza SS and Monza GT, and the
Chevrolet Astro II.

THE QUAIL, A MOTORSPORTS GATHERING
Carmel Valley, California, August 15

Every year during Concours week on the Monterey
Penninsula, The Quail, a Motorsports Gathering, celebrates
great sports and racing cars at the Quail Lodge in Carmel
Valley. It combines spectacular automobiles and the finer
aspects of life, including wonderful cuisine, wine and a
special selection of vendors. Attendance for this exclusive
event is limited to 3000 guests to ensure that there is the
right crowd but no crowding.

At The Quail, fine cuisine made with fresh local ingredients shares the stage with a fascinating array of cars. For 2008, the five distinct food experiences included Carmel Valley Farmer's Market, Portofino, Sebring, St Tropez and Havana.

Best of Show was awarded to the first production Cobra. Originally fitted with a 260 cid V8 and displayed at auto shows throughout the United States, it was uprated with a 289 cid Ford V8 by Lucky Casner and campaigned extensively in Europe. Now back in the United States, it is owned by well-known collector Bruce Meyer. Standing behind the car, on the right, is organiser Mathias Doutreleau.

One class at The Quail included production examples of Porsche's 959, as well as a rare 959S and Bernard Carl's 1985 factory-prepared Paris-Dakar 959 winner.

The Eagles soared at The Quail, with a full class of cars celebrating Dan Gurney's All American Racers. Gurney was also on hand to help observe the rare occasion when so many of his magnificent Eagles were gathered, from the Spa-winning Formula 1 Eagle, to this car, which was the very first Indy Eagle and now belongs to Douglas Magnon. It, two team-mates and a pair of customer cars debuted at the Speedway in 1966 powered by 265 cid four-cam V8s.

PEBBLE BEACH CONCOURS D'ELEGANCE
Pebble Beach, California, August 17

Jay Leno, the celebrated American TV star and a great collector, always providing much amusement, started a drawing during the concours saying: "Last year, we were very hot here. This time, we are freezing. Now that we have resolved the global warming issue, what's next on the agenda?" It was cold indeed, but it was another exceptional gathering of cars with, amongst several more highlights, a very comprehensive exhibition of General Motors dream cars, brought to celebrate the manufacturer's 100th anniversary.

To heighten the suspense, three finalists for the most coveted Best of Show award of the season are lined up prior to the final announcement. The 2008 contenders included (from left): the 1935 Hispano Suiza K6 Brandone cabriolet of Sam and Emily Mann, the 1934 Packard 1108 LeBaron sport phaeton owned by The Nethercutt Collection, and Jon and Mary Shirley's 1938 Alfa Romeo 8C 2900B Touring berlinetta. And the winner was…

…the Alfa Romeo! Sandra Kasky Button, chairman of the event, stated: "It takes an amazing level of elegance for a closed car to win here".

In recent years, unrestored vehicles have gained increasing importance at Pebble Beach. This stunningly original 1905 Royal Tourist G Touring owned by John and Heather Mozart was the winner of the Pre-war Preservation Class.

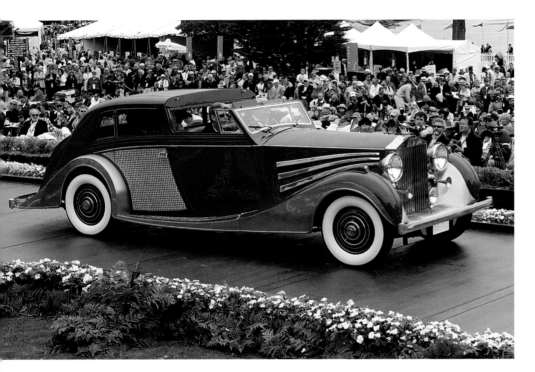

The winner of the class for Pre-war Rolls-Royces was the 1937 Phantom III Sedanca owned by Don and Janet Williams. Built by Freestone & Webb as a showcase of its skills, the PIII was constructed with copper fenders and brightwork, which it retains today.

The 1959 Ferrari 250 GT California Spyder of James Patterson, a superbly proportioned long wheelbase version bodied by Scaglietti, was the recipient of the Strother MacMinn Most Elegant Sports Car Trophy. MacMinn was an automobile designer and design instructor who served as the Chief Honorary Judge for many years.

On the occasion of its 100th anniversary, General Motors was honoured with a Cadillac V16 class as well as one for the cars from the famous Motorama road shows. The turbine-powered Firebird II (foreground), Firebird XP-21 and Firebird II Titanium were all shipped to California by the General Motors Corporation, which has had the foresight to retain a selection of some of its most memorable dream cars.

LOUIS VUITTON CLASSIC CONCOURS AWARD
Paris, France, October 6

The Louis Vuitton Classic Concours Award, now in its fourth year, goes to a car that won Best of Show in one of the major concours d'elegance in the world, all covered in the preceding pages. The 2008 recipient was Jack Croul's Ferrari 166 MM. The berlinetta, sporting coachwork by Touring Superleggera, did not only win one concours in 2008, it won two: first, Cavallino Classic and then, Villa d'Este. It has everything going for it: its lines, its mechanical specifications, its rarity, its authenticity, and a fabulous racing history. Jack Croul, a Californian collector, commented, "This is my year!"

The victory was not easy though, such was the level of the other nominated candidates. The Alfa Romeo 8C 2900 in particular, also with Touring coachwork, which had won Pebble Beach, was strongly supported by several jury members until the final vote was cast. The judges gathered on the occasion of the Mondial de l'Automobile show in Paris. They included designers, historians and collectors. Seated, from left to right, are Olivier Boulay (Mercedes-Benz), Laurens van den Acker (Mazda), Luc Donckerwolke (Seat), Anthony Lo (General Motors), Christian Philippsen (Automobile Year publisher and chairman of the jury), Lorenzo Ramaciotti (Fiat), Lowie Vermeersch (Pininfarina), and standing, still from left to right, are Roberto Piatti (Torino Design), Jean-Pierre Ploué (PSA Peugeot Citroën), Gert Hildebrand (MINI), Patrick le Quément (Renault), François Melcion (Artcurial), Matteo Fioravanti (Fioravanti), Shiro Nakamura (Nissan), Fabrizio Giugiaro (Italdesign) and Wahei Hirai (Toyota).

The curtain has now fallen on a season rich in exceptional shows.

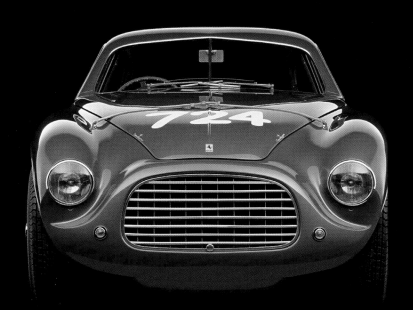

Original Thinking

This past year was an outstanding one for vintage car auctions. Let's enjoy a guided tour commented by specialist **Dave Brownell**.

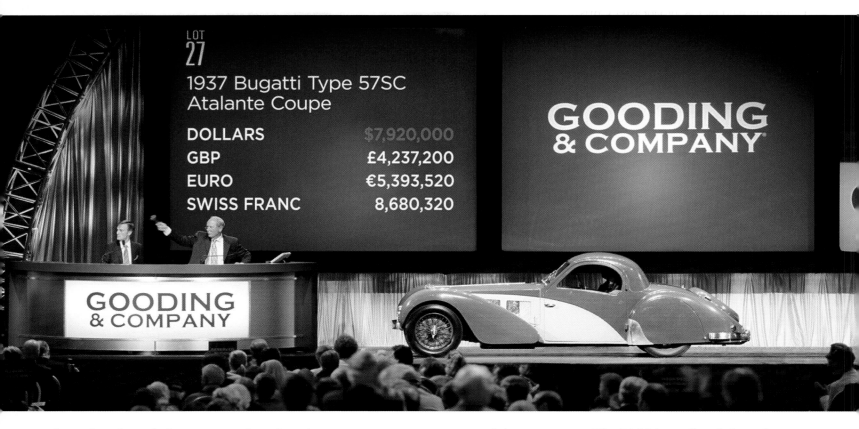

In reading through the entries in this edition's auction review, I am struck by just how many entirely or substantially original cars came to market and sold for very strong sums.
This is a notable shift in collector thinking, especially in the U.S. where the gospel of dazzlingly presented restorations has caused many fine original automobiles to be forever changed in the quest for awards at concours.

An automobile is only original once and no amount of restoration work can alter this fact. Take, for instance, two Rolls-Royce Silver Ghosts sold at the 2008 Gooding Pebble Beach auction. One, a 1920 Barker-bodied roadster had recently emerged from over 70 years' storage and was totally, marvellously original. The other, a 1926 Springfield Piccadilly roadster carrying an impressive professional restoration. The original car brought $110,000 more than the restored car. A few years ago quite the opposite result would have been likely.

Despite the gloom of escalating fuel prices, mortgage crises, bank failures and plunging corporate balance sheets in America and Europe, great models of the great marques continued to climb to record heights at auction. The Bugatti Type 57 SC Atalante hammered down for $7.9 million even

surprised the auctioneers. The RM Maranello sale brought some stratospheric Ferrari prices.

Veteran and Edwardian cars (called brass era in the U.S.) sold strongly, especially those that are London-Brighton Run eligible or cars that possess high horsepower engines and, ideally, chain drive. Post-war sports cars, too, from the ubiquitous MG to Italian exotics enjoyed strong collector demand, as did true racing cars with outstanding histories – witness the Jaguar E2A sold by Bonhams at Carmel for close to $5,000,000.

American muscle cars continued their retreat. A market glut of cars and a diminishing customer base combined to further depress this collector market segment at auction.

Where might the auction market head from here? Undeniably, more long-time collections like the Otis Chandler cars (sold by Gooding), or Dr Peter and Susan Williamson Bugattis (sold by Gooding at Pebble Beach) or the Paine Seal Cove cars (sold by Bonhams) will be offered as the heirs of those who assembled these cars have little interest.

1961 FERRARI 250 GT CALIFORNIA

€7,040,000, £5,605,200, $10,969,940
(RM, Maranello, 18/5/08)
World record price for a short wheelbase
California paid by UK broadcaster Chris
Evans. James Coburn ownership history
and all the right stuff, including covered
headlights. Checked and approved for
authenticity by Ferrari Classiche, like all
Ferraris included in the RM Maranello sale.

1937 BUGATTI TYPE 57 SC ATALANTE

$7,920,000, €5,132,160, £4,245,120
(Gooding, Pebble Beach, 16/8/08)
From the Williamson collection.
Magnificent low-chassis supercharged
Bug with memorable Jean Bugatti styling.
Older, slightly mellowed restoration on an
extraordinary, highly original motorcar. New
price record for cars sold at Pebble Beach
auctions.

1964 FERRARI 250 LM

€4,510,000, $7,027,620, £3,590,860
(RM, Maranello, 18/5/08)
Well-restored example of 32 built, it had seen
many racing miles, including a win at the '65
Austrian GP, and even more as a New York
City commuter car! Original chassis, engine
and gearbox. Ready for vintage events on
track or road.

VETERAN & EDWARDIAN CARS

1904 Pierce 15 HP Arrow
$165,000, £88,710, €111,870
(Gooding, Pebble Beach, 16/8/08)
One of two extant. Splendid restoration and
ready for London-Brighton and other early auto
events. A particularly good buy on this pioneer
example of a great marque.

1904 Rolls-Royce
£3,521,500, $7,242,915, €4,952,400
(Bonhams, London 3/12/07)
Double the previous top auction price for a Rolls
and/or a veteran car. Only existing pre-1905
Rolls-Royce and a London-Brighton veteran. A
most prestigious possession for the new owner.

1907 Thomas Flyer 36 60 HP
$1,028,500, €700,560, £551,365
(Gooding, Pebble Beach, 17/8/08)
Ex-William Harrah collection and one of his
favourites. Showing some honest wear but still a
hugely attractive Edwardian. Same mechanics
as 1908 New York-Paris race winner. Well
bought for prestigious California collection.

1909 Peerless
$170,500, €115,600, £91,390
(RM, Monterey, 16/8/08)
Astonishingly original 'barn find' carefully
brought back to operating condition while
preserving its patina and character. Should never,
ever be restored. Potential preservation class
concours winner.

1910 Pierce Arrow 48 SS
$632,500, €430,825, £339,075
(Gooding, Pebble Beach, 17/8/08)
Only 48 SS demi-tonneau extant. Excellent
restoration on a very original, unhurt car.
Handsome, stylish, powerful tour car with great
presence and superb engineering.

1911 Oldsmobile Limited
$1,650,000, €1,163,735, £809,675
(RM, Hershey, 12/10/07)
In museum for over 50 years. Completely original
'barn find' condition. Should be either gently
recommissioned or totally restored. Ultra rare and
desirable 707-cubic inch giant with 42" wheels.

1913 Isotta Fraschini
$1,492,000, €1,011,575, £799,700
(Bonhams, Carmel, 15/8/08)
10.5-liter monster with new period style
coachwork. Rescued from New York junkyard in
the 1940s. Restored through several iterations.
The ultimate Edwardian road locomotive.

1914 Peugeot 145 S
$172,000, €116,600, £92,190
(Bonhams, Carmel, 15/8/08)
Only known survivor. US and British owner
history, period-correct colours, original body,
reproduced fenders, in lovely condition and ready
for enjoyable, fast vintage touring.

1914 Stutz Bearcat
$1,375,000, €932,250, £737,000
(Gooding, Pebble Beach, 16/8/08)
Record price for the marque and first Bearcat
to top one million. Authentic example in same
family for 60 years. Older restoration still presents
well. 390-cubic inch engine has authoritative
bark, delivers impressive performance.

VINTAGE CARS

1929 Bentley 4 ½ litre
$880,000, €600,270, £447,500
(RM, Phoenix, 18/1/08)
Vintage Bentleys have been on a roll ever since the sale of the Green Hornet blower roadster for $4.5 million in 2007. Impeccable provenance and total originality for this Vanden Plas bodied tourer helped with this record price for a 4 ½.

1932 Bugatti 55
€2,097,500, $3,237,975, £1,658,450
(Bonhams, Monaco, 10/5/08)
Sold for nearly $1.5 million more than at Christie's 2003 Retromobile auction. Complete mechanical overhaul, used very sparingly since. Some patina but generally presents very well.

1929 Bentley 6 ½ litre
$561,000, €380,350, £300,700
(Gooding, Pebble Beach, 17/8/08)
Wonderful older restoration of an unmodified original car except for Speed Six engine upgrade. Rare one-off semi-enclosed coachwork, superb provenance, a fine example with just enough patina.

1929 Cord L-29
$1,078,000, €730,885, £577,800
(Gooding, Pebble Beach, 17/8/08)
Unique coupé designed by DeSakhnoffsky for Hayes Body Corporation. Numerous concours awards when new and now. Lovely, curvaceous style from every aspect. Record price for L-29 Cord.

1929 Duesenberg Model J
$1,650,000, €1,163,735, £809,675
(RM, Hershey, 12/10/07)
One of three dual cowl phaetons built by Murphy; ex-Swigart Museum collection, AACA and CCCA firsts, older restoration shows a bit of patina but still very impressive.

1931 Bentley 8 litre
$2,200,000, €1,430,400, £1,093,085
(RM, Amelia Island, 8/3/08)
Original-bodied tourer by Harrison; one of ten 8-litre tourers built. Older but still sharp restoration with new upholstery. Handsome vintage Bentley with a splendid appearance.

1932 Alfa Romeo 6C 1750 Series V Gran Sport
$1,540,000, €1,051,975, £784,010
(Gooding, Scottsdale, 19/1/08)
Zagato roadster in fine, fresh restored condition. Pebble Beach and Amelia Island concours winner that appeared to be in excellent running order. Very correct Alfa in all areas.

1932 Packard Model 904 Convertible Victoria
$1,210,000, €826,555, £616,000
(Gooding, Scottsdale, 19/1/08)
Dietrich bodied eight-cylinder car in one of the loveliest styles ever to grace a Packard chassis. Concours ready and a 2007 Pebble Beach class winner. One of four extant. Fairly priced.

1933 Rolls-Royce Phantom II
$2,310,000, €1,566,180, £1,238,160
(RM, Monterey, 16/8/08)
Sleek, elegant, formal yet dashing town car. Sole survivor of three originally supplied with this Brewster coachwork. Multiple concours winner, immaculate original interior and trim, irreplaceable classic and worth the money.

1934 Riley MPH
$308,000, €208,825, £165,090
(Gooding, Pebble Beach, 16/8/08)
1980 restoration, ex-Arthur Dobson, retains
Dobbs lightweight racing parts. Quick and
reliable vintage race and rally participant and a
genuine MPH. Strong price, strong car.

1934 Ford Model 40 Special
$1,760,000, €1,444,320, £874,470
(RM, Amelia Island, 8/3/08)
One-off boat-tail aluminum-bodied sportster
built for Edsel Ford. Designed by Bob Gregorie.
Very racy appearance, substantially original low
mileage car. Sold by Bill Warner of Amelia Island
Concours d'Elegance fame.

1935 Avions Voisin Aerodyne
€522,192, £388,935, $756,560
(Artcurial, Paris, 9/2/08)
Extraordinary original Aerodyne sold at no
reserve. One of seven built, this was probably
the best remaining example. Charming interior
patina, good repaint, amazing automobile.

1937 Mercedes-Benz 540K Spezial Roadster
£3,905,000, €5,896,875, $8,496,975
(RM, London, 31/10/07)
One of 25 ever built, ex-Brooks Stevens and
Bernie Ecclestone, beautiful interior, a few paint
and plating faults, ultra-clean chassis and engine
area, visually stunning in silver finish. Not in our
year's top three list because sale took place in late
2007.

1938 Alfa Romeo 6C 2300B Mille Miglia
$2,585,000, €1,752,630, £1,385,560
(Gooding, Pebble Beach, 17/8/08)
Part of famous Dovaz 'sleeping beauty' group
found in France. Restored several times, then
re-restored to its present concours-winning
condition. Matching numbers Touring-bodied
car, Pebble Beach and CCCA first. Faultless, fast
and fine.

1939 Talbot-Lago T150 CSS
$4,847,000, €3,286,270, £2,598,000
(Bonhams, Carmel, 15/8/08)
One of four built with Pourtout coachwork on a
Paulin design. Amazingly original Talbot with
a successful racing history. Owned by American
Talbot enthusiast for decades. Beautifully
preserved and a potential future best of show in
major concours.

POST-WAR CLASSICS

1948 Tucker
$1,017,500, €689,865, £545,380
(RM, Monterey, 16/8/08)
Famous post-war failure and a mythic motorcar.
Radical style and engineering; only 51 built. This
one brought a record price and was show and tour
ready.

1952 Lancia B52 Aurelia
$81,400, €55,190, £43,630
(Gooding, Pebble Beach, 17/8/08)
Three built, one of two remaining. Innovative
Lancia drivetrain coupled to Boano-styled,
Ghia-built Turin Show Car. Very American in
appearance with Nash/Willys overtones.

1952 Siata Daina
£74,100, $146,600, €93,150
(Bonhams, Goodwood, 11/7/08)
Sweet little matching number GT with highly
attractive coachwork design and Fiat 1400
power modified by Siata. Louis Vuitton Classic
'Bagatelle' concours and numerous vintage rallies
to its credit.

1955 Mercedes-Benz 300 SL
$852,000, €577,650, £456,670
(RM, Monterey, 16/8/08)
Rudge wheels and fitted luggage. Completely restored by SL specialist and still shows very well despite some road use. Sold at market-correct level for an excellent example.

1957 BMW 507
£423,500, €639,520, $921,500
(RM, London, 31/10/07)
New price record for these beautiful Bimmers. This was the 15th of 253 produced and was freshly and correctly restored. Gorgeous example sold for $100,000 above estimate.

1959 Cadillac Eldorado Biarritz
$231,000, €148,430, £117,025
(RM, Meadow Brook, 2/8/08)
Senior national AACA winner, 527 miles on superb restoration. Once considered outrageous, these '59s are now regarded by collectors as an automotive style icon of the '50s.

1959 Ferrari 250 GT California
$3,300,000, €2,254,240, £1,680,020
(Gooding, Scottsdale, 19/1/08)
At time of sale, this was a world record for a steel-bodied open headlight long wheelbase example. Repainted in factory correct but non-original Fly Yellow. Original cold air box. Superb inside and out.

1961 Ferrari 250 GT
$4,510,000, €3,057,780, £2,417,360
(RM, Monterey, 16/8/08)
Breathtakingly beautiful and totally correct. Cavallino Classic award winner. Minimal miles since restoration. Stunning example of one of Ferrari's legendary series.

1961 Jaguar XK 150
$181,500, €123,060, £97,285
(RM, Monterey, 16/8/08)
Perhaps the finest restored XK 150 coupé extant. Engine upgraded to S specifications. Unusual, highly attractive claret factory colour. Superb show and go Jag.

1963 Ferrari 400 Superamerica coupé Aerodinamico
$1,320,000, €901,695, £672,000
(Gooding, Scottsdale, 19/1/08)
One of only 18 Series 2 LWBs produced. Concours-ready condition throughout. Sold at Gstaad in December '05 for $560,921. Excellent return on investment for a true Ferrari supercar.

1965 Shelby Mustang GT350
$247,500, €167,800, £132,660
(RM, Monterey, 16/8/08)
Straight, low mileage GT350 with second but correct engine and transmission. Excellent appearance inside and out, shows obvious care. Sold at a whisker below low estimate.

1966 Ford GT40 MK I
£968,000, €1,386,300, $1,997,565
(RM, London, 31/10/07)
Low mileage street-legal GT40. Paint somewhat uneven, very good interior, uses 38-mm downdraft Webers, Halibrand alloy wheels in place of Borranis. One of 31 built for road use.

1967 Ferrari 275 GTB4
$1,320,000, €1,050,985, £2,056,865
(RM, Maranello, 18/5/08)
Matching numbers example done to highest
standards. First in class at Ferrari 60th
anniversary concours. Unusual but correct colour.
Sold for nearly $1 million more than a GTB2 at
Gstaad in December '07.

1971 Ferrari 365 GTB/4
$1,023,000, €693,595, £548,330
(Gooding, Pebble Beach, 17/8/08)
One of 124 Scaglietti factory-produced spyders.
Well sorted with recent engine and transaxle
overhaul. Full documentation; upgraded
drivetrain for higher performance gives top speed
of 180 mph.

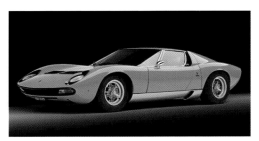

1972 Lamborghini Miura SV
$891,000, €604,100, £477,575
(RM, Monterey, 16/8/08)
One of only 150 SVs, LHD conversion, restored
to concours-winning condition by Lambo
specialists. Low mileage from new, very correct
and attractive Miura.

RACING CARS

1934 ERA
£359,000, €451,330, , $710,290
(Bonhams, Goodwood, 11/7/08)
Prototype R1A, important progenitor of highly
successful line of single-seaters. Well restored and
sorted, great racing history and active vintage
competitor. Sold for well under low estimate.

1950 Ferrari 166 MM
$2,200,000, €1,491,600, £1,179,200
(Gooding, Pebble Beach, 16/8/08)
Matching numbers; known provenance from
new; upgraded with triple carburetors and
195S engine specs. Recent four-year specialist
restoration has this Touring-bodied 166 equally
ready for important concours or historic rallies.
Well bought by a Chicago enthusiast.

1952 Glöckler-Porsche
$616,000, €420,190, £313,250
(RM, Phoenix, 18/1/08)
Coachwork by Weidenhausen. Third
Glöckler-Porsche built. Replacement engine,
clean and fine throughout. Auction circuit
veteran. Failed to sell for more money at two
previous sales.

1955 Jaguar D-Type
£2,201,500, €2,767,685, $4,355,710
(Bonhams, Goodwood, 11/7/08)
Full provenance from new, first production
D-Type, matching numbers, recent professional
mechanical work, showing some light and honest
patina. Marvellous race-ready example.

1960 Jaguar E2A
$4,957,000, €3,360,850, £2,656,950
(Bonhams, Carmel, 15/8/08)
Historically significant one-off raced by
Cunningham team drivers Gurney, Hansgen,
Brabham, McLaren. Originally 3 litre for LeMans,
now Jag 3.8 unit. Older factory refurbishment.
Auction record price for a Jaguar.

1962 Chevrolet Corvette
$1,485,000, €1,006,830, £795,960
(Gooding, Pebble Beach, 17/8/08)
Highly important US sports racing car from
leading privateer Gulf Oil team. Daytona and
Sebring winner, 1962 SCCA A-production
champ. Restored to highest authentic level with
multiple NCRS and Bloomington Gold awards.
Matching numbers, brutally fast.

1963 AC Cobra 289
$1,732,500, €1,181,780, £881,010
(RM, Phoenix, 18/1/08)
Shelby factory team car showing some battle scars
and interior wear. Extensive racing history and
undoubted authenticity. Should be a fearsome
vintage race entry in the right hands.

1986 Martini
€14,296, £11,325, $22,520
(Artcurial, Paris, 28/6/08)
Cheap entry to the 2010 Monaco Historic Grand
Prix. Yannick Dalmas's ex-Ecurie Oreca 1986
Formula 3 championship winning car. Won six of
11 races plus F3 Monaco GP. Displayed for many
years as a piece of art in a Parisian flat.

1986 Ferrari F1/86
$363,195, €252,055, £176,000
(RM, London 31/10/07)
Sold without reserve. Very tidy presentation;
placed third in 1986 Australian GP. Correct
drivetrain, well-detailed throughout.

OF SPECIAL INTEREST

1941 Chrysler Thunderbolt
$1,320,000, €900,400, £671,250
(RM, Phoenix, 18/1/08)
One of four extant; Pebble Beach award winner
in 1997. Retractable hardtop. A true dream car
and an important styling exercise of the time.
Presented very well.

**1959 Cadillac Eldorado Seville 'Elvis
Tribute'**
$302,500, €203,220, £161,822
(RM, Monterey, 15/8/08)
Professionally customized three position cabriolet
on gargantuan Eldorado drivetrain. A monument
to '50s excess writ large. Elvis would have loved
it. The buyer did, too.

1962 Citroën 2CV Sahara
$93,600, €63,460, £50,170
(Bonhams, Carmel, 15/8/08)
'Bimotore' Tin Snail built for Citroën by
Panhard. One of 694 produced. Rare survivor
with engines transplanted from another Sahara.
Quirky fun for a lot of money.

1963 Amphicar 770
$44,000, €29,830, £23,585
(Gooding, Pebble Beach, 16/8/08)
From a German museum with less than 3000 km
from new. Fine original condition throughout
and ready to make a splash wherever it goes on
land or water. Sold at no reserve.

1966 Volkswagen Microbus
$60,500, €41,325, £30,800
(Gooding, Scottsdale, 19/1/08)
Show winning restoration of a 21-window van
carrying optional 1500 cc engine, factory sliding
sunroof and walk-through interior, among other
extras. The most deluxe of Microbuses and
exuding '60s nostalgia.

1967 Baja Boot
$199,500, €135,260, £106,930
(Bonhams, Carmel, 15/8/08)
One of two built, looks like a moon explorer
but was first a Dune Buggy supercar. Driven by
Steve McQueen, boasts many racing victories,
extremely sophisticated engineering.

Automobile Year 1908

The year 1908 was one of beginnings says historian **David Burgess-Wise**, a year in which the first shoots of future greatness were planted. The award of the Britain's Dewar Trophy to Cadillac for a convincing demonstration of its mastery of standardisation showed the way ahead for the motor industry, Billy Durant's formation of General Motors marked the birth of a giant corporation, the launch of the Model T Ford ushered in an undreamt of era of popular motoring. The year also saw the opening of the first-ever concrete motorway with the completion of the first section of the Long Island Motor Parkway, though it would be many years before another such road was started. And the year also saw the end – for a while – of Grand Prix motor racing and the running of the longest motor race, a round-the-world affair that ended in controversy.

In 1904 America's leading wagon and carriage producer William Durant took over and revitalised the failing Buick Motor Company. On September 16, 1908 he incorporated the General Motors Company, into which he first absorbed Buick, subsequently buying Oldsmobile, Oakland and Cadillac. By 1910, the group accounted for some 20% of the American automobile production. But it had spread its net too wide and in September 1910, Billy Durant lost control of GM to an investment banking group.

The most significant car in motoring history, the Model T Ford, was launched in November 1908. It was a carefully-studied exercise in minimalism, built of fine materials. It was affordable, easy to drive, and backed by a worldwide network of service agencies. When the Model T was introduced, the motor car was a rarity; when the last Tin Lizzie was built late in 1927, over 16 million had been built in 50 factories in 19 countries on six continents and half the cars in the world were Fords.

1908 saw the running of the longest motor race ever attempted, a 170-day, 21,000-mile round the world contest that linked New York to Paris via San Francisco, Japan, Vladivostok, St. Petersburg and Berlin. Entries were sparse and came from Protos, De Dion-Bouton, Sizaire-Naudin, Motobloc, Züst and, at the last minute, E.R. Thomas. The race was beset by bad weather, controversy and chicanery, and retirements left only the Thomas and the Protos in contention. When the Protos reached Paris first, the Germanophobe French quickly adjusted the rules to declare the Thomas Flyer the winner on elapsed time.

Run over 10 laps of the same 77 km circuit outside Dieppe as the 1907 Grand Prix, the 1908 event followed a new formula that imposed a minimum weight of 1100 kg and attempted to limit engine capacity by restricting bore sizes, though most engines were still between 12 and 13 litres. The race was won by the novice driver Lautenschlager's Mercedes. German cars finished 1-2-3, rendering the French "livid with rage". There would not be another Grand Prix until 1912...

Automobile Year 1958

David Burgess-Wise remembers 1958 fondly, as it was a champion year for Great Britain, with Mike Hawthorn achieving the first ever drivers' World Championship for a Briton and Vanwall winning the Constructors' Championship. It was also a banner year for the introduction of significant new models and the first ever year in which Britain's motor industry produced more than a million cars. Against that, America suffered a significant downturn in sales, despite which Ford produced its 50 millionth automobile and Chrysler its 25 millionth. Ideas ahead of their time included General Motors' self-steering car that followed a magnetic wire buried in the highway, Ford's Glideair hovercar and Chrysler's flying Jeep; French manufacturer Arbel's atomic powered car proved to be a flight of fancy.

The Amsterdam Show in February saw the debut of the first new Dutch car for many years. The brothers Huub and Wim van Doorne were truck and trailer manufacturers who compensated for falling sales in their traditional products by introducing an economy small car that needed no servicing apart from oil changes. With an air cooled flat-twin engine of only 590 cc, the DAF featured an ingenious Variomatic transmission with continuously variable final drive ratios.

God created the woman and Ghia, with the advice of its old patron Virgil Exner of Chrysler, of Exner Jr who actually penned it, and of Frua who built the prototype, created the Floride for Renault. Eventually, the car was launched at the 1958 Paris Salon, with Brigitte Bardot for godmother. Almost 50,000 were sold before production ended in 1963.

Despite its bizarre styling – it was described as "a vehicle you might ride in to the astroport for a trip to the moon" by General Motors chief stylist Harley Earl – the turbine-powered GM Firebird III concept car was awash with technical innovations like cruise control, remote door opening by ultrasonic beam, electroluminescent instrument displays, anti-skid braking, automatic lamp illumination and air-conditioning. More debatable was the single lever that controlled acceleration, braking and steering and could be operated from either seat…

Aston Martin's DB4 unveiled at the 1958 Paris Salon represented the first absolutely new design produced under the leadership of David Brown. A new platform chassis was devised to accommodate 'Superleggera' coupé bodywork by Touring of Milan. Power came from an all-new 3.7-litre twin overhead camshaft six-cylinder engine. Soon after its launch, a DB4 achieved the remarkable feat of accelerating and braking from a standstill to 100 mph and back to zero in under 30 seconds.

After a career lasting 20 years, five times world champion Juan Manuel Fangio finally retired from racing in July 1958 after the French Grand Prix at Reims in which he finished fourth despite a burnt-out clutch on his Maserati 250F. It was, said an onlooker, "a demonstration of Fangio at his greatest and best". Earlier in the season, Fangio had travelled to Havana to compete in the Grand Prix of Cuba. The day before the race, he was kidnapped by Fidel Castro's '26 of July Movement' and held until the race was over as a protest against the ruling Batista regime. Despite Fangio's intercession, his kidnapper was later shot by the police due to "a regrettable bureaucratic error".

Britain had its first Formula One champion when Mike Hawthorn wrested the title from Stirling Moss by a single point by finishing second to Moss in the last race of the season, the Moroccan Grand Prix. In fact, during the season, Hawthorn had won only one Grand Prix against Moss's total of four, but had finished in the points more often. His sole victory had been in the French Grand Prix at Reims, in which his Ferrari led all the way from the mid-point of the first lap. But it had been a grim year for Formula One, with Luigi Musso crashing fatally at Reims, Peter Collins being killed at the Nürburgring and Stuart Lewis-Evans dying of burns at the Moroccan GP.

Vanwall didn't enter the Argentine GP, which opened the season, so Stirling Moss drove Rob Walker's 1.9-litre Cooper Climax. The car had bolt-on wheels rather than knock-offs, so Stirling chose to drive the whole race on one set of tyres. He took the lead in lap 35, but towards the end of the race, driving without a clutch, he could see the white breaker strip on the back tyres. When he crossed the finishing line in first place, his tyres had less than a lap of life left. It was the first ever Formula One win by a rear-engined car. In the third race of the season, the Dutch Grand Prix at Zandvoort, Stirling had led from start to finish in his Vanwall, breaking the lap record set by Fangio's Mercedes in 1955. This moved Moss into a convincing lead in the World Championship after three races, but there was the rest of the season to go, with disappointments like here in Monza, and, despite his vast talent, the title would escape him by a single point…

The 500 cc Formula 3 class, dominated by Britain and Germany, was declining in popularity by 1958, so Count Giovanni Lurani and the Italians devised a new Formula Junior based on 1100 cc pushrod production engines (Fiat for instance…). The first race held under the new formula, which didn't go international until 1959, took place at Monza on April 25 and attracted an entry of just eight cars, "with at least the same number nearing completion, so that the Italian idea has got away to a reasonable start". Indeed it had, for by 1960 Formula Junior had become the new international Formula 3. The eventual winner in Monza was Roberto Lippi, driving a Stanguellini 750 Corsa upgraded to 1100 cc (No. 18).

"Interminable, tragic, tempestuous" was how Autocar described the 26th running of the Le Mans 24-hour race, which saw 36 of the 55 starters eliminated by mechanical failure or accidents due to heavy rain. Unfortunately, one of the 15 crashes proved fatal, when the Le Mans veteran 'Mary' (Jean-Marie Brousselet) died after his Jaguar collided with the Ferrari of American Bruce Kessler in the seventh hour. Soon after midnight, the Ferrari of Olivier Gendebien/Phil Hill (who sadly passed away in 2008) went into the lead, where it remained "unchallenged and unchallengeable" to the end, having covered 4102 km (2550 miles) at an average speed of 170.9 km/h (106 mph). The second place Aston Martin was eight laps adrift; the Index of Performance went to the OSCA of Davis and de Tomaso.

Publisher
Christian Philippsen

Photo selection
Christian Bailly
Claudio Bari

Race results
Rein Luik
Philip van Osten

Translations
Geoffrey Day
Desmond Tumulty

Design & layout
Gattocubico/Gianluca Pace,
Modena (Italy)

Photoengraving
Vaccari Zincografica,
Modena (Italy)

The publisher expresses his heartfelt thanks
to the following persons for their invaluable
and friendly support to *Automobile Year*:

Yves Carcelle & Christine Bélanger
(Louis Vuitton Malletier), Karl Baumer &
Max Bauer (BMW Mobile Tradition),
Kenton Elliot (A1GP), Philippe Douchet
de Rouère (Audemars Piguet), Ginger
Ostle (CarMen), Luigi Macaluso
(Girard-Perregaux), David Gooding & Dawn
Ahrens (Gooding & Company), Kazunori
Yamauchi & Takuya Asano
(Polyphony Digital), Bastien Schupp &
Claude Hugot (Infiniti), Klaus Burger
& Stephan Mohr (Maha), John Francis
Marsh, Patrick Oliva & Jean-Pierre
Lamour (Michelin), Yves Junne (Motul),
Manrico Iachia & Alexandra Carvalho
(Europ Assistance), Douglas Freedman
(Motor Club Events), Benito Andrea
Benassi (Labirinto), Marie-France Bouillé,
Prof. Ing. Andrea Curami, Pierre
Dupasquier, Franck Guillou
(Fondation Brigitte Bardot), Karl-Heinz
Kalbfell, Margus Kuuse, Prof. Gordon
Murray, Peter Sachs (The Klemantaski
Collection), Ray Scherr, Simone
Steichen, Laurens van den Acker, Sven Xu

Photo credits

Page 5: Hugo Modderman • 6: Citroën Communication • 8-9: Volkswagen/Design LA (3x) • 10-11 Volkswagen/Design LA • 12: General Motors/Design LA (2x) • 13: Mazda Motor Corporation • 14: Toyota/Design LA • 15: Renault Design • 17: Archives Louis Vuitton • 18: • 19: John Francis Marsh •22: Mazda Motor Corporation • 23: Mazda Motor Corporation (2x) • 24: Honda (3x)• 25: Nisan (2x), Mitsubishi (2x) • 26: Toyota (2x), Nissan (2x) • 27: Nissan, Honda, Toyota • 28: General Motors • 29: General Motors (2x) • 30: Audi, Chrysler Group (2x) • 31: Land Rover (3x) • 32: Ford Motor Company (3x) • 33: General Motors (2x), Toyota (2x) • 34: Chrysler Group (3x) • 35: Toyota (3x) • 36: Chrysler Group (3x), Mitsubishi • 37: Mazda Motor Corporation (3x) • 38-39: Italdesign-Giugiaro (3x) • 40-41: Pininfarina (3x) • 42: Renault Communication/ Peter Keil (2x), Renault Communication/Benoît Chimenes • 43: General Motors (3x) • 44: Fioravanti, Hyundai (2x) • 45: Espace Développement, Magna Steyr 46-47: IAT • (3x) • 48: Guangzhou Honda, FAW (2x) • 49: Beijing Automobile, Sivax (2x) • 50-51: Venturi • 52-53: Citroën Communication (4x) • 54: Lamborghini • 55: Peugeot, General Motors • 56: Renault Communication/Karim Louiba (3x) • 57: Citroën Communication (3x) • 58: Mazda Motor Corporation (2x), Heuliez • 59: Nissan • 60: Bertone (2x) • 61: BMW (2x) • 62: BMW, Touring, Pininfarina • 63: Torino Design (2x), Mazda Motor Corporation • 64-69: CarMen • 71: Anna-Louise Felstead • 76-77: Pininfarina (3x) • 78: Think (2x), Ford Motor Company (2x) • 79: Renault Product Communications, Ford Motor Company (2x) • 80: Citroën Communication/Laurent Nivalle et Charles-Antoine d'Autichamp (3x) • 81: Alfa Romeo (3x) • 82: Renault Communication/Patrick Curtet, Renault Communication/Dominique Dumas, General Motors (2x) • 83: Lancia (2x), Citroën Communication (2x) • 84: Renault/Dominique Dumas, Audi, Ford Motor Company • 85: Daimler, Volvo, BMW • 86-87: BMW Group/ Rolls-Royce Cars • 88: VW (3x) • 89: Artega (2x), Lotus (2x) • 90-91: Ferrari (5x) • 92-93: General Motors (3x) • 94: General Motors (2x), Ford Motor Company (2x) • 95: Fisker (3x) • 96: General Motors • 97: Chrysler Group • 98: Toyota (3x), Chrysler Group • 99: Ford Motor Company (3x), VW • 100-101: Tata Motors (7x) • 102: Toyota (3x) • 103: Geely, Suzuki, KIA • 104: Roewe, Nissan, Hyundai • 105: Toyota, Honda (2x) • 106: Toyata (2x), Mazda Motor Corporation (2x) • 107: Okuyama (3x) • 109-111: Manufacture française de pneumatiques Michelin (5x) • 115: Daimler • 118-119: Prof. Gordon Murray • 120: Ferrari/Photo4 • 122-123: Photo4 • 124-125: LAT Photographic/Steven Tee/Renault • 126: DPPI/Thierry Bovy, Photo4 • 127: BMW, Ferrari • 128-129: DPPI/Jean Michel Le Meur • 130-131: Daniel Reinhard • 132: DPPI/ Jose Rubio • 133: Photo4 (2x), DPPI/Gilles Levent • 134-135: Photo4 • 136: AP/La Presse • 137: LAT Photographic/ Steven Tee/Renault • 139: Anna-Louise Felstead • 142: Ferrari (3x), DPPI/Eric Vargiolu •143: Paolo d'Alessio • 144: Photo4 (2x), DPPI/Eric Vargiolu, DPPI/Gilles Levent • 145: Paolo d'Alessio • 146: BMW (3x), DPPI/Eric Vargiolu •147: Paolo d'Alessio • 148: Toyota (3x), DPPI/Eric Vargiolu • 149: LAT Photographic/ Charles Coates/Renault (2x), LAT Photographic/Steven Tee/Renault, DPPI/Eric Vargiolu • 150: Scuderia Toro Rosso/Getty, Scuderia Toro Rosso//GEPA, Photo4, DPPI/Eric Vargiolu • 151: Red Bull/Getty (3x), DPPI/Eric Vargiolu • 152: Honda (3x), DPPI/Eric Vargiolu

• 153: LAT Photographic/Glenn Dunbar/Williams (2x), Williams, DPPI/Eric Vargiolu •154: Photo4 (2x), DPPI/Eric Vargiolu, DPPI/Thierry Bovy • 155: Photo4 (2x), DPPI/Eric Vargiolu, DPPI/Gilles Levent • 156: Photo4 • 157: Photo4 • 158: Photo4 •159: Photo4 •160: DPPI/Thierry Bovy • 161: Photo4 • 162: Photo4 • 163: Photo4 • 164: DPPI/Gilles Levent • 165: Photo4 • 166: Photo4 • 167: Ferrari • 168: Photo4 • 169: Photo4 • 170: LAT Photographic/Glenn Dunbar/Renault • 171: LAT Photographic/Andrew Ferraro/ Renault • 172: Photo4 • 173: DPPI/Gilles Levent • 174: DPPI/Gilles Levent • 176-181: A1GP (12x) • 182-183: DPPI/Vincent Curutchet • 184: DPPI/François Flamand • 185: Audi Motorsport (2x)• 186: Peugeot Sport, Graphic Images/Eric Metcalfe • 187: Photo4 • 188: Photo4, Graphic Images/Eric Metcalfe • 189: Graphic Images/Eric Metcalfe • 190-191: DPPI/Alexandre Guillaumot • 192-193: DPPI/Jean Michel Le Meur • 194-195: DPPI • 196: Graphic Images/Eric Metcalfe • 197: Graphic Images/Eric Metcalfe (2x) • 198: Audi Motorsport, DPPI/Alexandre Guillaumot • 199: Audi Motorsport (2x) • 200: DPPI/Alexandre Guillaumot, DPPI/Jean Michel Le Meur • 201: Graphic Images/ Eric Metcalfe, DPPI/Alexandre Guillaumot • 202: Graphic Images/Eric Metcalfe, Photo4 • 203: Graphic Images/Eric Metcalfe, Régis Lefébure • 204: DPPI/Jean Michel Le Meur (2x) • 205: Maserati (2x) • 211: Photo4 • 212-213: Photo4 • 214: FIA WTCC, Photo4 • 215: Photo4 • 216-217: Photo4 • 218: Photo4 • 219: Photo4 (2x) • 220-221: Photo4 • 222: Photo4 (2x) • 223: Photo4 • 224: Photo4 • 225: DPPI/Frederic Le Floc'h • 226-227: Photo4 • 228: Photo4 • 229: Photo4, DPPI/François Baudin 230-231: Photo4 • 232: Citroën • 233: Photo4 • 234: Pebble Beach Concours d'Elegance/Ron Kimball • 236-241: BMW (8x) • 242-247: Ann-Louise Noeth (9x) • 248: Archives Louis Vuitton • 250: Keith Bluemel • 251: Cavallino Classic, Keith Bluemel • 252: Hugo Modderman • 253: Amelia Island Concours d'Elegance/Rashba 254-255: Amelia Island Concours d'Elegance/Rashba (3x) • 256: BMW Group • 257: Johann Lemercier • 258: Johann Lemercier (2x), BMW Group • 259: BMW Group • 260-261: Meadow Brook Concours d'Elegance/Paul Cannon • 262: The Quail/Steve Burton • 263: The Quail/Notfarnow, The Quail • 264: The Quail/David Burton, The Quail/Notfarnow 265: Pebble Beach Concours d'Elegance/Ron Kimball • 266-267: Pebble Beach Concours d'Elegance/Ron Kimball • 268: Pebble Beach Concours d'Elegance/Ron Kimball (3x) • 269: Pebble Beach Concours d'Elegance/Ron Kimball • 270: Archives Louis Vuitton • 271: Scott Williamson (3x) • 272: Gooding and Co • 273: RM Auctions (2x), Gooding and Co • 274: Gooding and Co (4x), Bonhams, Bonhams and Butterfields (2x), RM Auctions (2x) • 275: RM Auctions (4x), Bonhams, Gooding and Co (4x) • 276: Gooding and Co (3x), RM Auctions (3x), Artcurial, Bonhams and Butterfields, Bonhams • 277: RM Auctions (7x), Gooding and Co (2x) • 278: RM Auctions (3x), Gooding and Co (3x), Bonhams (2x), Bonhams and Butterfields • 279: RM Auctions (4x), Artcurial, Bonhams and Butterfields (2x), Gooding and Co (2x) • 280: LAT Photographic • 281: General Motors, David Burgess-Wise Collection, Klemantaski Collection • 282: General Motors • 283: LAT Photographic, Fondation Brigitte Bardot, LAT Photographic • 284-285: Klemantaski Collection (2x) • 286: Klemantaski Collection • 287: Fondazione Negri • 288: Klemantaski Collection • 291: Hugo Modderman

Printed by Nuovo Istituto Italiano d'Arti Grafiche, Bergamo (Italy)